PORTRAIT *for* POSTERITY

William H. Herndon

PORTRAIT

FOR

POSTERITY

Lincoln and His Biographers

by

BENJAMIN P. THOMAS

Illustrations by ROMAINE PROCTOR

Biography Index Reprint Series

BOOKS FOR LIBRARIES PRESS
FREEPORT, NEW YORK

Library of Congress Cataloging in Publication Data

Thomas, Benjamin Platt, 1902-1956.
    Portrait for posterity.

    (Biography index reprint series)
    Bibliography: p.
    1. Lincoln, Abraham, Pres. U. S., 1809-1865.
2. Lincoln, Abraham, Pres. U. S.--Bibliography.
I. Title.
E457.T43 1972   973.7'0924 ⌈B⌉   72-38318
ISBN 0-8369-8130-8

PRINTED IN THE UNITED STATES OF AMERICA
BY
NEW WORLD BOOK MANUFACTURING CO., INC.
HALLANDALE, FLORIDA 33009

To Sally

PREFACE

THIS is the story behind the Lincoln books, based on the correspondence of Lincoln's biographers. These letters are personal, sometimes bitter, sometimes funny, sometimes gossipy, sometimes keen and penetrating. They were not written for you and me to read; but there is reason why we should examine them.

None of us knows Lincoln at first hand. Some of these people did; and the remainder knew him through long study. Our Lincoln comes to us through them.

For that reason it is important that we know what kind of people they were, what methods they used, what personal bias influenced their thought, whether they chose to tell all they knew, whether they aspired to truth or camouflaged their subject with protective coloration.

Their letters give the answers.

Why were both Holland and Herndon, who took widely different views, incapable of giving us an accurate idea of Lincoln's religion? Why was Beveridge so critical of Lincoln's opposition to the Mexican War? Why did Chauncey Black, Lamon's ghostwriter, make Lincoln's background so unattractive? Why did he wish to prolong the controversy over Lincoln's religion? What did men who knew Lincoln personally think about the merits of this controversy? Did Herndon ever give up the idea that Lincoln was illegitimate? What did Lincoln's friends think of the Ann Rutledge story; and of Herndon for revealing it?

Why did Ida Tarbell espouse the idea that Lincoln's mother was of legitimate birth in the face of Herndon's alleged information to the contrary from Lincoln himself? Was William E. Barton able to convince her that she was wrong? Was she?

How did the public react to the work of the various biographers? To what extent did they write to please the public? What did they say privately about each other? Were they willing to admit mistakes or did they have closed minds?

These are only a few examples of the sort of questions their letters answer. In them they express their real feelings. And since most of them were colorful figures, their letters are colorful, too. Behind the scenes they speculated, confided, argued and sometimes schemed.

From these letters the theme of the book emerges as a struggle between two conflicting schools of thought regarding the way to write about Lincoln. One school would depict him as a national hero with all the attributes a national hero was supposed to have. The other school thought he should be represented as he was. At first, public opinion was solidly behind the former view. Gradually it shifted. Now people want the facts. Yet, even those who tried honestly to show us Lincoln as he was, had a feeling of failure. There was something about the man that the most probing technique could not always penetrate.

The letters which are the foundation of this book are scattered over the country. Investigation of them has required long but pleasurable journeys, and has put me under obligation to many persons who gave willing and often enthusiastic help.

At the Henry E. Huntington Library, San Marino, California, Leslie E. Bliss, Librarian, allowed me to examine the Ward Hill Lamon Collection, the John Hay Collection, the Judd Stewart Collection, the William E. Lambert Collection, and other manuscripts. Miss Norma Cuthbert, who has charge of these manuscript collections, was ever ready to assist me in their use.

At the University of Chicago, Jesse Shera and Miss Gladys Sanders introduced me to the Barton Collection. At the Chicago Historical Society, Paul M. Angle and his staff made me feel like one of the family. At Allegheny College, Meadville, Pennsylvania, where Ida Tarbell's letters are deposited, I was welcomed as a guest of the college. Philip Mohr Benjamin, Librarian, aided me in every possible way and pointed out some things I might have missed.

The great Herndon-Weik Collection is at the Library of Congress in Washington, D. C.; but the Illinois State Historical Library has photostats of the entire collection, so I was able to "board at home, so to speak," as Lincoln once said, while I studied it. Here I also went through the Jesse W. Weik Papers, Albert J. Beveridge's correspondence with William E. Connelley, the John Hay Collection, and others; and I drew upon the Library's excellent collection of photographs for illustrations.

When I was stumped on obscure matters, Miss Margaret Flint, Reference Librarian, showed me where to look, or, with gracious donation of her time, and an ingenuity at which I never ceased to marvel, came up with what I wanted. Jay Monaghan, Illinois State Historian and head of the Library, also offered suggestions, encouragement, and assistance. The whole staff was eager to help.

The Illinois State Library has an excellent collection of periodicals, and the staff of the periodical room was most cooperative, as was everyone in the Library of whom I requested aid. William E. Baringer and Miss Marion

Dolores Bonzi brought out material in the Abraham Lincoln Association's files and Miss Bonzi earned my lasting gratitude by reading proof. Ralph Newman of the Abraham Lincoln Bookshop, Chicago, permitted me to examine the letters of George P. Hambrecht which are in his possession. William H. Patton loaned me the correspondence of his father, William L. Patton, with Albert J. Beveridge.

At sacrifice of their own valuable time, Paul M. Angle, Lloyd Lewis, and George W. Bunn, Jr., read all or large parts of the manuscript and offered good advice which I have tried to follow.

William P. Kilroy was indefatigable in digging out material in the Library of Congress. Nira C. Irwin did the typing.

Publishers were uniformly gracious in granting permission to quote from books upon which they hold copyright, and I wish to thank the following for such permissions: Dodd, Mead & Company for allowing me to quote from Tyler Dennett's *Abraham Lincoln and the Civil War in the Diaries and Letters of John Hay,* from Dennett's *John Hay: From Poetry to Politics,* and from James G. Randall's *Lincoln the President: Springfield to Gettysburg;* Harcourt, Brace and Company for permission to quote from Carl Sandburg's *Abraham Lincoln: The Prairie Years,* and from Karl Detzer's *Carl Sandburg: A Study in Personality and Background;* Harper and Brothers for allowing me to quote from Ida M. Tarbell's *In the Footsteps of the Lincolns;* Houghton Mifflin Company for similar permission with respect to Albert J. Beveridge's *Abraham Lincoln, 1809–1858,* Claude G. Bowers' *Beveridge and the Progressive Era,* and William Roscoe Thayer's *The Life and Letters of John Hay;* and the Macmillan Company for permission to quote from Ida M. Tarbell's *All in the Day's Work: An Autobiography.*

The illustrations were drawn by Romaine Proctor, who showed his usual interest and enthusiasm and was assisted in preparing photographs from which to work by N. E. Nilsson.

Many others aided in one way or another, and if I do not mention them individually I am none the less thankful for their help.

Springfield, Illinois   BENJAMIN P. THOMAS

CONTENTS

LIST OF ILLUSTRATIONS

PORTRAIT *for* POSTERITY

Chapter One

THE ISSUE IS JOINED

I HAVE endured a great deal of ridicule without much malice; and have received a great deal of kindness, not quite free from ridicule," wrote Abraham Lincoln to James Hackett on November 2, 1863. The averment was true, but an understatement. Lincoln was loved and hated, lauded and blamed, as few men have been before or since.

But with Lincoln's death, the clamor of his critics and detractors was stilled in a chorus of praise. Preachers did not fail to note that he was a carpenter's son and that his martyrdom came on Good Friday. Poets, some of whom had mocked, now laid their wreaths on his bier. Abolitionists who cursed him for his caution now claimed him as prophet and martyr of their holy cause. Politicians who distrusted and sought to thwart him now clutched him to their bosoms as an invaluable party asset.

Lincoln, almost overnight, became a hero-myth; and it was inevitable that his earliest biographers should so regard him.

The most important of the earlier biographies—that by Josiah G. Holland—appeared within a year of Lincoln's death. Born of pious parents, and reared in Puritan tradition, Holland was a typical New England moralizer. Edu-

3

cated for medicine, he found himself to be more deft with
pen than scalpel, and as editor of the Springfield *Republican* had attracted many readers with his "healthy maxims"
for the young and the poor in spirit which he wrote under
the pseudonym of Timothy Titcomb. Poetry, essays, and
novels also issued from his pen, and in everything he
wrote there was a sermon. Many persons knew him because
of "some high impulse given when perhaps the will was
faltering, some clear light shed when the path was dark."
His mother grieved that he had not become a preacher,
but he consoled her with the plea that essentially he was
one, commanding from his "lay pulpit" a larger audience
than any clergyman reached. He taught Sunday School and
sang in his church choir; at heart he was an evangelist.
Soon he would be editor of *Scribner's Monthly,* in which
capacity he would continue to purvey moral and intel-
lectual refreshment.

He believed Lincoln was "developed by the providence
of God"; and the life of such a man should point a moral.

Although many sources available to later writers were
still closed to him, he wrote an estimable book. Basing his
earlier chapters on the campaign lives of Lincoln and
using those speeches and documents which were in print,
he obtained additional information from Lincoln's acquaintances. His point of view was frankly partisan and
laudatory. "I have not attempted to disguise or conceal
my own personal partiality for Mr. Lincoln and my thorough sympathy with the political principles to which his
life was devoted," he confessed. "Though unconscious of
any partiality for a party, capable of blinding my vision or
distorting my judgment, I am aware that, at this early day
. . . it is impossible to utter any judgment which will not
have a bearing on the party politics of the time. Thus, the

Josiah G. Holland

only alternative of writing according to personal partialities and personal convictions has been writing without any partialities and without any convictions. I have chosen to be a man, rather than a machine; and if this shall subject me to a charge of writing in the interest of a party, I must take what comes of it." He knew that books like his, "though they satisfy an immediate want, and gather much that would otherwise be forever lost, can hardly hope to be more than tributaries to that better and completer biography which the next, or some succeeding generation will be sure to produce and possess."

Replete with anecdotes and folklore, his book depicted Lincoln as a model youth, rising through sheer merit and the force of high ideals to the highest office his admirers could bestow. Its eulogy was unadulterated; and the sale of more than 100,000 copies proved it to be what the public liked. It set a pattern to which writers for the next quarter-century found it expedient to conform, if their work was to win acclaim.

Other early biographies were in the same vein—*The Life and Public Services of Abraham Lincoln,* by Henry J. Raymond, editor of the New York *Times; The History of Abraham Lincoln, and the Overthrow of American Slavery,* by Isaac N. Arnold; *Six Months at the White House,* by Francis Bicknell Carpenter.

The one discordant note came from a surprising source —William H. Herndon, Lincoln's former law partner. He could not tolerate "finical fools" who sought to smooth out Lincoln's wrinkles. Why did they not write the truth, instead of what they thought the people wanted? A few more years of this and Lincoln would be unrecognizable. Take Arnold, for example. Lincoln often used the word "gal," but this "literary dude" insisted on changing it to "girl." Sometimes "these our nice sweet smelling gentlemen change whole sentences," Herndon complained, "and deaden things."

Herndon was no moralist, like Holland. He had little respect for form. In thought, in politics, sometimes in conduct, he was a nonconformist. Skeptical, opinionated, proud, he resented the condescension of "good" people. From the time Lincoln became a national figure he aspired to be his biographer and had studied him carefully. He prided himself on his clairvoyance, thought he possessed "mud instinct," "dog sagacity." His intuition saw "to the gizzard" of a man, enabled him, so he thought, to analyze his secret thoughts and mental processes. A professed infidel who scorned the dogmas of the church and leaned to pantheism, like most persons when they thought to fathom Lincoln's faith, he saw only what he wanted to see.

To his way of thinking, Lincoln was one of the greatest men that ever lived. He needed no embellishment at the hands of biographers. The world should know him as he really was. "If Mr. Lincoln is destined to fill that exalted station in history or attain that high rank in the estimation of the coming generations which has been predicted for him," he declared, "it is alike just to his memory and the proper legacy of mankind that the whole truth concerning him should be known. If the story of his life is truthfully and courageously told—nothing colored or suppressed; nothing false either written or suggested—the reader will see and feel the presence of the living man. He will, in fact, live with him and be moved to think and act with him. If, on the other hand, the story is colored or the facts in any degree suppressed, the reader will not only be misled, but imposed upon as well. At last the truth will come, and no man need hope to evade it."

At this time Herndon was in the prime of life, with saffron skin, black eyes pouched with "peculiar dark crater circles," and blue-black hair and beard soon to turn grey. Five feet nine inches in height, high cheekboned, thin, angular, erect, he was quick and nervous in actions and temperament. With his tall silk hat and patent leather shoes, he was something of a dandy in his younger years; but with age he had grown careless. His teeth were now tobacco-stained, and a visitor who saw him in his office, clad in bright yellow breeches twice turned up at the bottom, was reminded of "a wind-hardened farmer."

Born in Greene County, Kentucky, December 28, 1818, he had moved to Illinois with his family two years later. Here Archer G. Herndon, his father, farmed for six years, then moved to Springfield where he opened the town's first tavern, the "Indian Queen." Subsequently Archer Herndon served with Lincoln in the state legislature as one of the celebrated "Long Nine," and later became receiver of public moneys at the Springfield land office.

William was educated in private schools and at the age of nineteen enrolled in Illinois College at Jacksonville. Here the faculty and most of the student body were strongly antislavery, and with the murder of Elijah Lovejoy at Alton at the hands of a proslavery mob, the college became a hotbed of abolitionism.

The elder Herndon—violent in his politics as well as his personal friendships and antipathies—was a proslavery Democrat, highly resolved to have no part in the upbringing of a "damned Abolitionist pup." Consequently, he forced William to withdraw from college and come home. But the seed had taken root, and throughout the remainder of his life Herndon was an avowed Abolitionist, far more radical in his thinking than was Lincoln.

Herndon became acquainted with Lincoln before he went to college, and upon his return he came to know him well when he went to work for Joshua Speed and lived with Lincoln over Speed's store; for the rupture with his father was irreparable and from this time forth he was on his own. Herndon worked for Speed until 1842, when he entered the Logan & Lincoln law office as a student. Two years later, upon the dissolution of this partnership, his own partnership and real intimacy with Lincoln began.

Herndon's was a contradictory nature. A good lawyer, he never liked the law. Eventually he came to hate it, and gave it up for farming. A temperance advocate, he frequently fell into intemperance. A nature lover and well-read man—he accumulated an excellent library of literary, philosophical, and scientific works—he was nevertheless a companion of "the wild boys about town." Active in politics, he spoke frequently at rallies, did much of Lincoln's political "leg-work," helped organize the Republican party in Illinois, served as mayor of Springfield, and in 1856 was mentioned—not very seriously—as a candidate for governor.

Springfield people were surprised when Lincoln chose him as a partner; the two men seemed so incompatible. Lincoln was deliberate, easy-going, cautious, and conservative; whereas Herndon was precipitate, hot-tempered, rash, and unpredictable. Although at home with all kinds of people and devoid of social aspiration, Lincoln moved in Springfield's most respectable circles. Herndon's misadventures, on the other hand, had often shocked the staid and straight-laced group.

But Lincoln, weary of the dominance of an older partner, had decided to set up for himself; and in Herndon he thought he saw a promising young man.

The alliance had turned out agreeably. The two men had pulled well in double harness. While Lincoln traveled the circuit Herndon tended to the office business in Springfield and saw to those counties, recently cut off from the circuit, where Lincoln had built up a clientele. Both men had cases in the State Supreme Court although Lincoln took care of the business in the Federal Courts. Herndon was no flunky; both he and Lincoln not only argued cases in court but also shared the drudgery of routine paper work.

There were minor irritations, naturally. Herndon loathed the Lincoln "brats," who romped into the office, scattered papers helter-skelter, upset inkwells and stacks of books, and left the place a shambles. He would have prescribed and taken pleasure in administering a lusty larruping; but the indulgent father seemingly thought nothing of it.

Herndon got along with Lincoln's wife by keeping out of her way. She had disliked him almost from the day they met. Herndon ascribed her animosity to an intended compliment. At a social function he had admired her lithesome grace; but in trying to pay his respects he had used an ill-chosen word. Mary Todd resented comparison with a "serpent"; and her displeasure was abiding and intense.

How Lincoln tolerated such a termagant Herndon could never understand; and he suspected that on more than one occasion he came to the office to seek sanctuary. He conceded Mrs. Lincoln a large measure of credit for her husband's success, not only because she spurred him with her grim ambition, but because what, in Herndon's opinion, must have been an unpleasant home life, drove Lincoln out into the world of politics and business and made him widely known. And Herndon granted that the account was not all on one side. In his periods of moodiness and abstraction Lincoln was probably no darling around the house.

Herndon thought Lincoln should read more widely and had tried to introduce him to good books. But unless they dealt with politics or government or literature, more often than not he provoked Herndon by merely glancing through a page or two and tossing them aside. Philosophy and metaphysics, which Herndon thought so fascinating, Lincoln found too abstruse. He got more profit and entertainment from newspapers, which he would read aloud, a habit which, he explained, enabled him to bring two senses to bear at once, but which irritated Herndon almost beyond endurance.

But while Herndon read, Lincoln thought. Indeed, Herndon believed he must have read less and thought more than any man in America. He was very little influenced by others; he must think things out for himself. And his thought processes, while slow, were "cold, clear, and exact." Herndon often grew restless at Lincoln's slow movements and speeches in court when he was trying to think a proposition through. But time and again he saw him arrive at a right result. He was "pitiless and persistent in pursuit of truth," crushing the "unreal, the inexact, the hollow, and the sham." He took nothing on faith: to believe he must be able to analyze and prove, as Herndon saw him.

The world and its problems weighed on Herndon's tender conscience; but Lincoln often seemed indifferent to them. Herndon tried to convert him to abolitionism, but he would go no farther than to oppose the extension of slavery. Herndon jumped without hesitation into the new-formed Republican party; while Lincoln joined it reluctantly. Herndon believed he had finally brought Lincoln into the antislavery path, and although he never boasted of it—never wished to seem to "blow his own horn"—he was pleased when anyone gave him the credit.

The relation between the two men had been closer than a mere business arrangement. It had something of father and son. It held faithfulness, affection, and respect. With Lincoln it was "Billy" or "William"; with Herndon it was always "Mr. Lincoln." Athough they did not always see eye to eye politically, Lincoln could always depend on Herndon's active support; and more often than not, "Billy" did the necessary menial work the "big bugs" shunned.

In the earlier years Lincoln shared political confidences with Herndon; but later he became more reticent. Lincoln never knew what "Billy" might say in his cups, and as the election of 1860 approached and Republican leaders deemed it expedient to muffle the antislavery drums, Herndon disapproved vocally of "licking the dust." Not only did he lose step, but his precipitancy led him to abuse a prominent Illinois politician whose friendship Lincoln could not afford to lose. So Lincoln ceased to confide; and Herndon was so far outside the inner councils that his partner's nomination seems to have taken him by surprise.

But if something of confidence was lost there was no diminution of affection. On the last day that Lincoln spent in Springfield the two men had a talk. It was brief, but crowded with the memories of sixteen years. For the first time Lincoln referred to Billy's weakness when he asked how many times he had been drunk. Herndon was taken aback. Then Lincoln revealed how others had tried to supplant Herndon in the firm by reason of Billy's inebriety. It was the closest Lincoln ever came to chiding him.

Lincoln asked Herndon if he wanted a government job.

But Herndon had been nauseated by the droves of office-seekers who fawned and demanded and cajoled. He would retain his present position of state bank commissioner and continue with the law.

Lincoln was probably glad. As they parted he looked up at the "Lincoln & Herndon" sign. They would leave it there, and take up where they were leaving off when he returned.

From these sixteen years of intimacy Herndon believed he knew Lincoln better than any living man. Sometimes he thought he knew him better than Lincoln knew himself. Again he was doubtful, as when he wrote: "He never revealed himself entirely to any one man . . . Even those who were with him through long years of hard study and under constantly varying circumstances can hardly say they knew him through and through. I always believed I could read him as thoroughly as any man yet he was so different in many respects from any other man I ever met before or since his time that I cannot say I comprehend him." Nevertheless, if anyone could explain him, Herndon believed he could.

Hardly a month after Lincoln's death, perhaps even earlier, Herndon began to supplement his personal knowledge by gathering additional material about his partner's life. Determined to obtain every scrap of information which would assist in writing a true biography, he visited the Indiana and Illinois localities where the Lincolns had lived, interviewed anyone who could give information, and even advertised for material in the newspapers.

His records now filled three big volumes "bound in excellent heavy leather, spring back, strongly done . . . ," he said describing them, "each the size of Webster's dictionary on legal cap." The originals were in his house and

bound copies were in the bank vault, safe from fire and
rats. If he should die, the record was safe—"written vouch-
ers, evidences of good men and women in Kentucky,
Indiana, Illinois and other places, men and women whom
I know." The work had cost him some $1800; but the
documents were priceless. He did not believe a true biography of Lincoln could be written without them.

He had not been stingy with them. Indeed, he was too
generous. Few Lincoln autographs remained. And there
was no single Lincoln author whose request for help had
been denied. Holland, Arnold, Barrett, Raymond, Carpenter—all were under obligation to him. Yet, in view of
what they were doing to Lincoln, Herndon thought it high
time he bestirred himself.

Holland irritated him no end. The Lincoln he por-
trayed was not the man Herndon knew. If Holland had
known Lincoln as he did, he would never have credited
Newton D. Bateman's story of Lincoln's drawing a New
Testament from his breast, calling it "this rock, on which
I stand," and quoting it against Douglas and other political
opponents, among them the ministers of Springfield who
proposed almost *en masse* to vote against him.

Herndon could not imagine Lincoln talking that way or
asserting that he derived his political opinions from the
teachings of Christ, and that Christ was God. Herndon
knew Bateman; and he suspected that in recounting this
supposed conversation, five years later, "Little Newt" had
let his imagination go. Perhaps he too had been tempted
to give the people what they wanted. Herndon suspected
that somewhere along the line the story had been embellished, and when he tried to draw Bateman out, Bateman told him enough to confirm his suspicions, but swore
him to secrecy. If Lincoln were living, thought Herndon,

he would think that Bateman did him more injustice than the living and the dead combined.

And Holland was probably just as blameworthy. Herndon remembered when Holland came to see him shortly after Lincoln's death. "Holland came into my office," he told Isaac N. Arnold several years later, "and asked me many questions in relation to Mr. Lincoln. I answered all willingly and truthfully. He then asked me—'What about Mr. Lincoln's religion,' and to which I replied—'*The less said the better.*' He then made this expression—'*O never mind, I'll fix that*' with a kind of wink or nod."

No, Herndon didn't have much confidence in Holland.

Imagine Lincoln, an eight-year-old boy, with almost no schooling and probably no ink or pen, writing to a parson to come preach a funeral sermon at his mother's grave! Holland probably got that from Dennis Hanks, whom Herndon suspected of being a notorious liar. Holland exaggerated the amount of reading Lincoln did; he made him too popular with the folk in his home town. But these were errors of detail. Far worse was the mawkish sentimentality of the book.

Yes, Herndon must get to work to counteract this bosh. But how hard it was to begin! He was naturally lazy—he admitted it; always busy, too; and lately there had come financial worries.

If he could only have maintained the pace at which he did start! On December 12, 1865, he delivered a lecture—"An Analysis of the Character of Abraham Lincoln." December 26, he expatiated on the same theme. On January 23, 1866, his subject was "The Patriotism and Statesmanship of Mr. Lincoln." These discourses were well received. Newspapers made note of them and several acquaintances sent commendations. John Hay, who had been one of

Lincoln's private secretaries and was then in France as American secretary of legation, had requested a copy; and even Robert Lincoln "saw nothing . . . at which to take umbrage," although he had read only the first lecture, and that in abstract.

But it was characteristic of Robert to dislike this probing into his father's character. "While it is true that the details of the private life of a public man have always a great interest in the minds of some," he wrote to Herndon, yet in Robert's opinion, "it is after all his works which make him live & the rest is but secondary." "I would not judge a discourse by an abstract of it," he continued, "but more than all, even when I differ with anyone in his views of my father's character etc., unless it were something flagrantly wrong, I would not discuss the subject."

Herndon thought that Robert was not lacking in hauteur.

Indulged by his fond mother and his easygoing father, Robert had turned out to be proud, shy, and sensitive. Educated at Harvard, moving in high social circles by reason of his father's eminence, he preferred not to recall his father's humble beginnings. Never very intimate with his father, he probably never really understood him. Nor did he recognize obligation to aid others to understanding. By what right were people so inquisitive? His father was not public property. He would reveal only what he deemed discreet, and that only to those he knew to be prudent.

A competent lawyer, Robert was destined to be uncommonly successful. Yet he would never seek to capitalize upon his father's fame; and he was resentful when he suspected others of so doing. In his old age, after a career in business and government, he would become almost a recluse, shutting himself up in his spacious homes in

Georgetown or Manchester, Vermont, devoting himself to golf, shunning the limelight, yet sometimes acting privily but no less effectively to see that posterity got what he conceived to be the proper idea of his father.

When Herndon wrote to Robert inquiring if he had any of his father's letters, Robert replied that he had none that would be "of any interest whatsoever" to anyone; he did not leave home until his father became so busy in public affairs that he scarcely had time to write at all, he explained, and with one or two exceptions the letters he had were those enclosing money.

Herndon wondered if Robert was naive. Did he really suppose Herndon meant letters to him personally? Herndon suspected that he understood well enough what he wanted, but took this means of refusing to share the secrets of his father's correspondence.

Herndon's fourth lecture was a long time in preparation. Not until November 16, 1866 was he ready to deliver it, and when the time came, the crowd was small; for Josh Billings, the famous humorist, had spoken in Springfield the night before. But those who did hear Herndon went home puzzled, angry, or pleasurably excited; for on this occasion he gave the world the story of Lincoln and Ann Rutledge, presenting it as the only real romance in Lincoln's life.

If Herndon expected to cause a sensation he was not disappointed. The next mail brought a letter from Isaac N. Arnold, of Chicago, who had been favored with an advance copy. Arnold had known Lincoln as a fellow lawyer as early as 1840, and had been a stanch friend and supporter as a congressman. A cautious, conscientious, scholarly sort of man, his own book had been discreetly sketchy about

Lincoln's personal life. Herndon might have expected him to disapprove the revelation of this early love affair.

"I have just read *hastily, rapidly,* because I could not read *slowly,* your paper," gasped Arnold as he replied. ". . . This is a strange chapter in Mr. Lincoln's history—very strange.—Of absorbing interest—You verify what I have said of Mr. Lincoln, had he lived in the days of Mythology he would have been placed among the Gods. I know nothing of your facts. I think your treatment of them incomparably more 'poetic' than anything in my 'Introduction.' I mean *'poetic'* but if you read the word *pathetic* it will still be true."

He closed on a warning note:

"I have looked to you to give the world a picture of Mr. Lincoln's life. Especially his private life. You are wiser than I have been in taking more time. You do not need the caution, I know, but yet I cannot forbear, saying you are dealing with the fame of the greatest, take him all in all, best man, our country has produced. I know you could not intentionally do him injustice. I shall read the paper again . . ."

Herndon had also sent copies to former residents of New Salem, where the affair supposedly took place, and their replies were gratifying. One thought there was "nothing in it but what was strictly true"; another thought Herndon described the state of Lincoln's mind induced "by the shock of Miss Rutledge['s] death to the letter"; a third liked it "very much" and offered additional information.

Other intimates of Lincoln, who were favored with copies, reacted differently. Joshua Speed, who had be-friended Lincoln when he came to Springfield and had been his closest friend in his earlier Springfield years, avowed that it "is new to me—But so true is my appreciation of Lincoln's character that independent of my knowledge of you I could almost swear to it." But T. Lyle Dickey, a fellow lawyer and political favorite of Lincoln's, until he refused to follow him into the Republican ranks, was cynical. "Thank you for copy of that fancy lecture," he answered. "Romance is not your forte. The few grains of history stirred into that lecture—in a plain narrative would be interesting—but I dont like the garnishments."

Especially interesting were the comments of F. B. Carpenter, whose *Six Months at the White House,* appearing just a few weeks before, had described the author's experiences while he painted Lincoln's portrait. Carpenter had printed part of Herndon's first lecture in his book; and the two men began a friendly correspondence as a result of his writing to Herndon to apologize for using his material without first asking permission. Carpenter admired the "marvelous analytical power" displayed in Herndon's first three lectures; but when he received a copy of the fourth, he was somewhat at a loss to know just how he felt. "I was a good deal *disturbed* by it, I will frankly confess," he wrote. "It seemed to me an intrusion of a sacred *chamber*—a tearing away of the veil which conceals the 'holy of holies.' I could see the reason for this—the necessity the author felt of showing the secret springs of action in Mr. Lincoln's life—feeling as he did, that this unrevealed history was the key to his character.—But it seemed to me that the *fact* of this experience might have been given without treading so far upon ground which all felt intuitively to be sacred.

"You are decidedly a *pre-Raphaelite* in biography—the danger, I should say is that '*pre-Raphaelitism*' may become morbid, and abnormal in your case, as it has frequently done with art-students."

Herndon took this criticism in good part. "I like your style of a man," he said; and proceeded fully to explain his purpose. His passion was for truth; and he would burn up his Lincoln record—*"the finest in the world or ever will be"*—sooner than depart from verity. "The great, keen, shrewd, boring, patient, philosophical, critical and remorseless world will find out all things, and bring them to light, and the question is now: who shall do that—a man's friends or his enemies? Shall it be done *now* or left for the future world to wrangle over, and yet forever debate . . . The very existence of Christ is denied because he had no good truthful biographers . . . I want, and intend, to have the generous broad and deep sympathies of the universal heart for good and noble Abraham . . . My philosophy is to sink a counter nail and blow up my enemies—Lincoln's future traducers . . ."

Carpenter was convinced. "I think you are right. The *truth* is what the world wants," he agreed. "Lincoln's love for Ann Rutledge may yet loom up in history like Dante's for Beatrice, or Petrarch's for Laura."

Meantime Arnold had read the lecture more carefully. Now he was skeptical, and warned Herndon to beware of accepting gossip as fact. This roused Herndon's ire. He was satisfied that Arnold would properly use and interpret the material he had, and he hoped Arnold would have the same faith in him. "I do not deal in gossip, and will not," he declared; but he would tell truthfully and heroically everything that should be told to the end that "all doubts will die forever or rather they never will exist."

By this time the Ann Rutledge story had attracted the attention of the press. Herndon's friend Leonard Swett reported a great deal of talk about it in New England; and in New York, Carpenter heard Herndon both defended and abused.

Herndon stood up well under the flurry, parrying the lighter thrusts, rolling with the punches; but he must have been severely shaken by a long, looping wallop landed by Grant Goodrich. Herndon had written to him for information about a law case which Lincoln handled in Chicago. Goodrich, a Chicago lawyer and former associate of Lincoln's, gave the facts desired; then, with little warning, he swung from his heels.

"In my opinion," he wrote, "you are the last man who ought to attempt to write a life of Abraham Lincoln— Your long and intimate association with him, unfits you for the task. No one holding the intimate relations to another which you did to him ever has succeeded. There may be exceptions, but I cannot now remember one . . . In intimate association, we fix upon some characteristic or peculiarity, & fail to catch other lineaments. We can only regard them as the kind friend, amusing companion, & generous mind. In the distance we see the bold outline of the mountain; its summits wrapped in sunshine, or swathed in cloud. When we approach it, we catch a view of the deep, it may be dark gorges, the rugged cliffs, the lean rocks, and distorted outlines. So in the characters of our dearest friends. See how Boswell, with all his literary abilities failed in his Life of Johnson. No blow so severe was ever struck at Johnson. Think of these things.

"If I am to judge of what your production will be by the publication of a portion of your Salem lectures, I am more solicitous still. I fear you did not realize what an injury and injustice you did to the memory of your dear friend, & mortification you caused his friends, but especially his widow and children. Ask yourself, if he was living, whether he would not have revolted at the uncovering to the public gaze that drama of his life? And shall his friends exhibit what we know he would have preserved in sacred privacy. If the facts were truly stated, I should as soon think of exposing his dead body, uncoffined, to the vulgar gaze of the public eye. It should never have been dug up from the grave, where time had buried it.

"Besides, your style is not well adapted to such an undertaking. The want of practice is palpable. Your style is purely legal, such an one as is acquired by drawing legal documents and pleadings, and is decidedly different from one formed by familiarity with the best writers. It is rugged, abounding in adjectives and explications—full of climaxes and hard dry words. It reads as if it had been jerked out, word by word—it gives one the sense you have in riding in a lumber wagon over a frozen road—or the noise made in machinery when a cog is broken.

"Now, my friend, I have spoken plainly, but sincerely. I may do you injustice, but it is not intentional. I may lose your friendship by it, but I have only done what I would wish one to do to me under the same circumstances. And I have observed, in myself and others, that the very points in which strength is supposed, are the very points of weakness."

William H. Herndon was never a man to duck a punch or take one without retaliating. His counterblow was short, sharp, and devastating. "Mr. Goodrich, Sir," he wrote. "I thank you for the first part of your letter giving me an account of the patent case which Mr. Lincoln 'tended to. I say I thank you for it. As to the second part of your letter, I guess I shall have to treat you as Lincoln always did treat you, as an exceedingly weak-headed brother. The more he kicked you, the closer you clung to him. Do you remember? Analyze yourself."

Herndon was still smarting when, from the crags of far-off Scotland, came another billet-doux. He had written to the Reverend James Smith for information about Lincoln's religious beliefs. Smith had been pastor of the First Presbyterian Church in Springfield, where the Lincolns rented a pew, and Lincoln, after becoming president, had appointed the reverend gentleman United States consul at Dundee. There Smith had read Herndon's Ann Rutledge lecture; and when Herndon's letter came he was quick to reply. The lecture had evoked both his indignation and sorrow, and he did not choose, he said, to make any man who would do a former partner such a turn, his medium of communication. Herndon had placed the whole Lincoln family, both the dead and the living, in "a most unenviable light before the public." If Lincoln said and felt as Herndon said he did at the death of Ann Rutledge, he was not an honest man, for he vowed faith, love, and affection for his wife when, according to Herndon, he had no love or affection to bestow. Was not Mrs. Lincoln's grief at her husband's death sufficiently poignant without this malicious attack? And Herndon had not only wounded her; he had put "a public brand" upon the children.

Smith went on to assert that during his pastorate he had the "high honor" to place before Mr. Lincoln arguments supporting the divine authority of the Scriptures together with the counterarguments of infidels. Lincoln examined the contentions of both sides as a lawyer would, and his conclusion was that the argument in favor of divine authority and inspiration was unanswerable.

Herndon had done Lincoln a greater disservice than

John Wilkes Booth, the embattled divine asserted. Booth unwittingly sent him "to glory, honor, and immortality, but his false friend has attempted to send him down to posterity with infamy branded on his forehead, as a man who notwithstanding all he did and all he suffered for his Country's good was destitute of those feelings and affections without which there can be no excellency of character."

Herndon had foreseen trouble from "blind bat-eyed hero worshippers, timid souled creatures, orthodox theologians, and other frigid souled men who cluster around form and color—never touching substance"; but two such blasts must have been more even than he counted on.

Some time previous to this he had been warned to remember that no man is great to his "valet de chambre." This counsel came from Leonard Swett, an Eighth Circuit lawyer who had eaten, slept, and hatched political stratagems with Lincoln, taken a prominent part in his nomination, and who knew him as well as Herndon did. Swett was now living in Chicago; but he corresponded regularly with Herndon and knew of the latter's plans.

Swett was doubtful about the wisdom of Herndon's forthrightness. There was only one true history in the world, he pointed out—the Bible. And look what happened to its heroes. Because all the facts about "those old worthies" were told, they appear as bad men when contrasted with other historical characters. "If the history of King David had been written by an ordinary historian, the affair of Uriah would at most have been a quashed indictment with a denial of all the substantial facts." Swett wanted Herndon's history to be true but not too "rigid." There was a skeleton in every house. "The trail of the serpent touches all characters." Lincoln's character would bear the closest scrutiny; but even with him, the weaknesses should not be overplayed to the detriment of the graces and virtues. Dig to the bottom, adjured Swett, but be judicious. (But if he should find what that skeleton was with Lincoln, what gave him that peculiar melancholy, he should by all means let Swett in on the secret!)

Whether because of these admonitions and criticisms, or for other reasons, Herndon gave no more lectures. And while he continued to collect material, he seemed unable to begin his book. "I need kicking, scolding, cussing, etc.," he admitted, "in order to make me trot along briskly with head up and tail up, gaily snorting along the great road of life."

One day his lethargy was broken, however, when a big, bluff man with long, dark curly hair and drooping walrus mustache came striding into his office. It was Ward Hill Lamon, a former Danville attorney, who had been one of Lincoln's closest friends on the circuit and whom Herndon himself knew well. Lamon was now practicing law in Washington; and he came with a proposition to buy Herndon's manuscripts.

Herndon was startled. He had never considered parting with them. But he thought the matter over after Lamon left and later wrote to him explaining what he had. He could not believe that Lamon realized the value of his collection. "Ward, there is fame in this," he wrote, "there is money, too, my good friend."

He could not make up his mind. "I may sell, may finish the life myself," he confided to his friend, Charles Hart.

But Lamon kept worrying him and so did his debts. Lamon was financially embarrassed too, and apparently despairing of being able to buy, he seems to have suggested a joint venture. But Herndon would have none of that. "I should prefer to sell out horse, foot, etc., than to do otherwise," he replied. "I want money; still if you have no money, you can have [them] without money on time making me safe, etc., and paying down some few dimes, so that I can pay my debts."

On March 17, 1869, after consulting friends, Herndon offered to take $4,000 for the "use" of his material—$2,000 down and the balance in "one and two years," with interest at ten per cent. But Lamon must make up his mind quickly, for Isaac N. Arnold and "a biographer in Boston" were also making overtures. Lamon decided to risk it and persuaded two Springfield friends—David Littler and Milton Hay—to endorse his note to Herndon for $2,000, payable in two years with interest at ten per cent. There is doubt as to some of the terms agreed upon, but a contract was evidently signed. To obtain his money, Herndon discounted the note at the First National Bank of Springfield; and on December 2, 1871, the note being overdue, Stephen T. Logan, Lamon's father-in-law and Lincoln's second law partner, paid the note and sent it to Lamon, canceled, as a Christmas gift.

This $2,000 seems to have been all Herndon received; and Lamon never paid a penny of it. On the other hand, Herndon vexed Lamon when he kept the original manuscripts and sent him only the copies.

Thus, temporarily at least, Herndon stepped aside. But if he thought this marked his exit from the field of Lincoln controversy, he was sore deceived. The strife soon to rage would make all that had gone before seem tame and trivial, and as long as Herndon lived he was destined to be in the thick of it.

For already in the Lincoln field there were rival schools of thought.

Here, four years after Lincoln's death, it was as though two groups of artists had clustered about an easel, eager to paint a portrait for posterity. But they differed violently and volubly in concept. On the one hand were a few realists who would throw the highlights into bold relief against the shadows. Opposed were the far more numerous idealists who thought the features should be softened with refracted light—the kind peculiar to a halo. Already they vied, nudging each other away from the canvas, each side seeking to etch out the other's work or to overlay it with their own peculiar touches. At times the nudges would become shoves; and instead of merely flicking blobs of paint, the rivals would throw pigment, brush, and palette at each other.

Chapter Two

LAMON BREAKS THE SEALS

HAD Herndon really possessed the intuitive insight into human character on which he prided himself, he might have had some doubts of Lamon's competence; for the latter's bent had not been literary. A great hulk of a man, six feet two inches tall, who once drew the appellation "Jumbo" from a brazen woman at a race track, Lamon was born near Winchester, Virginia, January 6, 1828; at nineteen he moved to Danville, in Vermilion County, Illinois, and was admitted to the bar two years later. In 1852 he and Lincoln formed a partnership which, while restricted to practice in Vermilion County, seems to have been a bona fide partnership none the less, and which continued until 1857, when Lamon became prosecuting attorney.

Although competent in the law, Lamon attained greater prominence as a local sportsman and strong man. He was marshal of the first Vermilion County Fair, at which he had the only race horse on the grounds, a trotter, which he raced under saddle against time. The records of this gala event also show that he paid a fee for the privilege of exhibiting a trick monkey in a booth.

A tough and ready fighter in politics, in court, or in

a barroom brawl, when a city government was established in Danville, in 1858, he had the doubtful honor of seeing his name appear as the first entry on the police docket when he and "Chickamauga Jim" Kilpatrick, the editor of the Danville *Republican,* were booked for assault and paid fines. His office was conveniently located over a saloon, the remainder of the second floor of the building being occupied by a house of assignation.

Lamon worked assiduously for Lincoln's nomination and election to the presidency, went with him to Washington, and there constituted himself as his personal bodyguard. Armed to the teeth, he followed Lincoln about with a dog-like devotion, ever fearful of plots to take his life.

Despite Lamon's intemperance and braggadocio, Lincoln had a genuine fondness for him and liked to hear him spin his yarns and sing his songs. Trusting him implicitly, Lincoln made him Marshal of the District of Columbia, in which position he aroused animosity by his bluster and bravado and his rigorous enforcement of the fugitive slave laws. His zealous performance of this duty accorded with Lincoln's policy of appeasement to the border slave states and Lamon bore with patience, as a duty to his chief, the odium the policy aroused.

Early in the war Lamon succumbed to military ambitions. Appointed a colonel on the staff of Governor Richard Yates of Illinois in what has been called "a tribute of one drinker to another," he coveted the rank of brigadier general; and in October, 1861, he went West and ordered two regiments—"Lamon's Brigade"—to be sent to the Potomac theater. Assuming by reason of Lamon's intimacy with Lincoln that he had full authority to issue such an order, the commanding officers entrained the troops, only to find upon arrival at their destination that Lamon had

Ward Hill Lamon

no authority whatever. The troops were not needed in Virginia and were sent back to the West, the cost of the excursion being some $30,000. The House Committee on Government Contracts investigated and made a scathing report; and Senator James W. Grimes exposed the escapade in a blistering Senate speech. With that strange obtuseness which he sometimes exhibited, Lincoln took no notice of the incident, and Grimes, indignant at toleration of such turpitude, became extremely cool toward Lincoln, an attitude which the preoccupied president was never able to comprehend.

After Lincoln's death, Lamon resigned as marshal of the District and, after trying unsuccessfully to obtain the governorship of Idaho Territory and then that of Colorado Territory, he re-entered the practice of law, sharing a Washington office with Charles E. Hovey and Judge Jeremiah S. Black, the latter having served as attorney general and secretary of state under President James Buchanan. Here Lamon became a close friend of able Chauncey F. Black, the judge's son. Soon the two men, one a Democrat, the other a Republican, both of whom had inside information on the personalities and politics of the time, resolved to collaborate on what was to be the true life of Lincoln. Knowing that Herndon had a mine of material, Lamon undertook to get it.

Having acquired this material for $2,000, Lamon then sold Black a half-interest for $1,500, Judge Black providing the money. Black and Lamon then executed a contract whereby both would gather additional material and each would have an equal interest in the copyright and profits. Lamon was to be allowed to suppress names and facts "found in the documents furnished by him" whenever he was bound to do so by promises previously made. Other facts and names were to be used judiciously "to the end that the interest and value of the book shall be increased"; and in case of differences of opinion regarding insertions or omissions, the matter was to be submitted to Jeremiah S. Black and David Davis, former Eighth Circuit judge now serving on the United States Supreme Court, whose decision should be final. Chauncey Black was to do the writing; but since resentment would certainly be aroused by a Democrat's presuming to invade the Republican domain of Lincoln authorship—especially a Democrat with close connections with the odoriferous Buchanan regime—, Lamon was to appear as sole author of the book.

Black and Lamon went to work with vim, but soon encountered difficulties. Looking through Herndon's manuscripts, Lamon noted that they were not originals, but copies, and asked that the originals be sent on at once. The evidence was contradictory on some points and Herndon should advise him what witnesses he could trust and which were unreliable. Some of Herndon's notes were fragmentary, might be intelligible to Herndon, but needed amplification before anyone else could use them. Herndon had told him he was bound not to reveal the names of some of his informants and had bound Lamon to respect his pledges. To whom had he made such promises? "I want to possess myself of your *mind* in regard to Lincoln," Lamon wrote, "your theories respecting disputed points and facts, and your plan or scheme of life, and the influence of particular incidents on his subsequent character." There was contradictory evidence about Lincoln's religion; and the implications about his birth and that of his mother were startling! Was Lincoln a bastard? Was his mother?

Herndon never needed urging to expatiate on Lincoln.

His letters became voluminous. When he first encountered statements about Lincoln's illegitimacy he had dismissed them as lies, but "on further investigation, I now and have for many years believed him the son of Enloe," he asserted. Someone had told Herndon that Thomas Lincoln lost his procreative powers as a result of a case of mumps; and Herndon thought the story was confirmed by the fact that Thomas' second wife, Sarah Bush Lincoln, although prolific by her first husband, had never borne a child to Thomas. Just when Lincoln's father fell afoul of this mischance, Herndon had not been able to discover, but he had reason to believe he never had a child of his own. Abraham Enloe, a Kentucky neighbor of the Lincolns, tall, lank, cadaverous, was the very prototype of Abraham Lincoln, while Abraham's putative father was his physical opposite. Then there was the supposed fight in which Thomas Lincoln allegedly marked Enloe for life by biting a generous chunk off the end of his nose. Some witnesses averred that when Thomas Lincoln took his family away from Kentucky, shortly after this, it was to remove his wife from bad influences. Herndon still had some doubts of the authenticity of the story. *"The evidence is not conclusive,"* he warned, "but men have been hung on less evidence."

-As to Lincoln's mother, Nancy Hanks, he had no doubts. One day, about 1852, as he and Lincoln were driving to court in Petersburg, Lincoln himself had confided that she was born out of wedlock and that the whole Hanks clan, to quote Herndon, was *"lascivious, lecherous, not to be trusted."*

As for religion, Lincoln had told him "a thousand times" that he did not believe in miracles, or that the Bible was inspired, or that Jesus was the son of God. John T. Stuart, Lincoln's first law partner, James H. Matheny, the Spring-

field politician who was Lincoln's close friend, and Joshua
F. Speed would tell Lamon the same thing, except that
they would "make it blacker than I remember it." "On Mr.
Lincoln's Religion—his religious views be bold," Herndon
counseled. "Tell the truth—that Mr. Lincoln was an infidel
—a Deist . . . that sometimes in his fits of melancholy he
was an atheist . . . I know whereof I speak and so do you."

Lamon could quote Herndon personally as much as he
wished, but he had best not use other persons as references without their permission. Some of Herndon's informants had asked that their names be withheld, just
which ones he could not recall; but he knew enough about
human nature to be sure that "timids, cowards, policy men,
squeamish women, gray hard youths, fools and asses would
turn on me if they could make a dollar out of it or dodge
a consequence of irritating circumstances, and how could
I prove that I made no promise?"

If Herndon were writing the book, he would show Lincoln's *"origin and end* sharply contrasted," Lincoln the
penniless, uneducated boy, rising through sheer persist-
ence and honesty to the country's highest office. Then he
would "applaud this democracy" which made such progress possible, showing that such a thing could never happen in Europe and holding forth these things "to the young
in this world for all coming time as stimulants, as living
hopes urging them to a life of integrity, faith, and hope.
This all seems good to me; and whether you know it or
not, Lincoln's life was a grand life, knowing what I do
of him."

Black already had the same idea. "It is our duty to show
the world the Majesty and beauty of his character, as it
grew by itself and unassisted, out of this unpromising soil,"
he wrote to Lamon. "We must point mankind to the dia-

mond glowing on the dunghill and then to the same re-
splendent jewel in the future setting of great success and
brilliant achievements." If this were not done, the life
would not be that of Lincoln, but a "Sunday School edition—expurgated and abridged for little folks"; and Lincoln would emerge as merely a "prissy old Western fellow"
whom luck made president and a murderous fool gave renown.

As for Herndon, Black did not hesitate to say that without him no true life of Lincoln ever could be written.
Lamon should adopt any means to keep him "in remem-
brance of us—preserve the present flow of his thoughts in
our behalf, and induce him to keep his pen to paper as
much as possible." Black differed with Herndon only on
one point. Perhaps he welcomed anything sensational. In
any event, he did not share Herndon's doubt about the
conclusiveness of the evidence regarding Lincoln's illegitimacy. To him the proof was "absolutely overwhelming." But it was all the more creditable to Lincoln that "he
never hid his face like a craven, but steadily walked straight
forward and upward from the condition of his birth, until
he trod the earth a conqueror . . . Nor was he the first
bastard that did the like . . . If Tom *Linkhorn* could by
any possibility have got a child . . . it would have been
no child like this one . . . Nancy Hanks did the *world* a
great favor by receiving the embrace of somebody who
was not Tom Lincoln."

If Herndon was a pre-Raphaelite, Black was a surrealist!

On March 9, 1870, Lamon confided that some one else
was working on the book, when he sent Herndon the foregoing letter from his "literary editor," enclosed with a letter from himself. Lamon could not bring himself to Black's
enthusiastic view of Nancy Lincoln's alleged peccadillo. "I

am inclined to think like you that it *is not conclusive*," he wrote. And even if it were, and Nancy did the world "so great a favor by receiving the embraces of some body other than her husband, . . . that theory might do well enough in a private conversation . . . but would look damned ugly in print." Besides, there was one flaw in the reasoning. Could Herndon subscribe to the idea "that the Lincoln stock could be improved by mixing in the Enloe pasturage?"

As time passed, Black found that he must do all the work, for Lamon gradually withdrew and confined his activities to whetting the curiosity of his acquaintances with broad hints about the sensational findings he was about to reveal. Hitherto Black and Herndon had communicated only through Lamon; now they began to correspond directly. On February 27, 1871, Black wrote to Herndon: "Col. Lamon's first volume approaches the end and will soon be ready for the press . . . As we approach the close your lectures and letters become the most valuable and important material we have and I have been giving them a most thorough study. They impress me very deeply. You doubtless guess what my politics are, but I do devoutly honor a bold man of decided convictions. I believe religiously that *you* gave Lincoln his anti-slavery mind, that *you* made him President, and that *you* are chiefly responsible for his merits and demerits of which as a *man* he had many of the former, and as an administrator a few of the latter.

"Please tell me one thing," he continued. "I long to know your opinion about it. Was not Lincoln's inordinate love of the lascivious, of smut, something nearly akin to lunacy? Didn't he love it for its own sake, when there was neither wit nor humor in it? Was he not a man of strong erotic passions, which conscience prevented him from indulging physically, and which therefore revelled in the creations of a diseased imagination? I have studied him as I shall never study another human character, and this is the only question which remains in doubt."

But Herndon had stopped writing. Recently he had given up the law, which he always hated, and had moved to a farm north of Springfield, where he was engrossed in pastoral pursuits. The book was almost ready for submission to a publisher; only a few testimonials and other items, which Herndon had undertaken to procure, were lacking. Nor had he forwarded a picture of himself, as he had halfway promised. On April 27, 1871, Lamon wrote to him from New York, where he had gone to consult Black: "What is the matter? Are you away, sick, drunk or demoralized?"

More than four months later the book was still unfinished; nor had Herndon sent the picture. "I want your photograph," demanded Lamon. "I want it at once . . . I must have it. I can't do without it and I don't intend to do without it, if it costs me a trip to Illinois and a race with Blood hounds to chace [sic] you down and then carry you to town in these strong arms of mine, and hold you until we can get your darned old phiz in type . . . I start tonight for Boston with the manuscript."

Tentative negotiations with the publishing house of James R. Osgood & Company had begun some months before, Mr. Osgood himself having become interested in the work. The house was old, respected, and reliable, having formerly done business under the name of Ticknor and Fields. The *North American Review* and *The Atlantic Monthly* were published under its auspices. Despite the sensational character of the book, the publishers, up to this point, seem to have had no misgivings about it. On September 20, 1871, soon after Lamon arrived in Boston, a contract was signed whereby the copyright was turned over to Osgood & Company for $5,000, with $2,000 payable in advance and the balance upon delivery of the manuscript. The authors were to receive a royalty of one dollar per copy and the publishers were granted an option on the second volume. The same day the contract was signed, Lamon receipted for $2,000 and assigned a half interest in the contract to Black.

During the autumn of 1871 all the manuscript except the last chapter, the twenty-first, went forward to the publishers and was set in type, proof sheets being sent to Black as they were run. John Spencer Clark was in immediate charge for the publishers. As the proof sheets came to him, he noted "a lack of appreciation of the finer qualities of Mr. Lincoln's nature," and a disposition to overemphasize the coarser aspects of pioneer life; but there was nothing to which he could take positive exception until the chapter on the Kansas struggle came through. This was in a tone to make a good Republican see red. It simply could not be printed as written. Clark protested to Lamon that the account was not only untrue, "but was wholly inconsistent with Mr. Lincoln's position on the Kansas question." A conference was called with Black and Lamon, and after considerable argument in which Lamon sided with Clark, Black reluctantly agreed to change the text.

By this time Clark suspected Black's good faith, and when the final chapter, the twenty-first, was turned over, his worst suspicions seemed justified. This chapter covered the period from Lincoln's election to his inauguration, the crucial last months of Buchanan's regime; and as we now know, it was based primarily on notes prepared by Bu-

chanan himself and given to Judge Black. To Clark it
seemed that justice to Lincoln was completely sacrificed in
an effort to defend the policy of the Buchanan administration.

Jesse W. Fell, the Bloomington lawyer who had persuaded Lincoln to write an autobiography for campaign
purposes and had been instrumental in the backstage ma-
neuverings incident to his nomination, had been allowed
to read the manuscript; and Fell had similar misgivings.
On February 19, 1872, he wrote to Lamon, pleading with
him to take the chapter out. At first he had thought it
could be modified so as to make it "acceptable to the country and to the mass of that great historic party which placed
Mr. Lincoln in power"; but reflection had convinced him
that its whole drift and tenor was wrong. "I don't know
what spirit could have taken possession of you when you
wrote it, but if Stephens of Georgia had written it, it could
not have been in a manner more acceptable to the Southern mind. *By all manner of means take the whole thing
completely out,"* he adjured. "That it is a masterpiece of
composition so far from being a reason for not doing this,
is one of the strongest reasons why it should be done. It is
one of the worst possible indictments ever penned against
the party that placed Mr. Lincoln in authority and you
may imagine the savage ferocity with which the volume
will be criticised all over the world."

Convinced by this appeal to party fealty, Lamon instructed Osgood & Company to omit the chapter; and his
letter crossed one from them in the mail. They pointed out
that the chapter depicted the Republican Party of 1861,
with Lincoln at its head, as merely a group of "outs" want-
ing "in," supported by a few fanatics and a body of "cajoled" followers; and that the author argued that the party

should have compromised itself out of existence rather than threaten the country with division. "Already the impression has got abroad that the son of Mr. Black has had charge of the preparation of your MS. and if it should appear in your pages that in the discussion of national questions involved, or that in the comments on the acts of prominent men the peculiar views of Mr. Black are put forward, we are sure that exceptions would be taken to the work by the great body of the people of the North, to whom we must look as the principal purchasers of it; and their exceptions would not lie against this chapter alone. If they found in it evidences of a strong political bias against the principles of the party with which Mr. Lincoln was identified they would not be slow to connect this motif with the presentation of certain unattractive phases of Mr. Lincoln's life in the pages of the work as an adroit attempt to drag Mr. Lincoln down . . . and if the work offers any foundation for such criticism, its failure as a commercial success . . . can be safely predicted."

On March 2, Osgood wrote to Black, "As you will no doubt have learned from Mr. Lamon before this, he has decided to omit the last chapter from his book. I feel sure this will be for the good of the book and I think mature reflection will lead you to the same conclusion."

But it did not. Lamon had deliberately violated the contract in permitting this change to be made without Black's consent. Black was so enraged that he offered to sell his interest in the book; but his price of $25,000 did not appear to be a bargain rate. As a last resort Black threatened to sue Osgood & Company, and in informing Lamon of his intention asked if he preferred to be joint-plaintiff or joint-defendant. But this was mostly bluff. A suit would have revealed that the book was ghostwritten and that the ghost had Democratic antecedents; and any such revelation would have been ruinous to sales. In effect, Black's hands were tied; and he was forced to content himself with a castigation of the publishers and a curt note to Lamon advising that "You will hear from me next through my counsel." Judge Black also warned Lamon by telegraph: "Believe me, you are acting unwisely, unjustly, and illegally. Do not shipwreck the craft. This suit will be immediately commenced." But like the threatened suit against the publishers, this one also languished.

Lamon's manuscript contained other matter objectionable to the Lincoln inner circle. John Hay read it in part and thought "nothing heretofore printed can compare with it in interest, and from the nature of the case all subsequent writers will have to come to you for a large class of facts relating to the early life of Lincoln and the circumstances in which he, in common with all the children of pioneer families grew up." But he wondered if Lamon had thought about the criticism he would evoke by telling so much about the intimate, private life of Lincoln's forebears. He doubted if Lamon's sources of information were altogether trustworthy and thought this portion could be modified to advantage. The passages about Mrs. Lincoln added little and would offend many. He had not seen the chapter on Lincoln's religion, "but from what I have heard intimated, I doubt if the old settlers in Sangamon and Menard have quite appreciated the facts of the case—and I think it safer to follow Lincoln's own words in his maturity than the reports and rumors of what he may have said in his youth."

When Lamon seemed disposed to disregard this advice, Hay apparently induced others of Lamon's friends to intercede, for Lawrence Weldon wrote to Lamon, *"In haste.*

Have just re'd a letter from Hay that Hill Lamon will probably publish in his book that Lincoln was a bastard"— "This seems to me to be simply awful," Hay had declared. "Can't you stop him? For the grave of the dead and the crime of the living prevent it if possible. Its effects will be most disastrous and men occupying intimate relations to Hill will be held more or less responsible."

The last sentence had especial applicability to David Davis, former judge of the Eighth Circuit who was now a member of the United States Supreme Court by reason of appointment by Lincoln. At this time Davis was a candidate for the presidential nomination on the Liberal Republican ticket. He was looked upon as the "heir to the Lincoln tradition" and his friends feared that since he was an influential friend of Lamon's, it would be assumed that he concurred in anything Lamon might say. Endorsement of such statements as Lamon proposed to publish about the Republican idol would be equivalent to political suicide; and it was imperative to purify the manuscript for Davis' sake as well as Lincoln's. So when persuasion failed, Davis and his friends resorted to heroic measures.

Horace White, then editor of the Chicago *Tribune,* recalled many years later, that Swett came into his office late one day and told him that he and Davis had just had a session with Lamon. True or false, they told Lamon, the story of Lincoln's illegitimacy must come out; and when he proved stubborn they got him into a room, locked the door, and told him he would stay there forever before they would permit such slander to appear in print. "They kept him there nearly a whole day," White recalled, "& finally they extorted a promise from [him] that he would take it out. He did take it out but I believe that there was something left in by inadvertence which directed public attention to something mysterious in connection with Lincoln's parentage."

On July 3, 1873, Orville H. Browning had breakfast with Davis in Springfield—their first meeting after the book appeared. A former professional associate of Lincoln's, a Republican Senator during his administration with entree to the White House, the aristocratic, proper, and somewhat pompous Browning had served for a time as Secretary of the Interior under Andrew Johnson, but had now resumed his law practice in Quincy, Illinois. Questioned by Davis about his opinion of Lamon's book, Browning said he deplored some of its statements, whereupon Davis told him that "the first chapter of the book, as originally prepared was much more objectionable than anything it now contained, that it contained indubitable evidence of Lincoln's illegitimacy, and that it had cost him, Davis, over three hundred dollars to have it suppressed." Evidently Lamon had given in only on condition that Davis defray the expense of resetting the type. And he must have been surpassing firm; for the penurious Davis would have parted with three hundred dollars only under pressure of a great necessity.

Chauncey Black's own version of what happened to the book was given in a letter to Herndon dated August 18, 1873. "A large mass of very valuable matter was excluded by the treachery of the publishers and the timidity of Lamon," he complained. "The last chapter giving the startling *secret* history of the closing months of Mr. Buchanan's Administration, drawn from papers in the handwriting of Stanton, Buchanan, my Father, Gen'l Scott and others was suppressed wholly, and also a most precious and graphically written diary by Donn Piatt, which covers the sayings, doings and surroundings of Mr. Lincoln between the election and the inauguration. Many of the chapters were shamefully mutilated and the most creditable as well as the most interesting parts ruthlessly struck out. In some instances they contented themselves with merely mutilating or corrupting the text—In others they blotted it out altogether, and in others still, committed the intolerable outrage of intermingling their own base hog-wash with my honest narrative."

The book was published in late May, 1872, and had Black finished the projected second volume before publishing this one, and gone on to place the "jewel" in the "setting of great success and brilliant achievement," he might have muted the outcry which this volume, appearing by itself, aroused. For with his idea of contrasting Lincoln's earlier and later life, he overdid the "dunghill" thesis. Appearing by itself, this volume was rather heady stuff, especially for a public that had become accustomed to an unvaried diet of eulogy. Even to present-day readers some of its passages have an unpleasant tang. To Mid-Victorian idealists, it reeked.

Characterizations like "subtle," "secretive," "ungrateful," "selfish," "cold," "unsocial," "impassive," "neither a good hater nor a fond friend," were at shocking variance with contemporary ideology; and certain incidents and facts were treated with what amounted almost to a genius for putting them in the worst possible light. For example, after adverting to the strange fact that Lincoln's mother, Nancy Hanks, bore the maiden name of her mother, Lucy Hanks, who "became" the wife of Henry Sparrow, the author went on to quote Dennis Hanks' explanation that her real name was Sparrow, but she was called Hanks because of her resemblance to the Hanks side of the family— she was "deep in stalk" of the Hankses. Having cited Dennis Hanks' testimony, the author then proceeded to disparage it by opining that Dennis was "woefully weak on cross-examination."

Even stronger was the innuendo regarding Lincoln's own paternity. The Enloe theory was omitted; but even as revised, the book stopped just short of calling Lincoln illegitimate. After conceding that Kentucky neighbors were agreed that Thomas and Nancy Lincoln were legally married, the author pointed out that despite diligent search their marriage records had never been found, although the documents of Thomas Lincoln's second marriage, to Sarah Bush Johnston, were easily discovered, just where the law required them to be.

Farther on the author declared, "The lives of his father and mother and the history and character of the family before their settlement in Indiana were topics upon which Mr. Lincoln never spoke but with great reluctance and significant reserve. In his family Bible he kept a register of births, marriages, and deaths, everything being carefully made in his own handwriting. It contains the date of his sister's birth and his own; of the marriage and death of his sister; of the death of his mother; and of the birth and death of Thomas Lincoln. The rest of the record is almost wholly devoted to the Johnstons and their numerous descendants and connections. It has not a word about the Hankses or the Sparrows. It shows the marriage of Sally Bush, first with Daniel Johnston, and then with Thomas Lincoln; but it is entirely silent as to the marriage of his own mother. It does not even give the date of her birth, but barely recognizes her existence and demise, to make the vacancy which was speedily filled by Sarah Johnston."

From Herndon's material, Lamon depicted a Lincoln much less saintly than the one in Holland's book. Lamon,

or rather Black, quoted Sarah Johnston to the effect that
the Bible was not included among the books that Lincoln
read in his youth, and he cited certain early companions
as witnesses that Lincoln's interest in the exhortations
of the pioneer preachers, which Holland had depicted
as an indication of budding piety, was inspired more by
a desire to mimic than by appreciation of their homi-
lectics. According to Black, Lincoln derived almost a sa-
distic enjoyment from biting satire, as exemplified in his
ridicule of the bulbous nose of Andrew Crawford, an Indiana neighbor, and his authorship of the "Chronicles of
Reuben," a rollicking tale of a mix-up of brides following
the double wedding of two brothers—an incident in which
young Abe had been an impelling participant.

Upon a rather flimsy framework of known facts about
Lincoln's New Salem life, the earlier biographers had
reared a paragon of virtue and chivalry. Holland described
Lincoln's walking several miles to and from the store,
where he was a clerk, to rectify mistakes in weight and
change. He whipped a braggart who swore in the presence
of ladies, dissuaded his companions from their more brutal
pranks, was ever what the good young man should be.
"Miserably poor," without an influence "which did not
tend rather to drag him down than to lift him up," he was
ever engaged "in making the best of bad conditions and
untoward circumstances, and in meeting and mastering
emergencies." Ever studious, he became a lover of Shakespeare and Burns; and while not a professed Christian, he
had deep religious faith.

Covering this period in great detail, Black gave it a less
idyllic treatment. The Lincoln that Holland depicted
seemed too benign for a rugged community like New Salem; but Black made him at home in it. He recognized his

"just and humane temper," his championship of the weak and unfortunate, and the driving urge for knowledge which made him waylay every resident or visitor who could "explain something which he did not understand." But he also had Lincoln taking his dram with the boys, selling liquor at his store, and actively participating in the rough and boisterous sports. According to Lamon, New Salem's was not a pious atmosphere; and Lincoln, reading Volney and Thomas Paine, was moved to write a treatise in which he assailed the divine inspiration of the Bible and the divinity of Christ. As in his younger days in Indiana, his taste in verse and humor still tended to the erotic; yet his influence was for the right; for he quelled riots, compromised feuds, and exercised a moderating influence on the rugged natures of his undisciplined companions.

Black elaborated Herndon's story of Lincoln's love for Ann Rutledge, devoting twelve pages to it, and buttressing Herndon's evidence with the testimony of Isaac Cogdale, a mediocre lawyer who lived near Springfield, and who claimed to have heard the story from Lincoln's own lips. Then Lamon gave a full account of another of Lincoln's love affairs, hitherto unknown, or forgotten—that with Mary Owens. There could be no question of the authenticity of this affair, for the lady in question was still living, and three of her letters to Herndon, in which she described the affair, together with three of Lincoln's letters to her, were printed in full. Then followed a letter to Mrs. Orville H. Browning in which Lincoln gave a humorous account of the whole thing.

Less convincing, however, was another "revelation"— Lincoln's failure to appear for his wedding with Mary Todd on the "fatal first of January," 1841. Herndon claimed that Mrs. Elizabeth Todd Edwards, wife of Ninian

W. Edwards and sister to Mrs. Lincoln, had talked freely to him of this embroglio; and from her information, together with other bits of evidence, he had concluded that Lincoln's strange behavior was due to temporary insanity induced by aversion to the impending marriage, a counter-attachment for Matilda Edwards, niece of Ninian Edwards, and "a new access of unspeakable tenderness for the memory of Ann Rutledge"—surely a conjuncture of emotions calculated to confound a person of the utmost self-possession.

Black not only related this in full detail, but went on to describe Lincoln's marriage as an "affliction" such as would have moved the "shade of Socrates." "It touched his acquaintances deeply," Black affirmed, "and they gave it the widest publicity. They made no pause to inquire, to investigate, and to apportion the blame between the parties, according to their deserts. Almost ever since Mr. Lincoln's death, a portion of the press has never tired of heaping brutal reproaches upon his wife and widow; whilst a certain class of his friends thought they were honoring his memory by multiplying outrages and indignities upon her, at the very moment when she was broken by want and sorrow, defamed, defenceless, in the hands of thieves, and at the mercy of spies. If ever a woman grievously expiated an offence not her own, this woman did. In the Herndon manuscripts, there is a mass of particulars under this head; but Mr. Herndon sums them all up in a single sentence, in a letter to one of Mr. Lincoln's biographers: 'All that I know ennobles both.' "

With Lincoln dead only seven years and his wife and a son still living, such revelations, no matter whether true or false, were surely in questionable taste.

Moreover, there is reason to believe that Herndon was

guilty of bad faith in turning over material about Mrs. Lincoln to Lamon and Black without putting restrictions on its use. On December 24, 1866, Robert Lincoln had written to Herndon: "I *infer* from your letter, but I hope it is not so, that it is your purpose to mention my mother in your work—I say I hope it is not so, because in the first place it would not be pleasant for her or for any woman, to be made public property of in that way—With a man it is different, for he lives out in the world and is used to being talked of—one of the unpleasant consequences of political success is that however little it may have to do with that success, his whole private life is exposed to the public gaze—that is part of the price he pays. But I see no reason why his wife and children should be included—especially while they are alive—I think no sensible man would live in a glass house and I think he ought not to be compelled to do so against his will. I feel very keenly on this subject, for the annoyance I am subjected to sometimes is nearly intolerable. I hope you will consider this matter carefully, my dear Mr. Herndon, for once done there is no undoing."

There was surely something to be said for Robert's point of view. And, written only some six weeks after Herndon's Ann Rutledge lecture, the letter may have been intended as a rebuke as well as a plea. We do not know what Herndon wrote in reply; but evidently he made some sort of promise. At least Robert chose to assume so. December 27, Robert wrote: "Your letter of yesterday is at hand and I am very glad to find that I misunderstood your language and that you do understand my feelings on that subject. There is no need of saying anything more about it . . . ." Of course, a promise by Herndon did not bind Lamon or Black; but it implied discretion in implementing the pens of others as well as in using his own.

Some sixteen pages of the Lamon book were devoted to Lincoln's religion, the subject being treated in the manner of a lawyer arguing a case. Herndon was quoted at length, and to his avowal of Lincoln's unbelief was added the testimony of many persons who had known Lincoln in his Springfield years, among them James H. Matheny, John T. Stuart, David Davis, Jesse Fell, and even Mrs. Lincoln. Then to prove that Lincoln's earlier ideas had never changed, Black quoted a letter that Herndon had obtained from John George Nicolay, secretary to Lincoln during his presidency, in which Nicolay declared that Lincoln "gave no outward indication of his mind having undergone any change in that regard" while he was in Washington.

Having presented his own case, Black proceeded to demolish the opposition. After recounting Newton Bateman's conversation with Lincoln, as told by Holland, Black concluded that there was no dealing with Bateman "except by a flat contradiction. Perhaps his memory was treacherous, or his imagination led him astray, or, peradventure, he thought a fraud no harm if it gratified the strong desire of the public for proofs of Mr. Lincoln's orthodoxy." Black then adverted to the testimony of the Reverend James Smith, the former Springfield divine and Scottish consul, and without attempting to refute it, simply explained it away. According to Black, Lincoln, realizing the growing political power of the churches and not wishing to incur their hostility, had played a "sharp game" on the Christian folk of Springfield by permitting himself to be "misunderstood and misrepresented by some enthusiastic ministers and exhorters with whom he came in contact," among them the Reverend Mr. Smith. Because Lincoln, while never really changing his opinions at all, allowed them to think he had come over to the orthodox view. Here was real heresy on the part of Black! An imputation of hypocrisy to "Honest Abe"!

The first reviews of Lamon's book were not unfavorable. True, three of them, written by W. B. Reed, were inspired either by Chauncey Black or Judge Black, and were approved by them before going to press; and some others seem to have been written after mere scanning or at best a hasty reading. Later, some newspapers that had printed favorable notices, changed their tone of praise to one of criticism. At least one reviewer was willing to accept everything the book contained as truth. Licking his lips with pleasurable disgust and abjuring all partisan or sectional prejudice, so he claimed, this writer for *The Southern Magazine* pontificated: "The whole story of this career from beginning to end is so dreary, wretched, so shabby, such a tissue of pitiful dodging and chicanery, so unrelieved by anything pure, noble, or dignified, that even to follow it as far as we have done, has well-nigh surpassed our powers of endurance; and when, putting all partisan feeling aside, we look back at the men who once were chosen by their countrymen to fill the places that this man has occupied—a Washington, a Jefferson, a Madison, an Adams, or later, a Webster, a Clay, or a Calhoun—men of culture and refinement, of honor, of exalted patriotism, of broad views and wise statesmanship—and measure the distance from them to Abraham Lincoln, we sicken with shame and disgust."

The New York *Evening Mail* and the New York *Commercial Advertiser* thought Lamon was well provided with all the requisites of a good biographer except literary ability and character. The Chicago *Inter-Ocean* was shocked at the allusions to Lincoln's family life and love affairs, the treatment of his religion, and the assertion that he liked dirty stories. The Chicago *Tribune* felt a similar revulsion. Its critic thought that "A brief statement of his religious ideas would have been all that was necessary for general information, for a man's religious ideas are a matter between himself and his Maker. The story of his final engagement and marriage to Mrs. Lincoln can be read by no one except with the most painful feelings. Even if every word of it were true, no excuse can palliate the atrocity of its publication. It is an event in Mr. Lincoln's life which should have been kept secret. It will shock not Mr. Lincoln's family alone, but every person whose sense of propriety is not thoroughly blunted, and it shows that whatever else Mr. Lamon may be fit for, he is not fit for a biographer."

Strangely enough, the religious press, while coming to the defence of Lincoln's faith, did not, as a general thing, become as irate or as personal in its criticism as the lay journals. An exception was the *New Englander and Congregational Review* which thought that Herndon and Lamon between them had "produced a portrait as like that of the original as those frightful images which are given by a mirror that in being itself cracked and defaced, and soiled and uneven, are untruthful, just in like proportion to the minuteness of detail with which it reflects the palid form of a fair face or a noble form."

The *North American Review,* an Osgood & Company periodical, thought every American should read the book —a thing highly to be desired, from the publishers' point of view. The next volume would be better; but meanwhile "we recommend this volume as one that, with some revision, might be made indeed a model biography." There were roughnesses here and there, and offences against good taste; but the material was unsurpassed.

Osgood's other periodical, *The Atlantic Monthly,* was not so kind. It confessed to doubts about the book's wisdom, reliability, and propriety; and to something more than doubt regarding the justification of "dragging from the dead man's grave the miserable fact of his unhappy marriage, and thrusting it again and again before the reader." Lincoln's love affairs were treated with "maudlin insistence" and "fumbling melodramatic sentimentality." It was too soon to tell such things. Yet the book did show Lincoln continually outgrowing his faults, gaining knowledge and wisdom. This reviewer detected an antipathetic spirit toward Lincoln "which is only restrained when the facts put it to shame and which almost wholly disappears towards the end . . . It is as if the author had begun to write it with a dislike of Lincoln [was he privy to the secret of authorship?] which vanishes as he learns to know him better. With this improvement of the author's tone, there is also a great improvement of his literature . . . which often appears coarse and flimsy; but the material immeasurably gains in dignity towards the close, and the author rises with it."

The reviewer for *Harper's New Monthly Magazine* picked up the book with great expectations and laid it down with deep disappointment. "The three most characteristic features of the book," he complained, "are neither of them likely to commend it to the reading public, except to those who enjoy gossip more than history. Page after page is filled with legendary accounts of 'Abe's' exploits as an amateur pugilist, which, if they be not exaggerated, are foisted into a position of undue prominence.

The private history—if it be a history—of his courtship
and marriage, illustrated by the publication of a package
of confidential letters, is put upon the record, and publicity given to those domestic and personal relations which
every man has a right to demand shall be kept sacred from
the intrusions of the public. And, finally, sixteen pages are
devoted to an elaborate piece of special pleading, based on
no other evidence than reports of Mr. Lincoln's immature
doubts in his youth, to prove that he was an infidel and an
atheist, had no faith, not only rejected the Bible but ridi-
culed it . . . but it will take very different sort of evidence
from that which Mr. Lamon has accumulated to make the
American people believe that Mr. Lincoln was an infidel
if not an atheist, and that his strong and reiterated assertions of his faith in a prayer-hearing and personal God
whose providence rules the nation were the simulated utterances of a 'wily politician' employed for political effect."

The reviewer for the *Galaxy* almost beat his breast in
rage. Herndon had tried to "hawk" his material around
Illinois in lectures until Lincoln's friends made him quit
in the name of decency. Now he had the effrontery to publish it. Anyone who knew Herndon was aware that he was
too "egotistical" and "unbalanced" to be a reliable source
of information; yet Lamon tried to make him the teacher
and Lincoln the pupil. Space would not permit the reviewer to point out the many instances of "vulgar incapacity to understand," of "gross conceit," and of "misrepre-
sentation." Lincoln's religious faith was treated with "vulgar inveracity," the story of his birth was "raked out of the
mud" and trampled "by the feet of swine," the passages
about Mrs. Lincoln were "a crime against common decency," "a brutal pounding of sacred facts to thresh out a

few kernels of sensation." But he should not be too harsh. Lamon and Herndon were "too ignorant and conceited to know untruth from truth."

Only a few critics questioned the assertion of the title page as to the author of the book. The Boston *Daily Advertiser* suspected Judge Black; and the New York *Sun* printed an editorial under the caption, "The Strange Story of a Strange Book: Who Wrote Lamon's Life of Lincoln? And who mutilated it before publication?" Without naming names, the writer made such a keen analysis of what had happened to the book that one suspects him of having inside information. And since Chauncey Black was intimate with the inner circle at the *Sun*—he later went on its editorial staff—it is entirely possible that he took this means of getting some small measure of revenge upon his publishers.

A review which had been awaited with interest was that of *Scribner's Monthly*, where Josiah G. Holland, dean of Lincoln authors and favorite of the idealistic cult, held down the editor's chair.

Holland mulled over the book thoroughly; and finally, in his August issue, he made his feelings known. Beginning his summation with deceptive restraint, he built up pressure as he progressed and finally exploded like a blunderbuss.

The merits of the volume were in some respects striking and admirable, he thought. Then—with a touch of irony—it was so well done, in fact, that many persons were surprised that either the military or legal profession could produce such literary competence. The story of Lincoln's early life had never been depicted with such accuracy and zest, although he could not accept the author's opinion that the Clary's Grove boys, representing, as they did, the rougher and more boisterous element of the New Salem population, were a character-building influence.

Having offered this meed of praise, he came to his objections, and began to warm to his work.

The Lincoln that Lamon knew—or thought he knew—was just such a man as the uncouth environment of Lincoln's early years would have made of Lamon. "Thou thoughtest that he was altogether such an one as thyself," he rebuked. But Lincoln refused to conform to this pattern. No matter what he may have been in Illinois, he became, in Washington, a figure beyond the comprehension of such men as Lamon and Herndon.

His religion was a case in point. The eagerness with which the "authors" (with unconscious accuracy he used the plural, referring to Herndon, however, rather than to Black) sought to besmirch him as a hypocrite was one of the most "detestable" and "pitiable" exhibitions that he had ever witnessed. With a cogency difficult to refute, Holland gave his view of Lincoln's spiritual estate. "The question is not whether Abraham Lincoln was a subscriber to the creeds of orthodoxy," he affirmed, "but whether he was a believing—that is to say, a trustful Christian man; not whether he was accustomed to call Jesus Christ 'Lord, Lord,' but whether he was used to do those things which Jesus Christ exemplified and enforced . . . Mr Herndon and Colonel Lamon [he held them equally guilty] may strive to demonstrate that he was nothing but a heathen, and a somewhat vulgar heathen, at the best, that the Bible to which he reverently and often appealed was no more to him than the works of Confucius or of Mencius would have been if he could have read them; that the prayers which he declared he offered and which he solemnly asked

men to offer up for him were directed to a mere unforgiv-
ing destiny; but the result of the attempted demonstration
is injurious to no one half as much as to themselves."

The religion of Jesus Christ was in no more need of the
patronage of a great man than it was endangered by the
disparagement of a small one, proclaimed Holland. It
should not be unduly covetous of Abraham Lincoln's dis-
cipleship any more than it should fear the injury of Mr.
Herndon's enmity. But it should be respected and appreciated; and any ignorant, insidious, or malicious attack upon
it should be promptly noticed and repelled. And to use the
good name and great fame of Lincoln to cloak a dagger,
with which to attack it, was "an offence against good taste
and an outrage on decency of which it is difficult to speak
with the customary calmness of mere judicial criticism."

And this book contained other outrages on decency.
Even if Lincoln did have domestic difficulties, it were better that history should wait to know about them, or even
lose the knowledge altogether, than that backdoor scandal
and neighborhood gossip should be flaunted to the world
while the woman to whom Lincoln was a faithful husband
for a quarter of a century was still living. "A writer who
can show himself so reckless of decency and honor ought
not to complain if his readers should presume him equally
reckless of truth. There surely rests on us no obligation to
believe a story which is told in such a shameless way."

Holland thought the book was written on the theory
that Lincoln became the sort of man that Herndon would
have had him be; and the effrontery with which all conflicting evidence was disregarded or assailed was intolerable. "The violent and reckless prejudice, and the utter
want of delicacy and even decency by which the book is
characterized . . . will more than counterbalance its new

material, its fresh and vigorous pictures of Western life and manners, and its familiar knowledge of the 'inside politics' of Mr. Lincoln's administration; and will even make its publication (by the famous publishers whose imprint imparts to it a prestige which its authorship should fail to give) something like a national misfortune. In some quarters it will be readily received as the standard life of the good President. It is all the more desirable that the criticism upon it should be prompt and unsparing."

One can almost imagine Holland going to his washstand to purge his hands of the book's polluting dust; or see him leaning back in his chair, mopping his sultry brow, and emitting a most distasteful belch.

The book was as nauseous to some of Lincoln's friends as it was to the reviewers. Isaac N. Arnold was shocked. How could Lamon accuse Lincoln of being a wily politician, or of being cold, impassive, selfish, and ungrateful to his friends. He was just the opposite. "How could he charge him with irreverence and infidelity when he remembers the sublime prayer with which he left Springfield, and the deep religious feeling which pervades all his writings and speeches to the day of his death?" Arnold asked Browning in a letter dated November 22, 1872. "Do not you and I owe it to the memory of the dead to vindicate him of these charges? Most of this book, it seems to me is filled up with trivial and insignificant matters which only prurient curiosity would care for and without any appreciation of the noblest traits of his character." Then — in a somewhat chiding tone—how did Lamon ever get hold of that flippant letter of Lincoln's to Mrs. Browning in which he made light of his affair with Mary Owens? Arnold would like to have the history of that letter if Browning cared to divulge it. And he would also welcome Browning's opinion of Lincoln as he had known him at Vandalia, Springfield, and in Washington. "You were much with him, I remember, at the time of Willie's death. Do you know what his religious views and feelings were then? I have been of the impression from some things which occurred, that he was under deep religious feelings. Do you know whether the statement so generally made that he was, while at Washington, in the habit of prayer and frequent reading of the Bible, *as a religious book*, was true? I hope you may find time to write a full reply."

Browning answered immediately. He had read the whole book carefully and it contained many things he regretted to see in print. Even if they were true, their publication was "injudicious" and not at all necessary "to the elucidation, or full comprehension of Mr. Lincoln's character." It was now almost forty years since Browning first met Lincoln, and from that time until his death he had never known him to be treacherous to a friend. Of his religious opinions he was not so able to speak. He attended Doctor Gurley's church and read the Bible, but did not say grace at table. Browning knew nothing of his private devotions, if any, but he evinced no religious feeling at Willie's death. "I know Mr. Lincoln was a firm believer in a superintending and overruling Providence," he avowed, "and in supernatural agencies and events. I know that he believed the destinies of men were, or at least, that his own destiny, was shaped and controlled by an intelligence and power higher and greater than his own, and which he could neither control nor thwart. To what extent he believed in the revelations and miracles of the Bible and Testament, or whether he believed in them at all, I am not prepared to say; but I do know that he was not a scoffer at religion. During our long and intimate acquaintance I have no recollection of ever having heard an irreverent word fall from his lips."

As for the unfortunate letter to Mrs. Browning, both he and she had always supposed it related a fiction, until about 1862, when "a biographer" asked for a copy of it. At her first opportunity thereafter, Mrs. Browning asked Lincoln about it, and found to her surprise that it told of an actual occurrence. Some of the persons involved were still living, and Lincoln requested that she should not allow it to be published yet. Later on she could use her discretion. Lamon had asked and been permitted to make a copy, provided Mrs. Browning's name were not used (a promise he had not kept). Lincoln wrote it only to amuse a friend; and if harm had been done by publishing it, the guilt was chargeable to Lamon, not Lincoln.

About two weeks after this, Browning had dinner in Chicago with Leonard Swett and Lyman Trumbull. Trumbull won the anti-Nebraska senatorial nomination over Lincoln in 1854, became a Republican, was reelected in 1860 and 1866, was personally friendly to Lincoln but not always in political accord with him, and now was a lame duck because of opposition to the Radical Republican program. In the course of conversation someone mentioned Lamon's book, and Trumbull and Swett were both severe in their strictures. Neither of them "impeached the truthfulness" of Lamon's narration, but both "thought him inexcusable for publishing it."

Everyone that Arnold questioned thought the book was reprehensible. Senator Charles Sumner had not read it, but the extracts he had seen were "disagreeable and some of them indefensible." Gideon Welles, Lincoln's Secretary of the Navy, read it "with deep regret." "Much of the scandal and smutch, if true, should have been omitted," he thought, "and would have been by a faithful and friendly biographer. It was not necessary to state he could not find the marriage certificate of Mr. L's father and mother—nor to detail his love affairs, etc. etc. I have one of the earliest copies of the work, and said to my family it was written by no friendly biographer, and portions of it indicated personal and party animosity. I take it for granted Lamon was not the writer."

Some persons unburdened their feelings to Lamon— J. H. Wickizer, a lawyer friend of Lincoln's, and Joshua F. Speed, among others. Wickizer considered the book "a truthful statement of facts"; but he would have handled the material somewhat differently. "I think I would have passed over his plebeian birth and education very lightly," he tactfully explained, "and been more special and dwelt more largely upon the philosophy and greatness of his character, say from about 1846. And especially would I have lingered long and happily on his Divine Genius from the repeal of the Missouri Compromise down to the hour of his assassination. This would have placed him where he really ought to be in the hearts of all true Americans, without any dark shading in the background . . .

"You have no doubt given the exact truth respecting his religious views, but as the people who loved him are not sufficiently advanced to appreciate his philosophy, and as his greatness did not consist in any religious ideas or labors, would it not have been better to have spared the good pious religious people the pain and shock of his unbelief? This does not shock you nor me nor Judge Davis nor Leonard Swett, who knew him but to love him, but those who drink the milk of the Word, and 'know it is so'—to them it is cutting off their rations, and they will insist, if

Lincoln really didn't believe their Religion, he has gone to hell. Would it not have been better to have spared them this sad calamity?"

Speed's estimate of Lincoln was very different from Lamon's, so different that he could not hold his patience as he read. "If he as you say damned with faint praize [sic] —well is he repaid in this biography," Speed thought. "For it does seem to me that he is damned without praize." Some time when he felt better he would give Lamon his opinion of Lincoln's character.

Only Herndon offered consolation. The book was good and Lamon should not feel too badly about the criticism. Unworthy books were never noticed. "I do not agree with you when you say a man is a fool for writing the truth. Your reward is in the future." Lamon should take "a good horn" in Herndon's name, and "when you feel jolly and good give my best respects to your partner, though a stranger to me."

In the face of all this furor, Lamon sulked in his tent. He could not admit it, but after all the book was only his stepchild. He had not really fathered it, and he seemed to lack either the inclination or the capacity to come out and join the joust. Battling with words was not his forte; and it was left for Black and Herndon to present the case for the defence.

Chapter Three

TWO AGAINST THE WORLD

Busy and isolated on his farm, Herndon was oblivious of the flogging he and Lamon were receiving from the magazines and press; and whatever irritation Black felt was probably assuaged by the thought that a book that was attracting such attention must be selling well. Black's resentment at Lamon had been sharpened by his recent discovery that the material for which he had paid $1,500 for a half-interest had cost Lamon only $2,000, instead of $4,000, as he supposed. Moreover, Black thought he was acquiring ownership of the originals, which were sure to have historic value, whereas, as it turned out, only copies were involved in the deal. So it may have been with something of a smirk that Black, secure in anonymity, beheld his erstwhile colleague buffeted by maledictions.

But when he wrote to Osgood & Company for an account of sales, he was shocked to learn that only 1,900 copies had been sold. Had he bungled the work? He wrote to learn Herndon's opinion.

"The Life is true," came the gratifying reply, "true to the letter and spirit of your Hero—Lincoln—When you give an opinion—express a judgment it is sound. There never was as true a biography written in this world. The

Life is an honest one telling 'flat-footed' all the facts of Lincoln's history." There were a few mistakes, as was inevitable in almost any book, and Herndon would be glad to correct them, if Black so desired, before the next edition was printed.

Black "prized" this opinion more than anything that had been said or could be said "by any living man." In writing the book, he had studied Herndon as well as Lincoln, he explained, and believed he knew Herndon well enough to be sure he would say nothing insincere. He would welcome corrections. His only ambition had been to write a true life; but he must necessarily have committed errors, "having no acquaintance with local history and local characters, and having no one to assist me in the slightest degree . . . I think I caught your spirit and I tried to develop your plan. If I have failed it was from lack of ability—and nothing else. I was never disposed to claim anything on the score of 'literary merit,' but I am very certain that the just claims on that score would have been greater, if the book had not been tampered with, after it left my hands, had been entirely revised, printed and ready to be stereoptyped [sic]."

In a letter of February 5, Black brought Herndon up to date on the reviews. *Harper's* was "short but bitter," the *Galaxy's* even "meaner and courser." The religious press treated the book "decently," and among newspapers, the New York *Times* was "the most appreciative." Holland's review in *Scribner's* was "ably written, but disingenuous and malignant—Spiteful as might be expected from an author with his book torn into shreds, or a lover with his mistress in another fellow's arms."

Many of the arguments of the reviewers would have been vitiated if Lamon had not permitted the book to be altered "at the bidding of mere sickly sentiment." This was a misfortune. "It broke the otherwise overwhelming force of the book; showed a disposition to violate truth for the sake of conciliating popular prejudice, and conciliated nobody after all—If it had been printed as it was written these fellows would have been as mute as if their tongues had been slit. My idea was that if they were to be hit at all, they should be hit hard, and knocked dumb. This sentimental lying is utterly degrading, not only to the liars but to the great man they have chosen to lie about."

As months passed and sales did not improve, Black became convinced that the publishers had sabotaged the book. Besides mutilating and corrupting the contents, they had overpriced it, made it unhandy and cumbersome, brought it out at a time when public attention was diverted to two exciting political conventions, never advertised it, and reviewed it in a derogatory manner in their own periodicals. It was planned as a subscription book but never sold that way. Their eagerness to get it was in strange contrast to their attitude "after they got control of it and Lamon." Sales were so meagre that Black was inclined to believe, as he had been told, that "some party or parties, either personally or politically interested, have bribed the publishers, thus to practically suppress the book while ostensibly complying with their contract."

One of Lamon's most persistent critics was the Reverend James A. Reed, pastor of the First Presbyterian Church of Springfield, who delivered a lecture on "The Later Life and Religious Sentiments of Abraham Lincoln" to numerous audiences throughout the West. The burden of his discourse was a refutation of Lamon's "dark and unfounded insinuations" about Lincoln's legitimacy, a confutation of Lamon's evidence regarding Lincoln's unbelief, and an attempt to prove Lincoln's essential Christianity. Holland was so impressed with Reed's dialectics that he printed the lecture in *Scribner's*. This was bad judgment, for had he only realized it, his quarry had holed up: Lamon inarticulate, Herndon preoccupied, and Black, although eager, perforce mute.

Black could not appear in the controversy himself; someone must front for him; and Herndon was the only person privy to his authorship with sufficient knowledge and standing in the Lincoln field to qualify as his mouthpiece. Somehow he must be induced to enter the lists; and on June 23, Black wrote the following letter, which was calculated to smoke him out:

"The Rev. J. A. Reed of Springfield has it appears been delivering to numerous audiences in the West, a lecture on the 'Life of Lincoln,' which paints *Lamon* as a mercenary libeller, and you as the forger of the documents paraded in support of the libels. This latter charge is very distinctly made, and manifestly intended, although not put in exact words. The substance and effect of Mr. Reed's elaborate performance is that you, being an infidel and therefore an immoral man yourself, have resorted to the basest means of proving that Mr. Lincoln was like you. He conveniently ignores the long list of respectable witnesses called in the book, and . . . fishes out of them weak statements that they did not *write* the language attributed to them. Nobody ever said they did, it was given merely as the substance of their evidence like a lawyer's notes, and that *it is the substance* of what they said they do not deny. But I do not propose to review Mr. Reed; you will do that better than I can.

"Now this lecture . . . is to be sure a flimsy, libellous, fraudulent concern. But it is well calculated to deceive the public mind which naturally leans to the priest as against an independent thinker, and unless it is answered and exposed it disgraces us all. Lamon you know is incapable of writing anything—or conducting any controversy, however trivial; and he has taken away from me all the books and papers we got from you, or anybody else, and thus left me as helpless as himself . . . Unless therefore I attempt to use voluminous materials from unassisted memory I can do nothing. The responsibility of meeting this flood of falsehoods and calumny rests therefore upon you, who are of all men the most competent to repel the lie and maintain the truth. Unless you rise to the occasion Mr. Lincoln's real character will be lost in oblivion, and a false one will live in its stead. You are the only person living who is able to rescue him from destruction. They are combining against us everywhere—Holland, Arnold', the preachers, and the press. They mean to drown us out with false clamors. They will suborn half of Springfield, where public opinion terrorizes the truth; and they will get all the preachers that ever saw Lincoln to lie about his supposed religion . . . Our publishers are no better than our avowed enemies; and Lamon whose name is on the book, being an imbecile from the first, and wheedled into emasculating his text, now cowers before the storm, as useless as a cross baby.

"Please write me what you are likely to do . . .

"One thing you ought to know and you will observe it when you come to examine things closely. The testimony of Matheny, Stuart and others, was somewhat mutilated by the publishers—a word left out, or altered for a gentler one, here and there—a circumstance which gives them an excellent opportunity to deny the language. Curses on those dishonest publishers—They have done everything to dishonor the book—Cowardice is generally more disastrous than knavery. I don't care a red cent how hard you hit them."

A month passed; and since Herndon showed no disposition to defend the book, Black himself wrote an article which he persuaded Manton Marble, editor of the Democratic New York *World,* to print. Marble was probably easy to persuade; he was no Lincoln lover. His paper had been consistently hostile to Lincoln, and the Lincoln administration had suppressed it for two days when it printed a spurious presidential proclamation calculated to give aid and comfort to the South.

Black informed Herndon that his article, which he had signed only with the initials "C. F. B.," would probably provoke an answer from Reed or Holland, in which case he was ready with a "crushing rejoinder," for he had fortified himself with additional evidence which he would hold back until the "preachers" made themselves "a little more conspicuous." He could get all the testimony he needed to prove that Lincoln never changed his views while in Washington, but he must depend on Herndon to show that he was an unbeliever before that. "Dr. Smith ought to be destroyed—He must have been a most impudent rascal," he observed; and Bateman's case also needed "serious attention." He had hoped to see Herndon lay the opposition "out cold" before this; and he again pleaded for support, anticipating that he might get into "a very deep fight."

Herndon was not the man to forsake a friend. His dander was up; and he was already at work on a lecture to be delivered very soon. Black was heartened. "I began to feel as if I was almost alone in this fight for historic truth," he rejoiced, "but if you enter the lists actively I am sure of ultimate success . . . Marble offers me room to smash these fellows up if they have the temerity to reply . . . If I can get Reed or Holland both to answer, I am able to make it an ugly job for them, and convince the world—if the world will deign to read—that historic truth cannot be trampled down forever by a gang of associated preachers and politicians."

Herndon should prepare his lecture in such manner as to make it suitable for publication, he suggested. *Scribner's* probably would not touch it, but Osgood might print it in the *Atlantic,* or, if he wouldn't, there were other editors who would give it space.

In fomenting this controversy Black was inspired by something more than ardor for truth. He still had hopes of the book's success; and for some time had been negotiating with Osgood & Company to obtain all rights, so that he could republish it under different auspices. "You tell me you are in pecuniary trouble," he wrote to Herndon, "and it strikes me that this book might avail for your speedy relief. If we could get joint control of it . . . there is no doubt of our being able to make an independent fortune." Osgood seemed disposed to sell, if Lamon would agree. But Lamon was "sour and sulky and ugly-tempered" and must be handled cautiously. "He is a dog in the manger and very snappy."

He would probably not sell to Black or his friends, but he might be induced to sell to Herndon or his friends. Black surmised that "he is heartily sick of the whole business. He has not succeeded in convincing anybody that he really wrote the book, and as a speculation it seems to be very poor, and he don't know how to redeem it. In fact he takes his opinions about the matter ready-made from Osgood & Co., who take care that he shall think nothing but

ill of me and my work. He expected to realize a great
fortune from the book and I verily believe he would have
done so, if he had stood by me and compelled these publishers to do their duty. But in betraying me he betrayed
himself and lost the golden opportunity."

If Black and Herndon could get control and obtain a
publisher who was "more intent upon money than politics"
and was not amenable to "Boston criticism or Yankee public opinion," Black believed they could make the magazines
and newspapers "ring with this Holland-Reed-Herndon-
Black controversy about Mr. Lincoln's religion, and thus
indirectly advertise the book indefinitely." Holland or
Reed must reply; and if they did, Black meant "to make
fine hash of them" or any other meddlesome "clerical gentlemen."

"But you and I both have other than a pecuniary interest in the fate of this book," he asserted. "We want to make
a *perfect* life of Mr. Lincoln which will endure forever. I
am already known as one of the authors of it and you are
supposed to be another. It is in fact in a peculiar sense *your*
book. It was written on your plan, from your materials,
and largely on your authority. Your fame—which your
family will prize more than money—is inseparably bound
up in it. Lamon did not compose a line of it, or furnish the
data upon which any five lines were based. In very truth
you and I alone are responsible for it, as we alone were the
intelligent agents who produced it. It is therefore of the
last importance to us that it should prove a successful and
permanent work."

For a time Black considered bringing out a new book
under a different name, but concluded that it would be
difficult to do so without infringing on the copyright.
Moreover, it would be cheaper to buy out Lamon and to

purchase the plates from the publishers and make whatever changes were desired—and Osgood & Company's good will was worth something. They were willing to accept $2,600 for the plates and the stock on hand; but Black declined this offer on the ground that the stock was a "debased and spurious edition of my book—a lie and a fraud—and therefore *dead* stock." Osgood then suggested that Black make a counterproposition; but he declined to do so unless Osgood & Company would first acquire Lamon's interest. This might be difficult, he thought, for besides the matter of price, there were other obstacles. Lamon would probably want assurance that Black would "never reveal the insignificant part he took in getting up the book. He always had a mortal dread of such an exposure," Black confided to Herndon. "He had the preface altered to read that *his* stores of information had been added to *yours*—for he said 'if it comes out that *Herndon* furnished all the materials and *Black* wrote the book where in the hell will *I* be?' "

Black thought Lamon suspected him of ill will, but he did not wish to injure Lamon if he could help it. Despite his "outrages," Black avowed a "sneaking kindness" for him. "I once loved the fellow and I can't quite get over it. I feel that he sinned ignorantly and under bad advice."

As autumn came, Black was still "hammering" at the publishers, and they were still "hammering" at Lamon. Black was delighted that Herndon had expressed willingness to enter into his plan, and was sure that "if we manage the business well there is a young fortune in it." He feared someone had "choked off" Reed and Holland; but a lecture by Herndon would *"goad* them thoroughly."

If negotiations should fail, he and Herndon would have to write a new life, "one which shall be as nearly perfect as our joint knowledge and experience can make it," but whether they did this or merely revised the present text, Black thought it imperative for Herndon to dissociate himself as much as possible from Lamon's biography. He should not approve or disapprove any part of it, express any critical judgment upon it, or hold himself responsible for anything within its covers, except what was specifically credited to him. A good deal of the part relating to Lincoln's religion should be rewritten; and it would diminish Herndon's authority to anticipate any portion of that work. "When we get out *Herndon's* Life it will be purged of the errors and mistakes of *Lamon's* Life, and that purging and those corrections will constitute the *new* value and *increased* power of the book. *Altered, corrected,* and *amended,* it will have the biggest run any book ever had in America, if it is pushed by the publisher with energy and judgment," he predicted.

To this end, Black wrote a "card" for Herndon to sign and publish, in which Herndon was to deny that he wrote any part of Lamon's book or even saw any part of it before publication except the first six or seven chapters. He thought these were good, the card affirmed, and told the author so; but that was the only opinion he had expressed. "Upon matters of propriety and taste I was not consulted and gave no opinion." The sketch of Lincoln's religious views was based on his material and was "true to the letter, but I couldn't help it. I couldn't substitute a lie for the fact merely because the fact might not be agreeable to some people. It is abundantly proven, but I did not create the proofs. I only gathered and authenticated them for the future historian . . . Yet Dr. Holland and the Rev. Mr. Reed have opened in full cry upon me as the chief offender, and I may yet find it necessary to show them that the truth is immortal and that a falsehood, like the one to

which they cling so pertinaciously, can live only by suf-
ferance. But not now; it will be time enough when they
have mustered courage to answer 'C. F. B.'s' reply to their
several articles in Scribner's Monthly . . ."

Black explained that the "fling" at Reed and Holland
was designed "solely as a provocation." Holland seemed
to realize that he had nothing to gain by re-entering the
controversy; but Reed was "quite fool enough to believe
in himself and his cause." His friends were probably re-
straining him, but if sufficiently angered, he might break
loose and give tongue.

Dutifully following Black's advice, Herndon copied and
signed the card, and sent it to the Chicago *Tribune,* where
it was published on November 24.

Meanwhile, Herndon informed Black that when he sold
his material, he had promised Lamon not to write a life of
Lincoln for five years. Black was surprised; Lamon had
never told him; but it would make no difference if they
could buy him out. If they could not, they must wait until
the time was up. Or they could follow another course; and
Black was inclined to favor it. If no deal should be made by
January 1, he proposed to notify Osgood & Company
that since they had refused his every offer he no longer felt
obliged "to keep my child at nurse with those who care not
for it." He would not sue, but would simply take his manuscript and publish it as originally written. Osgood & Company would not dare enjoin him, for to do so would result
in publicizing the whole history of the book. *"They will
never draw that fire. They know better."*

Black would send a copy of this notification to Lamon,
who "will curse himself black, drink himself blind, and go
to bed under a heap of blankets to sweat out his wrath."
Then he would write Black a "courtly letter containing

two separate and distinct propositions—(1st) that I may kiss his backside and go to hell and (2) that he will upon sight give me a much deserved 'body-beating.' But in the long run I won't do the one and he won't do the other." Then, when Lamon was beginning to cool off, Herndon should write him a letter, stating that his five-year period of silence was almost over, and that Herndon's mission on earth would not be fulfilled until an acceptable life of Lincoln had been published. He should concede that part of Lamon's work was well done and that he wished to incorporate it with his own; and should then suggest that Lamon sell him his interest in the copyright as he had previously sold Lamon his materials. He should also say that he had heard that Black had some interest in the book and suggest that Lamon use his influence to prevail upon Black to sell out also, or at least put Herndon in communication with Black. This would afford Lamon a graceful way out. True, he was the most suspicious man Black ever knew, and as obstinate as a mule. He might not succumb to this intrigue; but it seemed the only hope of "an easy accomodation."

Herndon finally delivered his lecture in Springfield on December 12, 1873, and the *Illinois State Register* printed it in full as a broadside. Then Herndon waited eagerly for the reaction, requesting Alfred Orendorff, his former law partner, Dr. William Jayne, a Springfield physician who had served as governor of Dakota Territory by Lincoln's appointment, and James H. Matheny to inform him what they heard about it.

Orendorff reported that, as might be expected, the sympathies of the people generally were with "what is thought to be the popular side," and since the newspapers had to satisfy the people in order to sell their wares, several of them had printed "scurrillous" comments, mostly to the effect that if what Herndon said about Lincoln's religion were true, he never should have said it. Some papers accused Herndon of seeking notoriety, but none of them, so far as Orendorff had read, presented any contradictory evidence. A great many people thought Reed and Holland unwise in reopening the argument.

Jayne had heard the lecture commented on a great deal. A majority of those who expressed themselves thought Herndon told the truth, but even some of those who agreed with him thought his revelations unbecoming. "The orthodox world is determined to claim Abraham," said Jayne, "& are not willingly going to give up one of their idols." Jayne had recently seen Ninian W. Edwards, Mrs. Lincoln's brother-in-law, who had been quoted by Reed, in a barber shop, and found that Edwards was not so good an orthodox witness in private as in the public prints. "So I guess with all if they would tell the *whole* truth," Jayne observed.

Matheny had been quoted variously by Black, by Reed, and by Herndon; and he saw nothing in Herndon's lecture at which he could take offense. No speech ever delivered in Springfield had excited so much comment; and the critics could be divided into three classes. First, there were those who would never believe otherwise than that Lincoln was a saint; and these denounced the lecture bitterly. The second group was glad to believe anything that could be said against Lincoln; and they were lavish in praise. The third group sought truth; yet the majority, even of these, Matheny regretted to report, saw no reason why Herndon should demolish "a very beautiful 'Air Castle' . . . They ask the question *'what good'*—Why disturb a beautiful faith, which, 'tho unfounded was still a pleasure to hold and enjoy."

Black thought the lecture "mighty bold," and would not have changed a line. If Holland or Reed had any self-respect, they must reply, although he feared they had had enough.

No sooner had he written this than a copy of the New York *Herald* came to his hand in which Herndon's lecture was summarized and Herndon was flayed editorially as a modern Judas Iscariot. Black sent Herndon a marked copy. "It is an outrageous outpouring of what Carlyle calls 'hog wash,'" he commented. "It is too much overdone, however, to have any effect. It shows only that your pole has reached the monkeys this time and stirred up the cage. The more discussion and the more abuse the better. The truth can't suffer. When they resort to mere personal denunciation it shows they are at their wits ends and have nothing else to say."

Black thought this "monstrous" editorial presented too good an opportunity to overlook. Herndon should reply; and if the *Herald* deigned to publish his answer he would get the benefit of its vast circulation. If it abused him further, its abuse would do no harm. So Black thought. He was like the manager of the prize fighter who, safely outside the ropes, urges his battered protegé to greater efforts with the assurance that "they ain't laid a glove on us."

If Herndon agreed with Black, he should act at once, and not let the subject grow cold. "I would use plain language and smoke the rascals out." With his predilection for ghostwriting, Black took the liberty of penning Herndon's reply. And he had a novel approach. If Herndon must be a Judas, Black would put Judas in a new and favorable light.

"Do you know that there is a lingering question about the nature of Judas' heart," began the letter which Herndon was to subscribe, "and that it is maintained with some show of reason that he was the most devoted and loving of the apostles? It is said by some that poor Judas believed his Master should never die, and he betrayed him to the law merely to see the decisive test applied, the welcome triumph achieved, and the perfect day dawn. When he saw his Master crucified, he naturally concluded that he had made a fearful mistake, and went and slew himself. But I reckon nobody but you [the *Herald's* editor] will accuse me [Herndon] of any partnership with that unfortunate. So let us pass him."

The truth was, the argument proceeded, that Herndon had collected a mass of evidence and had let others, including Lamon, use it without restriction. All these gentlemen knew the truth about Lincoln's religion, and those who were joining the hue and cry against Lamon were trying to save themselves by shouting "Stop thief!" after an honest man. For his part in trying to make known the truth, Herndon was now "likened to Judas, and half suffocated by the foul emanations of the New York *Herald*, which are proverbially laden with the peculiar stench that could possibly arise from no other embodiment of moral putridity."

Black thought Herndon's lecture lacked only one thing —"a broad eulogy on Mr. Lincoln['s] character as a patriot and a man"—and the letter to the editor went on to set this right.

Although Lincoln never made any false pretenses to

faith in the Christian creed, Black affirmed (and this was at variance with what he said in the book), he was nevertheless "an *eminently religious man*—as unaffectedly pious as Mahammet [sic], George Washington or Theodore Parker." And because his name would be held in "awful veneration by all coming generations of men," Herndon would not permit it to be "enveloped in fables, and clouded with lies." Posterity must know the selfsame "Honest Abe" that he had known; and in order to appreciate the "glory of his crown," must realize the "heaviness of his cross."

It was a masterpiece of casuistry and vituperation; but if Herndon ever chose to send it, the editor tossed it aside.

Nor did Herndon's lecture elicit a reply from Holland or Reed. But Mrs. Lincoln was less discreet. Herndon had alluded to a conversation he had with her in Springfield about a year after Lincoln's death in which she allegedly confirmed his opinions of Lincoln's lack of faith in the accepted sense; and at this juncture she wrote a letter to John T. Stuart denying that any such conversation about Lincoln's religion ever took place, and declaring that Herndon's allegations were totally inconsistent with every word that Lincoln ever uttered on the subject of religion. Herndon thought Stuart was instructed to "show this letter around." At any rate it attracted wide notice and was commented upon by the papers.

Black thought "the old lady shows a great deal of temerity in obtruding herself into this controversy," and when Herndon replied to her in a letter to the *Illinois State Register,* which was reprinted in the *World* (probably at Black's instigation), Black was gratified at his "good tone and temper" and more especially at the large heading, calculated to attract attention, under which the reprint appeared. Doctor Jayne also congratulated Herndon on his restraint. "In this affair with the 'First Ladie of the Land' you do not like a clod hopper call her a d—d old liar & hussy," he commended, "but like a country gentleman & lawyer you say that the good poor woman crushed beneath a mountain of woe with her bruised heart & failing memory, she is not altogether a competent & trustworthy witness. William, your intellect & diplomacy does not seem to have rusted by a few years of country life. I have heard no two opinions about this denial—everyone I have heard speak of it pities the woman for again obtruding herself before the public."

In some quarters Herndon's lecture was having effect. The New York *World*—possibly again inspired by Black—believed Herndon had adduced enough evidence to discredit those authors who would make Lincoln a pattern for the Sunday Schools; while the New York *Tribune* thought it went far to invalidate much of the testimony relied upon by the champions of Lincoln's orthodoxy. And the *Tribune's* own conclusion showed that the matter was becoming incandescent, in that at last from all the heat was coming light. "Mr. Lincoln was one of the most reticent men who ever lived in regard to his own spiritual exercises," it declared. "He had a deep respect for religion and for its outward symbols and forms. He had also a profound religious sense, sometimes approaching mysticism. But it will be as impossible to prove that he was a Christian as to prove that he was not, and historians and biographers will divide upon this question, as they are divided now, according to their personal beliefs or disbeliefs."

To convince the public that what he wrote about Lincoln was in no unfriendly spirit, Herndon wrote a letter to Black in which he made only incidental reference to

Lincoln's religion but expounded on the theme of Lincoln's standing "up against the deep blue sky the greatest figure of the age . . . as near a perfect man as God generally makes." Black thought this was "conceived in the right spirit and was a capital piece of work for you to do right now. It places you where you ought to be—at the head of Mr. Lincoln's friends and defenders." Without using his own name, Black had Herndon's letter inserted in the New York *Tribune* and the Pittsburgh *Chronicle.*

While the argument proceeded, Black continued to negotiate for control of the book. Osgood & Company were willing to sell, but could get nowhere with Lamon. A friend, whom Black prompted to "pump" Lamon, reported that the Colonel trusted nobody and suspected Osgood & Company of trying to "freeze him out."

Since there seemed to be no other solution, Black now instructed Herndon to try his luck with Lamon; but he should be careful not to mention Black, nor to say anything about paying Lamon anything unless the Colonel brought that matter up himself.

But Lamon, sour on the world, turned his back on every overture; and, as months passed, Black finally gave up. In 1874 he became an editorial writer on the New York *Sun,* and in 1882 was elected Lieutenant Governor of Pennsylvania. The whole affair left him unscathed, except in the minds of a very few insiders; but the attacks on Herndon continued intermittently for years. In 1882, when the Cherryvale (Kansas) *Globe News* carried an article headed "Lincoln's Old Law Partner a Pauper," Herndon was moved to reply. For years he had seen "floating around in the newspaper literature" such charges as "Herndon is a pauper"; "Herndon is a drunkard"; "Herndon is in a lunatic asylum, well chained"; "Herndon is a vile infidel

and knave." And now this "rich and racy article" added
a new charge—infidelity to his clients. In "A Card and A
Correction," published November 9, 1882, Herndon defended himself. He was no pauper and never had been,
but was working on his own farm, making his living with
his own muscle and brain. Nor was he ever a common
drunkard. On the contrary, he was, and had been for years,
an ardent temperance man, "though opposed to prohibition by law." "Once," years ago, he declared with magnificent understatement, he "went on a spree; and this I now
deeply regret." He had not fallen, he had risen; and
everyone except a few so-called Christians applauded his
rise. He may have "slid out" of a law case now and then,
when he had no faith in it; but he did so in order that his
lack of enthusiasm might not disparage his client's case.
Much of this libeling he attributed to the influence of the
Reverend James A. Reed, "pastor and liar" of Springfield;
and the whole thing resulted from Herndon's zeal for
truth.

Ensconced in a comfortable political job, Black viewed
with some uneasiness the possibility of the controversy's
breaking out afresh. He stood to gain nothing from it now.
January 1, 1883, he admonished Herndon that if he got
into a dispute he should quote "Col. Lamon not *me*, the
book and not the writer. It would be unfair to Col. L. for
me to state over my own hand that I had written his book
so long as he chooses to let the contrary be understood."
But Black was still generous with advice. "Your knock-
down argument," he counseled, "is . . . to challenge the
other side to state which church Mr. L. belonged to, or else
[make them] take the ground that a man can be a Christian
and repudiate the Church."

Despite all the odium that Herndon incurred by reason

of his connection with Lamon's book, he never felt ill will toward the reputed author. He did regret selling his manuscripts to Lamon, and claimed that he tried to dispose of them elsewhere before closing the deal with him; and he suspected that Lamon was "no solid, firm friend of Lincoln," especially during the latter part of his administration. But he blamed Black, not Lamon, for the bitter tone of the book. He never wounded Lamon's feelings by so much as hinting to him that he knew who really wrote the book, and he never changed his opinion of its essential veracity.

Replying to a letter from Lamon, on December 1, 1885, he expressed regret that the Colonel was "laid up on the drydock for repairs," and hoped "the good old hull is sound to the core." He recalled the happy circuit days, his first meeting with Lamon at Danville, and Lamon's unfailing kindness to him as a young lawyer. "I am glad to know that you are writing a second life of Lincoln entitled 'Abraham Lincoln, his Administration,' "[1] he said, ". . . I am glad to be informed by you that you intend to write it under, and in the same spirit of independence and truth that moved you in writing your first life . . . Why Lamon, if you and I had not told the exact truth about Lincoln, he would have been a myth in a hundred years after 1865. We knew him—loved him—had ideas and had the courage of our convictions. We told the world what Lincoln was, and were terribly abused for it. We were hated, but all this is wearing away gradually. The good people see that we were honest in our convictions and had the moral and physical courage to stand by them . . ."

---

[1] The book was never published. The manuscript is in the Huntington Library.

And in a postscript: "Come give us a 2d Edition of your first Life with the rough corners chiselled off." Herndon reported that Robert Lincoln had been in Springfield the previous day to attend the funeral of John T. Stuart; and from what Herndon had gathered, Robert hated both him and Lamon "with a kind of savagism."

Herndon did not know that Robert Lincoln had already achieved a measure of revenge on Lamon. Upon the advice of friends, who wished to spare him personal annoyance, Robert had not deigned to read the book, he said; but from newspaper paragraphs, which he could not avoid seeing, he was aware of its tenor. But it was beneath his dignity to protest publicly. Meantime he had advanced steadily at the bar, and in politics, and in 1881 was appointed secretary of war in the cabinet of James A. Garfield. When Garfield was assassinated, Robert Lincoln was the only member of his cabinet to retain his portfolio under President Chester A. Arthur. By 1883 he was being prominently mentioned for the presidency.

About this time Lamon, having failed in his efforts to obtain a territorial appointment, and as a candidate for Congress, tried to obtain appointment as postmaster at Denver, Colorado. Seeing a notice of Lamon's candidacy in a Washington newspaper, Robert Lincoln hastened to the office of Postmaster-General Walter Q. Gresham and protested against Lamon's appointment on the ground that it would be "personally offensive" to him.

Robert's opposition was sufficient to thwart Lamon; and when the Colonel heard what had happened, he wrote to Robert for confirmation or denial. He could not believe Robert was responsible for his rejection, he said. He was the last man on earth he supposed would do such a thing

—and it was so unlike anything his father would have done. Nevertheless, if Robert did not reply he would construe his silence as acknowledgment.

Lamon did not need to fear that Robert would not reply. Robert was only too eager to have an opportunity to tell the Colonel what he thought of him. He took full responsibility for keeping Lamon off the Federal payroll and gave his reason gladly. Despite all the kindness his father had shown Lamon during his life, Lamon had not scrupled to blacken him after death. Robert had finally read the book before drafting his letter, for he wished to be sure "in a matter which, to my amazement, you seem to have forgotten," namely, Lamon's insinuations about his father's birth. "I cannot believe," said Robert, "that you acted by inadvertence, merely using carelessly material bought from Herndon; for it was told me, before the publication of your book, that you had resisted the importunity of at least one good friend of my father, who begged you to omit some offensive statements which he had seen in the proof sheets, and of which I believe this was one."

Robert had reason to believe that Lamon knew the insinuation to be without foundation, but however that might be, it was nevertheless "an astonishing exhibition of malicious ingratitude on your part towards your dead benefactor." Robert could not say whether or not his action in blocking Lamon's appointment was unlike anything his father would have done; his father was charitable and forgiving in the last degree. But he thought that "no man ever attempted while he was living to give him such a wound as you tried to deal him when his friendship was no longer of practical use to you except to be advertised to increase the sale of your merchandise."

Lamon admired Robert's candor, he said in reply, but that was the sum total of his esteem. "President Garfield constituted you the American Mars—the God of War," he replied, "and it would seem that this elevation has prompted you to constitute yourself Lord Almoner of the Postoffice Department also." Robert should improve his understanding by perusing Shakespeare's account of the hallucinations of Jack Cade, who thought he had a birthright to be king of the realm during the reign of Henry VI. But Cade "was satisfied to wait until he became King before exercising his damnable policy, while you enforce yours during the time you are in training for the promotion." Lamon thought there was no accounting for some of nature's freaks, for he could discern no single quality in Robert that could have been inherited from the male side of his house.

Lamon went so far as to admit that his book was not written in the best of taste; and that the language was unnecessarily blunt, sometimes bordering on "reprehensible harshness." No one regretted this more than he did; and if it were to be done over, "these faults and blemishes would not appear." But not one fact would be changed; for the book was truthful, if not polite.

Lamon denied that it reflected on Lincoln's legitimacy. He supposed Robert referred to the recent discovery of the alleged marriage records of Lincoln's parents when he intimated that Lincoln's legitimacy could easily have been established, if Lamon had cared to take the trouble. Robert could accept this new discovery as authentic, if he cared to do so; but Lamon rejected it. If it were genuine, Lincoln's parents were married on September 23, 1806, only four months and nineteen days before Abraham's elder sister was born, on February 10, 1807.[2] "I am not disposed to permit you, or any other man to misrepresent the truth of history when it reflects on the virtue of the family without contradiction," Lamon moralized.

Lamon went on for pages, unburdening his soul, mostly on the theme of Robert's unfitness for the presidency as demonstrated by his vengefulness toward him. He feared for the country. It had been plagued by many isms—communism, nihilism, agrarianism, socialism—now it faced the threat of sentimentalism or "Bob Lincolnism."

If Robert could reconcile his charge of ingratitude "with what God has implanted within your bosom as an apology for a conscience, be it so. It will only demonstrate the fact that you have lived without virtue and will die without repentance." Because Lincoln would have been murdered long before he was if it had not been for Lamon's incessant watchfulness. And he might have escaped Booth's bullet if Lamon had been in Washington instead of Richmond, where Lincoln had sent him, on that fatal night.

Lamon concluded with a conciliatory growl. He hoped Robert would do what every gentleman was pleased to do when convinced of error and when shown he had done injury to a person who had never wronged him. In that case, Lamon would apologize for the contents of this letter. But—and his hackles rose again—if Robert preferred to continue the fight, Lamon was perfectly willing that their whole correspondence should be published to the world.

Thus ends the story of the first efforts of the realistic school—with no one happy at the outcome. Looking back,

---

[2] The New York *Christian Advocate* announced the discovery on May 25, 1882 under the headline, "A lie of Lamon's nailed to the counter—Lincoln's legitimacy established." In copying the entry a clerk ascribed the wrong date to the marriage. Actually, as was later ascertained, it took place on June 12, 1806.

it is apparent that the book was ahead of its time. Probably a fair judgment from the modern point of view would describe it as a mine of information which must be used cautiously—which is to say that Herndon's valuable but not altogether reliable material was maltreated by Chauncey Black.

The controversy over Lincoln's religion seems now to have been a bandying of words. Neither side defined its terms. Had they done so, they might have found they were not too far apart. But, in its later stages, what was originally an honest—if violent—difference of opinion, degenerated into a promotional intrigue with Black the venal prompter and Herndon his gullible stooge.

Unfortunately, no one knew or remembered that Lincoln had once made a public avowal of his religious beliefs. In fact, this was not discovered until 1942. It occurred in 1846, after his campaign for Congress against the Methodist preacher, Peter Cartright, who tried to make Lincoln's religion, or lack of it, an issue of the campaign. Lincoln held his peace until after the election, then set the record straight with a public statement printed in the *Illinois Gazette* of Lacon, Illinois. A letter to the editor explained his reasons, and an accompanying handbill, prepared during the campaign but not used, set forth his views. "A charge having got into circulation in some of the neighborhoods of this District, in substance that I am an open scoffer at Christianity, I have by the advice of some friends concluded to notice the subject in this form," the handbill stated. "That I am not a member of any Christian Church, is true; but I have never denied the truth of the Scriptures; and I have never spoken with intentional disrespect of religion in general, or of any denomination of Christians in particular. It is true that in early life I was inclined to believe in what I understand is called the "Doctrine of Necessity"—that is, that the human mind is impelled to action, or held in rest by some power, over which the mind itself has no control; and I have sometimes (with one, two, or three, but never publicly) tried to maintain this opinion in argument—The habit of arguing thus however, I have entirely left off for more than five years—And I add here, I have always understood this same opinion to be held by several of the Christian denominations. The foregoing, is the whole truth, briefly stated, in relation to myself, upon this subject.

"I do not think I could myself, be brought to support a man for office, whom I knew to be an open enemy of, and scoffer at, religion.—Leaving the higher matter of eternal consequences, between him and his Maker, I still do not think any man has the right thus to insult the feelings, and injure the morals, of the community in which he may live.—If, then, I was guilty of such conduct, I should blame no man who should condemn me for it; but I do blame those, whoever they may be, who falsely put such a charge in circulation against me."

The book and the ensuing controversy had one salutary effect in serving to warn romanticists that there were bounds which they must not transgress without expecting to be challenged and made to adduce proof. Thus the trend toward hagiography was checked. Lincoln was not to become at once a counterpart of the statuesque, too perfect Washington of "Parson" Weems. His figure was still vital, human, ductile, not brittle and hard-cast.

Chapter Four

ROMANTICISM IS THE VOGUE

THE feelings of the Lincoln devotees were gradually assuaged by the numerous magazine articles, reminiscences, and books that poured forth in a swelling stream, and especially by the biography written by Isaac N. Arnold.

A tall thin man of scholarly mien, with high-domed forehead and close-clipped mustache, which was augmented in his later years by a goatee, Arnold was a native of Hartwick, New York, born on November 30, 1815. Moving to Chicago he was admitted to the bar, later serving as city clerk, representative in the state legislature, and Republican congressman, in which latter capacity he was a leader in the enactment of the thirteenth amendment abolishing slavery. An effective public speaker, he frequently addressed literary and historical gatherings and was president of the Chicago Historical Society for many years. In 1866 he published *The History of Abraham Lincoln and the Overthrow of American Slavery,* a forerunner of his *The Life of Abraham Lincoln,* published in 1885.

Arnold knew Lincoln intimately, "revered him as one of the greatest and best of men," and "loved him as a brother." He corresponded regularly with Herndon and frequently solicited his advice while writing his books. Like Herndon he distrusted Bateman. He "does not stand up squarely," he said. "I wrote to him once to ask him if Holland had reported him correctly & he replied—as I recollect 'substantially.' His letter was burned up in the great fire." But Arnold could not agree with Herndon's conception of Lincoln's religious views. Arnold believed that Lincoln subscribed to "the great fundamental principles of Christianity—but as to creed & dogma, he was not strictly *orthodox*." "I do not call him an '*Evangelical*' Christian, but a *broad rational* Christian," he explained. But he would not quarrel about it. "I don't know, but if you & I were to sit down & compare our opinions about Mr. Lincoln's religion I think we should not be so far apart as we seem," he asserted. ". . . If we differ—it will be an *honest* difference—& we shall not cease to believe each means to be truthful."

Herndon thanked Arnold for his "good natured note." "I guess it is true that, if you and I were to sit down together we could nearly agree about Lincoln's religion," he admitted. "Once define what was a *rational* Christian— what are the great *fundamental* principles of Christianity, then we could agree or disagree and say—yes or no."

Herndon invited Arnold to examine his manuscripts. He was glad Arnold planned to devote most of his space to Lincoln's presidential life, "the period which you say you know the most about. This is probably wise. You can and no doubt 'will aid those who come after us to a more just conception of Lincoln.' I hope so—believe so. It will require nerve to tell the truth and the whole truth."

Arnold agreed with Herndon that Lincoln had real, generous affection for very few men, although he had many warm friends. "But take men as a whole," he wrote, "I think he thought better of them than they deserve. He had more *faith* in mankind, the masses than any other man I ever knew. He was never directly acquainted with the vice, corruption of our great cities—Man as he knew him best on the frontier—was as Lincoln believed—disposed to do right—but in the great corrupt cities—there has always been a large class far below Lincoln's general estimate of humanity."

Arnold's book was in keeping with the growing Lincoln tradition, its theme Lincoln's supposed lifelong ambition to free the slaves. Characterizations such as "magnanimous," "affectionate in all his family relations," "honest," "cordial," "simple," served as antidotes to the unflattering adjectives found so frequently in Lamon's book. As for Lincoln's stories, it was always clear to the listener that they were told for their wit; and if they were sometimes vulgar, vulgarity was not their purpose.

To many contemporaries, Arnold's was the most "satisfactory" biography that had yet appeared; and even today it has value because of Arnold's intimacy with Lincoln and its contemporaneous material.

For the most part, however, the flood of Lincoln books was frothy. John P. Usher, formerly Lincoln's Secretary of the Interior, found himself "saluted almost daily by the d—est lot of trash and fiction." In fact, he was so sickened by it that he thought it would almost be a comfort for those who were intimate with Lincoln to die rather than be assailed with any more of it. He had mentioned this to Judge David Davis, and the judge, while expressing no desire to seek comfort in the manner prescribed, had agreed with his opinion of the quality of Lincoln literature. But he saw nothing to be gained by trying to correct it. For the public seemed to find it succulent and satisfying.

Thus, by the middle 'eighties, the "ignoble" performance of Lamon had been largely counteracted. And now came a mammoth work beside which all others paled—the long-anticipated project of Nicolay and Hay.

Nicolay and Hay conceived the idea of writing a biography while they were Lincoln's secretaries. Hay kept a diary, while Nicolay made notes; and Lincoln, who knew of their plan, allowed them to keep some papers of historic interest. After Lincoln's death, they hoped that Robert Lincoln would give them access to his father's papers, and were seriously disturbed to hear that Arnold was to be allowed to publish them. "That dishes our chances," wrote Hay to Nicolay. But later they were gratified to learn that Arnold was working "on his own hook." "Bob encourages it," Hay discovered, "but will not give him the key to the boxes. He will keep them for the present & still hopes for our assistance in classifying them."

This was not the only difficulty. Publishers were not encouraging, would not "talk turkey," said "the market is glutted etc." Hay feared the book would have to be a "labor of love that we will do when we get rich and idle."

Soon after Lamon's book came out, Hay wrote Nicolay that they should get to work. It was not yet time to publish, "but the time for preparation is slipping away." They should have talked to Seward before he died. Gideon Welles had a mass of material, but was publishing it himself in the *Galaxy*. Gustavus Vasa Fox, Lincoln's assistant secretary of the navy, could tell them a great deal; and so could Henry Sanford, Norman B. Judd, and "all the Springfield luminaries."

By 1875 they were at work, Orville H. Browning noting in his diary under date of June 17 that Nicolay called on

John G. Nicolay

him in Springfield where they talked about Lincoln for two hours, Nicolay taking notes all the while.

So far as technical competence was concerned, both Nicolay and Hay were eminently qualified. The former, a native of Bavaria, born February 26, 1832, was industrious, conscientious, and possessed of that mental discipline that characterized nineteenth-century German scholarship.

With the passing years his dark hair and mustache turned grey, while the tufted whiskers of his younger days shredded forth luxuriant from his chin. Always somewhat delicate, with lean face and thin nose, he was sometimes rendered testy by his ailments.

Coming to the United States with his father in 1838, he lived and attended school in Cincinnati, moved to Pittsfield, Illinois, at sixteen took a job with the *Pike County Free Press,* and before he came of age was its owner and editor. In 1857 he went to Springfield as assistant to the secretary of state of Illinois, leaving that position to become Lincoln's private secretary. Hoping to write the campaign biography of his chief, he had been "filled with a jealous rage" when others were delegated to that task.

In 1865 he became American consul at Paris, returning after four years to become editor of the Chicago *Republican.* Now he was marshal of the United States Supreme Court, a position affording him ample time to indulge his literary penchant.

John Hay was traveled, erudite, and gifted with the poet's touch. Glib, dapper, and goateed, a country boy become cosmopolite, he was born in Salem, Indiana, October 8, 1833, graduated from Brown University, studied law and was admitted to the bar in Springfield, but left for Washington as Nicolay's assistant before ever practicing. After the Civil War he served in various diplomatic capacities in Paris, Vienna, and Madrid, then became an editorial writer on the New York *Tribune* under Whitelaw Reid, acting as editor-in-chief for several months while Reid was abroad. In 1875 he moved to Cleveland only to return to Washington four years later as assistant secretary of state under President Rutherford B. Hayes. Later he would be ambassador at the Court of St. James's and secretary of state under McKinley and Roosevelt. Already he had attained literary repute with his "Pike County Ballads" and "Castilian Days."

Before starting their work, Nicolay and Hay made an agreement with Robert Lincoln whereby they were to have the use of his father's papers provided they allow him to approve their manuscript before publication. The papers were turned over to Nicolay; and both he and Hay added what additional material they had or could obtain. Hay bought many books for their joint use. Nicolay outlined the general plan of the work. Then each chose the topics he preferred to write about; and as chapters were finished, each criticized the other's work. Often they found it necessary to reconcile Nicolay's passion for thoroughness with Hay's "artistic craving for proportion"; but no serious disagreements seem ever to have arisen.

Hay was the stylist, and warned Nicolay against his propensity for split infinitives. "I believe this is condemned by all the authorities," he warned. "Lincoln used it, I know, but I don't think it wise for us to." His own work, too, he frequently revised. Having used the expression "mopped up the floor with him," he suggested that the publishers delete it. "When I first heard it, years ago, it seemed very racy," he observed. "Since then it has got to be a regular bit of newspaper slang. If it has grown banal to your ear strike it out."

John Hay

All the while they were at work, they feared they would be "scooped" of some of their choice gems and tidbits. Gideon Welles' magazine articles were especially perturbing. "Do you understand Mr. Welles' references to a 'Memorandum' written by Lincoln in 1864 in anticipation of defeat—in Atlantic?" Hay asked Nicolay, referring to the document in which Lincoln expressed a purpose to call in his successor for a joint effort if he failed of reelection, and which, sealed, with contents undisclosed, was signed by the cabinet members so that if the contingency arose it would bear witness to his decision. "I have the original Mem: he [Lincoln] gave it to me in the presence of the Cabinet, after his reelection. I have the whole occurrence in my note-book. As I was leaving the room with it, Judge Bates asked me for a copy. I cussed silently—then Welles asked for one, and then everybody. Charlie Philbrick made the copies, and I have been dreading their reappearance and felt a little relieved that our old friend had finished his work [1] without an allusion to this matter when lo! in the very last Article, he refers to it. If he has not left other articles in MS. we are still safe; but if he has, he will be sure to copy this precious document in full in the next one."

When the Comte de Paris' *History of the Civil War in America* came out, Hay read it with great interest; and despite a hearty prejudice against the author and his "outrageous unfairness" to Lincoln, he admitted it was "a splendid piece of work." He was envious of the author's complacent discursiveness. "He cares no more for time than McClellan himself," Hay grudged. "He goes plodding peacefully along and tells 'everything.' His chapters

---

[1] Welles died on February 11, 1878.

average 180 pages. He makes me ashamed of my feverish anxiety to boil down and condense, but when your job is to get the universe into 8 vols., you must not make two bites of an atom."

Very early, the writers learned an important precept— that reminiscences are unreliable. They thought to gain much by interviews with Lincoln's contemporaries; but soon found that the memories of even the most intelligent and truthful men were apt to play tricks. They encountered so many instances of this that they came to distrust their own recollections, unless they were confirmed by memoranda or other written evidence.

As the work progressed, the very material threatened to engulf them. Memoirs, reminiscences, diaries, biographies, and histories, not to mention official publications, were pouring from the presses in a torrent with which they could scarcely keep pace. "We shall never get through in a million words, I fear," Hay groaned, and he feared that those who began to read the book "in the flush of youth would go tottering down to their graves" before finishing it. From their original conception of what they termed "the Lincoln book," their work expanded into a history of the times; and rather than the pleasurable exercise they had anticipated, it became an irritating and exhausting responsibility. "They had become," in the words of Hay's biographer, "the guardians of the Lincoln tradition"; and their work must be completed at all costs.

Both had trouble with their eyes, and recurring headaches forced Hay to dictate to a stenographer—"a dull young Englishman who has nothing in the world but a handwriting." Even with pen in hand Hay found that he was rusty, and feared that he would "never write easily and fluently again." "I write with great labor and difficulty," he complained, "my imagination is all gone—a good rid-dance." When forced to dictate, he feared he was through. But he discovered that by taking time, correcting, some-times going back to start afresh, he could dictate about as well as he could write. Indeed, he was surprised at his speed; but "the rapidity is only in the writing," he ex-plained to Nicolay. "The study has taken years."

By the spring of 1885 they had three volumes well in hand and were ready to negotiate for publication. "All the publishing houses in the country want it," wrote Hay to Robert Lincoln; "Children cry for it," he exulted to Nico-lay. Eventually competition narrowed down to the Cen-tury Company and Harpers. Hay conducted the negotia-tions; and when the Century Company offered $50,000 for serial publication, in addition to royalties on the book, the deal was closed. Publication in the *Century Magazine* was scheduled to begin in November, 1886, and to con-tinue month by month. "The only contingency in which we should not be able to keep up would be death," Hay wrote to Nicolay. "If we live we can do it."

This was a period when historical scholarship was in mid-passage between the old school, which wrote from a preconceived point of view, be it laudatory or critical, partisan or sectional, and the cult of modern scholarship with its ideals of objectivity and detachment; and the point of view of Nicolay and Hay was coeval with their time. They aspired to technical accuracy; yet they acknowl-edged a strong pro-Lincoln bias. On August 10, 1885, Hay wrote to Nicolay: "The war has gone by. It is twenty-years ago. Our book is to be read by people who cannot remem-ber anything about it. We must not show ourselves to the public in the attitude of two old dotards fighting over again the politics of our youth . . . We must not write a stump speech in eight vols. 8mo. We will not fall in with the present tone of blubbering sentiment of course. But we ought to write the history of these times like two ever-lasting angels who know everything judge everything, tell the truth about everything and don't care a twang of our harps about one side or the other. There will be one exception: We are Lincoln men all through. But in other little matters, let us look at men as insects and not blame the black beetle because he is not a grasshopper. Salmon Portland Chase is going to be a nut to crack—so is Stanton."

Hay's "one exception" would make a modern historian look at him askance. Pro-Lincoln bias connoted prejudice against every Southern leader and many persons in the North. Another portion of Hay's letter, which referred to General McClellan, made this evident. "I have toiled and labored through the chapter over him," Hay declared. "I think I have left the impression of his mutinous imbe-cility and I have done it in a perfectly courteous manner. Only in Harrison's Landing have I used a single injurious adjective . . . Gilder [editor of the *Century*] was evidently horrified at your saying that Lee ought to be shot—a simple truth of law and equity. I find after a careful reading of a dozen biographies and all his own reports that Stonewall Jackson was a howling crank."

McClellan was their particular *bête noire,* more espe-cially so because a recent writer, the Comte de Paris (and also the Prince de Joinville) had defended him. Hay was "riled" and disgusted. "They have built up an impudent fiction which I fear the plain truth will never destroy," he complained. Their output affected him physically, made him so nervous he feared he must stop reading them. And he was disgusted when Alexander S. Webb, who criticised McClellan in *The Peninsula: McClellan's Campaign of*

1862, "winds up by abusing Lincoln and Stanton like pickpockets for not supporting him."

Hay's attitude toward McClellan was to *"seem* fair to him, while we are destroying him." And the same for Jefferson Davis. "If you can see your way to soften your *tone* toward old Jeff . . . it would be politic," he suggested to Nicolay. "Let the facts make him as despicable as he is—*we* do not want to appear to hate and despise him." And in a postscript: "But we do, and I presume we can't keep it from sticking out."

Hay felt almost as strongly about Chase. "There is enough in Chase's letters abusing Lincoln behind his back for a quiet scorcher," he thought. But unlike Chauncey Black, Hay had regard for the feelings of living relatives. They must think of Mrs. Hoyt, Chase's surviving daughter, he warned. Yet, when they came to deal with Chase, they did not think of her too much.

Sometimes their publishers restrained their animosity. Hay thought that if there was ever a ridiculous character in our history it was James Shields, a Civil War general and an early political opponent of Lincoln's with whom Lincoln almost fought a duel; and Hay also thought that "if there was ever an unprincipled politician it was Douglas." But he was willing to placate "the indignant shade of Paddy Shields." He would strike out everything "that is true and offensive" about him, if the *Century* editors insisted; and he would also suppress his abomination of Douglas. "It would suit me to write nothing but taffy about the Devil himself," he averred with a touch of sarcasm, "in fact there is much in his character to admire. But we are forced by our consciences to tell the truth sometimes, and every time the truth is told you will hear a yelp . . . If I have anywhere called Tom Thumb undersized or insinuated that the onion is less sweet than the rose, I am ready to draw my pen through it."

In view of this privately expressed opinion about Douglas, it is interesting to note how tenderly Nicolay and Hay treated him in print. They agreed with Lamon that a questionable skill in false logic was his main reliance in his forensic duels with Lincoln; yet seemingly they forgave him much for his support of Lincoln in the secession crisis, where they thought he stood forth like a beacon. In the years between the passage of the Kansas-Nebraska Act and the outbreak of war, everyone of his party rivals "disappeared in obscurity, disgrace or rebellion . . . [while] Douglas alone emerged from the fight with loyal faith and unshaken courage, bringing with him through treachery, defeat, and disaster the unflinching allegiance and enthusiastic admiration of nearly three-fifths of the rank and file of the once victorious army of Democratic voters at the North. He had not only proved himself their most gallant chief, but as a final crown of merit he led his still powerful contingent of followers to a patriotic defense of the Constitution and government which some of his compeers put in mortal jeopardy."

As soon as the publishing contract was signed, the Century Company accorded the authors its aid. A. W. Drake, superintendent of the art department, traveled through the Lincoln country collecting pictures, and was able to obtain a photograph of the marriage records of Thomas Lincoln and Nancy Hanks. Richard Watson Gilder, editor of the *Century*, reported that "Herndon, poor old fellow, has been extremely kind to Drake and has been of actual service to us." He furnished an excellent photograph of Lincoln's stepmother, among other things. "Of course he comes up smiling now with a proposition of an article on

Lincoln. He does not know what it is we are going to publish. I shall deal kindly with the old man."

Gilder waxed enthusiastic as the work progressed. "I tell
you, old boy," he wrote to Hay, "you have done and are
doing—a great thing! Somewhere have you given any *personal description* of the man as he was in the White House?
Yes I think I remember a description somewhere.—You
mention in a chapter just read his tenor voice. Such points
are pictures of gold in frames of silver." And C. C. Buel,
an assistant editor, wrote: "I've had a great deal of entertainment out of these three chapters—particularly the last
two; they are great."

The publishers were not chary of expense. Hay was
urged to make changes in proof as freely as if it were
manuscript. "Perfection is what we are after!" Gilder
declared. Even after the plates were cast, Hay should send
on all changes "that are dictated by the Muse of Verity and
the Spirit of Fancy. If you are diffident in this matter you
will never be quite satisfied with the book when you see
it on the shelves of Walhalla."

Buel was in immediate charge for the *Century*. He had
helped edit the *Century's* series on "Battles and Leaders
of the Civil War," which ran serially and which was now
almost completed and ready to be published in book form.
"In reading the MS I'll try to be of a little service, without hypercriticism," Buel promised. "Editorial habit has
kept me at the neutral point of view, and it may be of
some use to you now and then to get a look from that
quarter." He made few suggestions regarding the early
chapters; but when the authors got into the war period,
he noted an undue amount of detail about battles and
campaigns, much of it inaccurate.

Nicolay and Hay were simply not abreast of the work

of military historians; yet they kept obtruding their ideas of military matters until it became necessary for Gilder himself to intervene and put the foot down. "The War Editors have just been going over the October instalment, and have made some suggestions," said he in a letter addressed to both authors on July 12, 1888. "From what they have read of the war part they feel very strongly that it will be necessary for you to take more into account the full result of their labors as shown in the War-*Book*.

"It will not do to depend, so far as their material goes, upon the Magazine publication. Things have been much more thoroughly sifted in coming to book publication. They have a certain feeling of dismay that you should be going to such an extent into the details of the War in 'The Century' itself after the wheat has been threshed so exhaustively in the Magazine and in the book; and they feel, as I suppose you do, that the treatment cannot be the same in any subsequent publication to what it might have been before their labors and the publication of the immense amount of material recently called forth.

"As this is a matter of the most enormous importance to all of us, I think I ought to say that the war-editors feel that the chapters on the War, so far as they have seen them, are, in view of all the circumstances, somewhat inadequate. Your History of course will now be judged by a different standard from what it would have been five or ten years ago,—because *many* persons are now experts where but few were before, and because the material is now so abundant. They suggest that if it were possible, it would be better to cut the military portion down to a smaller scale, because if you go so much into detail the work would have to be perhaps even more exhaustive as well as impeccably accurate.

"But the practical point now is that I must ask you kindly to curtail, so far as the Magazine goes, all that you possibly can with regard to the purely military part, so that we will not be publishing simply a new War Series. What I wish to ask you now definitely is to cut all you can, and we will assist you in doing that . . . In a few months Messrs Johnson and Buel will have finished the War-Book, and they can then turn to and give you the whole benefit of their knowledge of the subject. I assure you they are extremely anxious about the matter. They feel that it would never do to let it go out as now written. It would not satisfy, scientifically speaking, the contemporary audience."

But Hay was mulish; and to the end Buel continued to fret that "Lincoln and his relations to the events is the absorbing thing. Here and there, as in the McClellan chapters, Lincoln's personality and views are strongly intermingled with military events. Aside from those I find most interesting those chapters which deal with Lincoln and the personalities of the commanders, and that give the slightest synopsis of military movements."

As time went on, it became necessary to cut the magazine material in order to get on to publication of the book; and, since it was the military matter which Gilder inevitably wished to take out, Hay became petulant, and told him to cut as he pleased. To Nicolay he wrote: "You may do as you choose about *your* military chapters, but, for my part, I am perfectly willing to have him cut out every military chapter I have written. I am sick of the subject, and fancy the public is." But he would not rewrite. Gilder must so make his elisions that this would be unnecessary. Leaving out a chapter here and there or "retrenching an adjective" would do no good; Gilder should decide which *topics* he wanted and reject the rest. The authors could not materially shorten the work by rewriting chapters. "This is in the nature of a caveat," Hay warned Gilder. "If you hereafter tell us the infernal thing is too long, we will sweetly answer, 'I told you so.' "

Hay thought this cutting was botching the work. They "have whacked about all the life out of the November instalment," he complained; but he, too, became anxious to wind up the serial publication and get on to the book, believing that the more original material it contained the better it would sell. So serial publication was ended in February, 1890, the *Century* having published something between a third and a half of the manuscript.

The *Century* editors were not alone responsible for alterations. Robert Lincoln made the work possible by giving Nicolay and Hay access to his father's papers, and he also helped them obtain access to Gideon Welles' diary and to genealogical data. In this latter matter he was zealous; for Lamon's insinuations had nettled him no end. But his aid was given at a price—his approval of the manuscript.

When Nicolay had looked over Hay's work on the first forty years of Lincoln's life, Hay told him to send it on to Robert; and Hay himself wrote to Robert: "I need not tell you that every line has been written in a spirit of reverence and regard. Still you may find here and there words or sentences which do not suit you. I write now to request that you will read with a pencil in your hand and strike out everything to which you object. I will adopt your view in all cases whether I agree with it or not. But I cannot help hoping you will find nothing objectionable."

Yet, as Hay reread his work, he was doubtful about Robert's probable reaction to three or four things, and wrote to Nicolay to scratch them out before sending Robert the manuscript. But his letter came too late. Hay tried to see Robert to explain, but was unable to get in touch with him. When the manuscript was returned, "I found you had marked every one of the passages," Hay informed Robert. "I will do what you suggest in final revision," he promised. "It is better, even as a matter of taste and without regard to your wishes which would of course be conclusive."

But Robert was distrustful; and Hay hastened to reassure him. "I was very sorry to see by a letter you wrote Nicolay the other day that you were still not satisfied with my assurance that I would make those first chapters all right," he expostulated. "Even before you read them I had struck out of my own copy here nearly everything you objected to & had written Nicolay to make the changes in his which he had not had time to do. Since then I have gone over the whole thing twice again reading every line so far as possible from your own point of view and I don't think there is a word left in it that would displease you. But of course before final publication I shall give you another hack at it with plenary blue pencil powers." Two years later, when they were much farther on in the book, Hay wrote: "Thank you for your corrections—all of which I have of course adopted. The MS of all the articles goes to the publishers today. I was sorry to bother you but I thought it best in every way to consult you—and it was."

In the light of this correspondence, it is interesting to discover that the original manuscript of the first four chapters of volume one has been preserved, with the changes that were made. One of Robert Lincoln's changes can be positively identified. It concerns the story of how his father sewed up the eyes of a drove of hogs, when he found it impossible to get them aboard a flatboat by driving them in the usual manner. On the margin of the manuscript, beside the story, was written, "leave out (?)"; and underneath this notation, "I say leave out—R. T. L." The story had already been published by Lamon; but Robert seemingly thought it in bad taste.

The hand that altered the other passages cannot be identified; but from the foregoing correspondence, it is certain that if they were not censored by Robert Lincoln, they were changed by John Hay when he read them from Robert's "point of view." All of them pertain either to Thomas Lincoln or to the conditions of pioneer life. Those parts of the manuscript that were altered are given below, with the passages that were struck out in italics and those that were added in brackets. It seems safe to conclude that the original version represents John Hay's opinions when he wrote without restraint.

Chapter One

. . . Thomas, to whom were reserved the honors of an illustrious paternity, *appears never to have done any else especially deserving of mention. He was an idle, roving, inefficient, good natured man, as the son of a widow is apt to be according to the Spanish proverb. He had no vices so far as we can learn but he also had no virtues to speak of. He* learned the trade of a carpenter *but accomplished little of it.* He was an easy going person . . .

. . . he seems to have resembled his son in appearance. *Men like him may be seen every day in Western rural towns, fond of story-telling, of talking things over by the red-hot stove of tavern bar-rooms, or in the cool door ways of livery stables, according to the season. He was a Jackson Democrat, as those of his kind usually were. He was dis-*

Robert Todd Lincoln

cursive in his religious affiliations, changing his church about as often as he changed his residence, but died a member of the Disciples or "Campbellite" Baptist Church. He was generally called an unlucky man . . .

. . . It required full as earnest and intelligent industry to persuade a living out of those barren hillocks, and weedy hollows covered with stunted and scrubby underbrush, as it would amid the rocks and sands of the Northern coast. *But neither the will nor the intelligence was there.* Thomas Lincoln settled down in this dismal solitude to a deeper solitude than ever; and there in the midst of the most unpromising circumstances that ever witnessed the advent of a hero in this world, Abraham Lincoln was born on the twelfth day of February, Eighteen Hundred and Nine.

Four years later, *the unlucky farmer seemed about to belie his baleful reputation, for by one of those spasmodic efforts not unknown to men inherently indolent, he* [Thomas Lincoln] purchased *without money as usual though not without price* a fine farm of 238 acres on Knob Creek near where it flows into the Rolling Fork, and succeeded in getting a portion of it into cultivation. The title, however, remained in him only a little while, *and the spurt of enterpise died away into the habitual languor of the man,* and after his property had passed out of his control, he *betook himself to the last resort of restless inefficiency, and* looked about for another place *where he owed no debts and could get fresh land for little or nothing* [to establish himself.] . . .

Chapter Two

. . . The old barbarous equality of the earlier times was gone. *Industry and thrift had had space enough to achieve their usual result in increased comfort and respectability. A difference of classes began to be seen, and this was as usual resented by those who from defect of energy or capacity naturally remained at the bottom. Of course Thomas Lincoln was not among the successful ones, and of course he attributed his lack of success to the conditions of life around him. He thought that this was no country for a poor man. Incapable of earnest competitive work, he was always trying to better his chances by escaping competition. He had heard from some of his cronies that there was plenty of good land and no rich neighbors in Indiana, and thither he determined to go. The easiest and most natural way for him to make the journey was by water for it was down stream all the way, down Knob Creek to Rolling Fork, down Rolling Fork to Salt River, down Salt River to the Ohio and down that beautiful stream to Perry County, Indiana, which was his destination.* [A difference of classes began to be seen. Those who held slaves assumed a distinct social superiority over those who did not. Thomas Lincoln, concluding that Kentucky was no country for a poor man, determined to seek his fortune in Indiana. He had heard of rich and unoccupied lands in Perry County in that state, and thither he determined to go.] He built a rude raft, . . .

. . . He arrived safely at the place of a settler named Posey, with whom he left his odd invoice of household goods for the wilderness, while he started on foot to look for a home in the dense forest. *It was not in his nature to go far and he* [He] selected a spot which pleased him in his first day's journey . . .

. . . *He accepted the goods the forest provided for him with little care for anything beyond. He never really owned his farm. He took steps a year after his arrival 'under the old credit system' to enter a quarter section. He afterwards gave up to the government half of this quarter, and did not get his patent for the eighty acres he retained, for ten years. This he accomplished at last, probably with borrowed money, for he gave it up the next year and moved West again carrying his ill-luck with him.* [His cabin was like that of other pioneers.]

When we consider that a weeks work was all that was required to make a cabin habitable, and that Thomas Lincoln was a carpenter by trade, we can form some idea of the hopeless indolence which allowed him to live two years in a house without a door and without a floor. A few three-legged stools . . .

. . . The Sparrows, husband and wife died early in October, and Nancy Hanks followed them after an interval of a few days. *Life was so undesirable that there was little occasion for mourning.* Thomas Lincoln made the coffins for his dead "out of green lumber, cut with a whip saw," and they were all buried, with scant ceremony, in a *little* clearing of the forest.

. . . *It is possible that Thomas may have painted his home in the greenwood in rather too flattering colors, for we are told that his wife was "surprised" at what she found; the signs of inefficient farming, the disgraceful state of the cabin, the wretchedness of the little Lincolns, and of Dennis Hanks, who had been thrown, in helpless orphanage, upon the family, but it* [It] took little time for this energetic and honest Christian woman to make her influence felt even in these discouraging surroundings, and Tom Lincoln and the children were the better for her coming all the rest of their lives. The *scandalous* lack of doors and floor was at once corrected. Her honest pride *made* [inspired] her husband *ashamed of his shiftlessness* [to greater thrift and industry.] The goods she brought with her compelled some effort at *decency* [harmony] in the fittings of the house. She dressed the *forlorn* children in warm clothing, and put them to sleep in comfortable beds. With this little addition to their resources, the family were *utterly changed* [much improved] in appearance, behaviour and self-respect . . .

. . . It is touching to think of this great-spirited child starving for want of the simple appliances of education which are now afforded gratis to the poorest and most indifferent *of the laboring class.* He did a man's work from the time he left school . . .

One more change, in addition to the omission of the hog story, appears in Chapter Four:

. . . His final move was to Goose Nest prairie where he died in 1851 at the age of seventy-three years. After a life which, though *a complete and utter failure in every* [not successful in any] material *and moral* [or worldly] point of view, was probably far happier than that of his illustrious son, being unvexed by *industry* [enterprise] or ambition . . .

Hay explained to Gilder that they were purposely curtailing their treatment of Lincoln's ancestry. There was information to show that the Lincolns in Virginia were thrifty and well-to-do; but if they said too much about that they would run up against the problem of Thomas Lincoln, upon whom they must not dwell. "His grandson is extremely sensitive about it. It is not an ignoble feeling in R. T. L. He says he feels sorry for the old man, and does not think it right to jump on him, in the broad light of his son's fame."

The revised version was in better taste than the original; but to a modern historian such truckling to the whims of Robert Lincoln would seem intolerable. Yet it is not without a feeling of sympathy that we see Robert striving to maintain his forebears' status. And 'strangely enough, he was unconsciously doing history a service. For, even in its diluted form, John Hay's characterization of Thomas Lincoln was too severe in the light of modern discoveries.

We may well regret that more of this manuscript was not preserved so that we might know what changes were made with respect to other controversial matters. As printed, it added nothing new about Lincoln's boyhood, youth, and early manhood, for Nicolay and Hay relied largely on Lamon and other earlier biographers for material for this period. In contrast to Lamon, however, their accent was upon the more attractive features of Lincoln's character, although they did not deny his fondness for the satirical and indiscreet. They conceded the Ann Rutledge incident only eight lines and made no mention of the "fatal first of January"; although they did describe Lincoln's misery of indecision preceding his wedding. They had a unique explanation of his melancholy, attributing it not to shame of family background, thwarted love, or infelicitous domestic relations, but to the fact that he "was poisoned by the enervating malaria of the Western woods, as all his fellows were, and the consequences of it were seen in his character and conduct to the close of his life."

Surprisingly enough, in view of Robert Lincoln's censorship, Nicolay and Hay were frank regarding Lincoln's mother. Without evading the controverted issue of her birth, they stated the facts, as they understood them, without calling undue attention to their apparent meaning. They accepted Dennis Hanks' affirmation that Nancy Hanks' mother was Lucy Hanks, and that Nancy was reared by the Sparrows and called by their name. But they did not mention Lucy's later marriage to Henry Sparrow, and essayed no explanation of Nancy's bearing her mother's maiden name. The whole Hanks family, they said, "was

composed of people so little given to letters that it is hard
to determine the proper names and relationships of the
younger members amid the tangle of traditional cousin-
ships."

The serial publication of Nicolay and Hay's book evoked
tremendous interest. Genealogical addicts were prolific
with suggestions, many of which were designed to establish a connection between themselves and the Lincolns. A
son of General O. M. Mitchel and a daughter of General
Irvin McDowell were thankful for friendly treatment
vouchsafed their fathers. One diffident informant hoped
his contribution was worth while; but if not, he assumed
the authors kept a wastebasket.

Some criticism went to the publishers, who sent it on
to Nicolay and Hay. "Here is Archibald Forbes [2] reaching
quietly for your top-knot," grinned Buel, as he wrote to
Hay. And again, "Doctor McClellan of Minnesota and
General [John] Gibbon have been going for you, in points
of the Fitz-John Porter case." Hay was vacationing in
Europe, and Buel enclosed Gibbon's article "just to remind
you that there is a land of pure despite, where work and
discord dwell."

General Porter himself complained of the way they
treated him,[3] and demanded a public retraction; but the
authors stalled by promising to review their conclusions
before publication of the book. And when Porter would
not brook procrastination, and threatened to take his "own
course to direct attention to these errors," Hay talked the

---

[2] Archibald Forbes (1838–1900) was one of the foremost British war correspondents of his day.
[3] Porter had been court-martialled and cashiered for his conduct at Second Bull Run, but was subsequently vindicated and reinstated. Nicolay
and Hay ascribed the reinstatement to political influences.

matter over with Buel and devised a "double-backaction-reversible statement of the Porter muddle that will hit him if he is a deer, and miss him if he is a calf."

Hay showed no great solicitude for Porter; but he was astonished and concerned to learn that Thomas T. Eckert was "outraged" by his account of the Hampton Roads conference.[4] Eckert said "all his friends tell him it is infamous," Hay wrote to Nicolay, "that reporters have been to him offering their columns to defend himself against us!! I listened, dumb with wonder. I will tell you the details when I see you. In the meantime I told him, if he would make a memorandum and send it to us, we would be glad to correct anything which was inaccurate etc. etc. We shall not have a friend left on earth by next fall."

Some objections were exasperating. Charles A. Dana, former assistant secretary of war and now editor of the New York *Sun,* could not concur in Hay's account of what took place at the War Department on election night in 1864 and insisted, reported Hay, "that I was not at the War Department that night, in the face of my diary which says I was. You see the sort of pig-headed contradiction we have to go through on the part of conceited old men with bad memories, who have been lying for twenty years." Probably before they finished they would "be contradicted by every dead-beat with a bad memory between the two oceans."

So many living persons had participated in the events Nicolay and Hay described that the minutest errors were picked out. Hay marveled that misnumbering a Massachu-

---

[4] Eckert was head of the telegraphic department of the war office from 1862 to 1864, when he became Assistant Secretary of War. At this time he was general manager of the Western Union Telegraph Company. From the account of the conference in both book and magazine it is difficult to determine what Eckert objected to.

setts regiment "has set the continent on fire. What would happen to us, if we made a serious mistake?"

Yet, when the articles had been running for sixteen months, Hay had to admit: "We get thus far very little abuse and most of that is clearly motivated." On one occasion he presided at the unveiling of a statue of Horace Greeley in New York. "I had built a monument to him myself," he told Henry Adams, "but *l'un n'era empêche pas l'autre*. His daughter was there, on the whole the prettiest woman in America (outside of your breakfast table), and she smiled at me so good naturedly that I am more than ever convinced no human being has read a word of my calumnies." But when he met Miss Mildred Lee, the daughter of General Robert E. Lee, at a dinner, she intimated "that I had better never have been born," although she was very nice.

From the first the publishers exulted. Circulation was up, and criticism denoted public interest. "I hope the criticism of Century Editors, correspondents, newspapers etc will not annoy you unduly," wrote Gilder to "My dear Authors." "The life is a great success.—All the world has its eye upon it: and it will be a d––d sight better for having had the benefit of a million criticisms. No history ever published had such observation. This is hard on you— but it is also your glory & opportunity.

"From a magazine point of view it is all I hoped—so keep stiff upper lips—& accept again, the congratulations of
Your grateful,
R. W. Gilder"

Back at "Chinkapin Hill," on the Sangamon River, a man, who once hoped to write "the" life of Lincoln, confided his opinions to another man, who was now writing

that book for him. As the articles appeared in the *Century,*
William H. Herndon wrote a running commentary to
Jesse W. Weik. He thought the first article "very good,"
and truthful on the whole; but in the second installment
Nicolay and Hay seemed to be suppressing facts. They
knew all about Lincoln's ancestry—A. W. Drake had intimated as much to several persons in Springfield—but they
weren't telling what they knew. Herndon would lay a bet.
"I will bet you a chicken cock that Nicoly [sic] & Hay's
book will tire out the public by its length and unimportant
trash. You mark what I say unless a change is made by
N & H."

"Have you read the Jany no. of the Century?" wrote
Herndon, when the third installment appeared. "If you
have you will see that N. & H. have suppressed many facts—
material facts of Lincoln's life; and among them are L's
genealogy—paternity—the description of Nancy Hanks—
old Thomas Lincoln—the Ann Rutledge story—L's religion
—L's insanity—the facts of L's misery with Mary Todd—L's
breakdown on the night that he & Mary Todd were to be
married, etc. etc. I do not say that they did not mention
some of these things in a round about way, but I do say
that the kernel—"nib" & point of things have been purposely suppressed . . . No wonder that L had a contempt
for all history and biography; he knew how it was written:
he knew the motives & consciences of the writers of history
& biography. Lincoln wanted to know the whole truth &
nothing less. *This I know.* N. & H. write correctly as far
as they go, or probably *dare* go . . . N & H handle things
with silken gloves & 'a camel hair pencil': they do not
write with an iron pen. If some sharp critic knew what
you and I know he would shiver the future of N & H's
biography in a minute."

It was plain to Herndon that "the boys" were "smothering up in words" some things they did not wish to make too evident. This was a mistake. They should either tell the whole truth about a subject or not mention it at all. If they piqued people's curiosity, someone would dig the matter out. He had once written an article on this subject and sent it to the *North American Review*. He wished they would publish it now. It would be timely; and would convince people that there was one man in America "who was not writing the life of Lincoln under the surveillance of 'Bob' Lincoln. H & N, in my opinion, are afraid of Bob: he gives them materials and they in their turn play *hush*. This is my opinion and is worth no more than an honest opinion." For once the old man's intuition was right.

Herndon scoffed at Nicolay and Hay's "miasmatic idea." Forest life made people thoughtful, reticent, and contemplative, but not sad. Pioneer folk were happy, as "the boys" would have known, had they lived with them. Their theory of Lincoln's melancholy did not fit the facts as Herndon's did. But they were right when they said Lincoln received everybody's confidence but rarely gave his own, and that he had individuality that always made him stand forth from the crowd. On the whole, however, theirs was weak and wordy stuff. People in Springfield were tired of it; and in Menard County, where New Salem used to be, "they laugh at it."

Possibly this was so, but the public seemed to find it appetizing. Gilder thought his readers wanted more, especially of the sort of thing that illumined Lincoln's personality. Before this book was finished he was suggesting another which would describe Lincoln's personal traits.

But the authors would not promise. First they must complete this work. Then they planned an edition of Lincoln's writings and speeches. Beyond that they would not commit themselves. Perhaps the "Personal Traits" would grow out of the writings. If so, well and good. Gilder hoped it would. He was sure they were full of that sort of thing if they would let themselves go.

Meantime Hay was working like a "dray-horse," correcting proof. "You know nothing about proof-reading," he wrote to William Dean Howells, an editor of *Harper's*, "with you it is the perusal of a charming author—no more; —with us it is reading an old story, musty and dry, and jumping up every instant to consult volumes still mustier, to see if we have volume and page right on the margin,— and the dull story right in the text. I am aweary of it."

But at last the work was done; and the book sold well, considering its size and relative costliness. Five thousand copies were disposed of by subscription in a short time, and it has enjoyed a steady, if slow, sale ever since.

Although Hay considered it *"a tour de force* of compression," some reviewers criticised its length. The man assigned to appraise it for *The Critic* must have hefted it and winced. With lowering brow he made some rapid calculations: It must contain at least 1,500,000 words; 300,-000 more than Gibbon had lavished on twelve centuries of the Roman Empire; as many words as Bancroft had employed in recounting the whole history of America from its discovery to the end of the Revolutionary War; as many words, dealing with the four and one-half years of Lincoln's presidency alone, as Green had used to narrate the whole history of the English people for thirteen hundred years. What prodigality! The reviewer was evidently not a Lincoln zealot. Whipping his statistics into shape, and adding a few general observations, he went home—probably to a novel.

The Athenium believed the book would be accepted as a standard work, although it too was repelled by its bulk. It would have been better, its reviewer thought, if the authors had been willing to sacrifice some of their material, no matter how laboriously acquired, instead of permitting it to overpower them. But the editors of *Harper's New Monthly Magazine* did not agree. They thought the writers had thoroughly assimilated their material and had done the most significant historical job of a generation, and their treatment was so impersonal that the facts seemed to make their own record.

On this latter point the *Political Science Quarterly* took issue. It agreed that the book was the most valuable contribution to American history in many years, but it conceded it this high tribute despite its partiality. Nicolay and Hay's affection for Lincoln "was so great and their devotion so blind that they instinctively resent the approach of a possible rival as if he were a positive enemy." They seemed to fear lest there be too many great men during the period of the Civil War and whenever anyone had the temerity to intrude, they proceeded to magnify his weaknesses and mistakes until he was reduced to an object of suspicion, pity, or contempt.

The Nation also objected on this score, especially since Lincoln needed "no such belittling of others to stand as the central figure." Perhaps the authors' canvas was too large and they thought they must maintain the dominance of their hero by throwing him into high relief against a lackluster background.

Lyman Trumbull wrote privately to Lamon that he much preferred Lamon's book to that of Nicolay and Hay. He saw no necessity of magnifying Lincoln's virtues or exaggerating his abilities, or especially of disparaging others, as Nicolay and Hay had done, "in order to hold him up as a noble example of mankind." And to Lamon, too, the picture seemed too perfect. The Lincoln he knew was "flesh and blood—human," while the Lincoln of Nicolay and Hay "from the time he was rocked in the cradle . . . never deviated from . . . the golden stairs."

On the whole, Hay was surprised that the critics found so few "weak joints in my armor." "Laws-a-mercy! If I had the criticising of that book, what a skinning I could give it," he confided to Henry Adams.

Some weak joints were probed at once, while others were detected with the passing of time. Upon the death of Hannibal Hamlin, in 1891, A. K. McClure, editor of the Philadelphia *Times,* printed an article asserting that Lincoln discreetly used his influence to have Andrew Johnson nominated as his running mate in 1864 in place of Hamlin. The latter was entirely unobjectionable to Lincoln; but the President thought the nomination of a Southern man would remove the taint of sectionalism from the administration and lessen the peril of foreign recognition of the Confederacy.

This was at variance with Nicolay and Hay's account. When they wrote, Andrew Johnson was in ill repute, and according to them, Lincoln took no position whatever on the vice-presidential nomination, but left the matter wholly to the decision of the nominating convention, although Hamlin was his personal preference. When McClure's article appeared, Nicolay wrote to Mrs. Hamlin, declaring it erroneous and referring her to what he and Hay had said.

McClure heard about this letter and replied publicly in his issue of July 9, presenting his argument in full and characterizing Nicolay as "ignorant," "arrogant," and no more familiar with backstage happenings "than any other routine clerk about the White House."

Nicolay scorned such "personal abuse." It proved nothing except McClure's "rage and wounded vanity at being exposed in a gross historical misstatement" that imputed intrigue and falsehood to Lincoln. "That might be your conception of Abraham Lincoln," he chided, "but it is not mine. That may be your system of politics, but it was not his."

McClure waxed wroth; amplified his argument, and concluded with a flash of verbal pyrotechnics. "Instead of speaking truth, you flung your ignorance and egotism with ostentatious indecency upon the bereaved household of the yet untombed Hamlin, and when brought to bay by those better informed than yourself, you resent it in the tone and terms of a ward-heeler in a wharf-rat district battling for constabulary honors. I think it safe to say that the public judgment will be that it would have been well for both Lincoln's memory and the country had such a biographer been drowned when a pup. Dismissed."

Nicolay would not permit McClure "to retreat in a cloud of vituperation." He wrote one more letter, which McClure answered by printing the testimony of several Republican party leaders. Horace White, who accompanied Lincoln as a reporter for the Chicago *Press and Tribune* during the great debates, and who had followed this controversy carefully from the *Tribune* office, where he now held forth as editor, was ready to concede that McClure "made out his case," although he had not thought so "until this last batch of evidence came out."

White himself found weak joints when he wrote his life of Lyman Trumbull. The more he studied the sources, the more he was convinced that Nicolay and Hay were more loyal to Lincoln than to historical truth. He found, for example, that Lincoln agreed to evacuate Fort Sumter provided the Virginia secession convention would adjourn *sine die*. Hay's diary showed that Hay knew all about this; but when he and Nicolay came to write, "it did not tally with the prevailing notion of the best way to meet the crisis impending in 1861. So they omitted it from the history but forgot to erase it from the diary." White also objected to their distortion of the facts relating to Simon Cameron's expulsion from Lincoln's cabinet. They did not advert at all to his "scoundrelism" and "rascality," but made it appear that he departed in consequence of Lincoln's repudiation of his official report recommending that slaves be freed and employed as soldiers, a policy that Lincoln was not ready to adopt. Actually, as White well remembered, Lincoln was forced to let Cameron go because the House of Representatives censured him for dubious awards of War Department contracts. Lincoln eased the pain by appointing him minister to Russia; and White recalled how Lincoln fell in the estimation of the more high-minded men in Congress when he continued to confide in Cameron upon his return from Moscow.

Later scholars have been even more critical. The book "exasperated" Nathaniel Wright Stephenson, a latter-day historian, while Albert J. Beveridge considered it "atrocious." But both these men ignored the march of time. A fairer estimate is that of John Spencer Bassett, who appraised it in the *Cambridge History of American Literature* as "one of the best historical works of the generation in which it was written."

Nicolay and Hay's two-volume edition of Lincoln's *Works* appeared in 1894, and made available a mass of original material from which readers and investigators could draw their own conclusions. Again, if we judge by the standards of their time, they did an estimable job; although they did not scruple at emendations in spelling, punctuation, and occasionally grammar; and there is evidence of carelessness and haste. And here, as in the *Life*, Robert Lincoln had the final word regarding what went in and what stayed out.

With the *Life* and *Works* completed, Hay had had enough. "You were kind enough to make some inquiry about the big book of N. & H.," he wrote to Henry Adams. "It is out and out of my thoughts." His career as a historian was over. He was surfeited and wanted no more of it. But Nicolay made Lincoln his lifework. For years he kept the Lincoln manuscripts, and from time to time wrote articles. In 1901 he wrote a one-volume abridgement of the *Life*, which sold 35,000 copies. He looked upon the Lincoln field as his demesne, and trespassers were unwelcome.

Close scrutiny of Lincoln enhanced his stature in the eyes of Nicolay and Hay. When they were two-thirds through, Hay wrote to Robert Lincoln: "Year after year of study has shown me more clearly than ever how infinitely greater your father was than anybody about him, greater than even we imagined while he lived. There is nothing to explain or apologize for, from beginning to end. He is the one unapproachably great figure of a great epoch."

And so they pictured him. A grand figure, their Lincoln. Yet, to some who were realistically inclined, the finish was too smooth, the expression too ethereal. "To the younger generation Abraham Lincoln has already become a half-mythical figure," wrote Carl Schurz, reviewing their book in *The Atlantic*, "which, in the haze of historic distance, grows to more and more heroic proportions, but also loses in distinctness of outline and feature. This is indeed the common lot of popular heroes; but the Lincoln legend will be more than ordinarily apt to become fanciful, as his individuality . . . was so unique, and his career so abounding in startling contrasts."

And while Nicolay and Hay toiled, the realists were not idle. Before their portrait was ready to be taken from the easel, William H. Herndon and Jesse W. Weik placed their sketch beside it. The product of the "camel's hair pencil" contrasted sharply with that of the "iron pen."

Chapter Five

THE MARK OF THE IRON PEN

THE financial troubles that forced Herndon to sell copies of his Lincoln manuscripts were aggravated by the panic of 1873 and the years of depression which followed. "My poverty keeps my nose to the grindstone and it is now raw," he lamented. The bucolic occupations he once craved had now become a necessary drudgery. Hating the law, he was forced to take it up again to augment the fruits of husbandry. Once a voracious reader and cognizant of what was going on, he now had little time for books. Had it not been for his customary graciousness in responding to a request for a Lincoln autograph, his dream of writing a biography of Lincoln would have remained illusory.

The request came from a young student at Asbury College, in Greencastle, Indiana. Herndon promised to see what he had, and searching through his papers, found a couple of legal documents, written and signed by Lincoln.

Enthusiastic and enterprising, the young man continued

to correspond with Herndon, and after graduation came to see him. Herndon took him to the old law office, the room where Lincoln wrote his first inaugural, the State House, where Lincoln delivered his "house-divided" speech, and other Springfield shrines. Then they repaired to the young man's hotel, where Herndon spent the remainder of the day in reminiscence.

The young man was Jesse W. Weik, who from that time forth was a Lincoln devotee.

Returning to Greencastle, he planned to write two articles, one dealing with Lincoln as a lawyer, the other with Lincoln as a politician. Herndon approved the idea and wrote long letters giving Weik what information he possessed. As Weik plied him with questions, his flagging spirit quickened, and he wrote until he was "pumped dry—dry as a sand desert." "Pick out what you like," he suggested, "and throw the balance to the dogs."

Weik planned investigations in Indiana and Kentucky, and Herndon told him whom to see. And Herndon continued to write, stealing moments in court, driving himself till late at night after working all day on the farm. If he could not write about Lincoln himself, he seemed to hold it a duty to encourage one who could and would. Often he inscribed two long letters in a single day. "It is now late at night—am tired from my daily toil," was a characteristic ending.

As time passed, it seemed he must have furnished enough material for a biography and he suggested the idea to Weik, who was keeping everything Herndon wrote. Herndon was glad his letters were being saved. They contained much that the world would want. "I am willing to be tested by them during all coming time, by the severest criticism," he asserted. "If I misrepresent willfully the world will know it, & if I am honestly mistaken the world will know that; and if I am true they will know that too."

Weik was grateful for Herndon's help—he was the only one of Lincoln's intimates who was frank and unreserved. Herndon was not surprised at this. Few people who claimed familiarity with Lincoln really knew or understood him, he explained, and many of those who did were strangely taciturn. "The ruling people here—say from 1856 to 1861 —do not, as I think, do right, they are mum about him except they are forced to say something good of him occasionally . . . I feel it my duty to state to all the Peoples my idea of Lincoln and my knowledge of the facts of his life so far as I know them. This is my religion—has been for 20 years and will be probably for 10 more years. I want the world to know Lincoln."

He recurred to the idea of a biography. He and Weik could do it. His letters were half of it, "ready made to hand," and he still had the originals of the material he sold to Lamon. If Weik would do the writing, Herndon would keep him primed.

Thus was the biography conceived, and thus it was eventually completed. Herndon sent letter after letter, rambling, discursive, unorganized. Sometimes when he yawed off toward the psychoanalytical in an effort to probe the processes of Lincoln's mind, Weik would suggest that they eschew the fanciful and stick to things mundane. But Herndon was hard to restrain. He had tried so hard to fathom Lincoln's soul.

Judging by the response to Nicolay and Hay, the public had an omnivorous appetite. People seemed to relish Lincoln's thoughts and feelings; they wanted to know what books he read, what "girls he hugged," and his earlier years

Jesse W. Weik

seemed no less stirring than the period of his greatness. Well, Herndon would tell all. "The truth and the whole truth about Lincoln will never injure him. He will grow larger under the blaze of truth and the sharpest criticism of the iron few. He was too great, too good, and too noble to be injured by truth." Herndon acknowledged a sort of mania on this point.

Yet, there must be bounds. Herndon had no wish to reopen the controversy on Lincoln's religion, for example. He had said enough about that. But it was too important to omit. Perhaps they could treat it briefly and in generalities.

And there was the riddle of Lincoln's birth. Herndon had pondered it for years without solving it. If Weik went to Kentucky, he should "scratch out the facts as a dog digs out a rabbit—coon or ground hog." Herndon had modified his previous opinion about Thomas Lincoln's loss of manhood only to the extent of ascribing it now to castration rather than mumps, or perhaps castration resulting from mumps. But he could not fix the time of this mishap and time was of the essence in the nature of the case. Until he had positive knowledge on that point, he would give Nancy Hanks the benefit of doubt, but he was not ready to reject the Enloe story. "It is a curious story, and may all be true," he wrote to Weik.

But the lashing Herndon suffered as a result of Lamon's indiscreet insinuations had cut deeper than he realized or would admit; and even with his zeal for truth he hesitated. He would see what some of his friends advised as to how far he should go.

John M. Palmer, Civil War general and former governor of Illinois, thought the question too delicate to answer offhand, and with a politician's caution, he pussyfooted, begging for time to think. Alfred Orendorff believed the people wanted the matter cleared up, and so did Senator Shelby Cullom and Dr. William Jayne. But James Matheny advised against touching it, unless the facts cleared both Lincoln and his mother of any offensive taint. Richard J. Oglesby, Illinois war-time governor now serving again in that office, declared that the people's good sense had already settled the question to their satisfaction.

Henry C. Whitney, a former Eighth Circuit lawyer, who was now living in Chicago, hoped Herndon would not go beyond the marriage record. It was one thing to talk about such things "among ourselves," and quite another to proclaim them to the world. "I as a friend should very much dislike to see any doubt cast upon Lincoln's legitimacy for the public eye," he said, "and I have no doubt his friends generally would do so. You are aware what a great deal of trouble Davis Swett & Fell had to induce Hill Lamon to suppress or change one chapter of his book. That affords an example of how Lincoln's average friends regard the matter."

Leonard Swett agreed with Whitney, and cited Lamon's experience as an example of what happened when an author was too brash. And that was as it should be, he asserted. History should perpetuate a man's virtues or hold up his vices to be shunned. "The heroes of the world are its standards, and in time . . . they are clothed with imaginary virtues." Take Washington and the cherry tree, for instance.

Surely, in writing a biography of Grant, thought Swett, one should not tell about the time, on the Western plains before the war, when Grant got so drunk he "did his business" in a brother officer's mess pan. His biographer should dwell rather on "the glories of Appomatox," and leave "this little episode" to oblivion.

Swett had heard that a certain publishing house had "got on to" a story of George Washington's mistress and illegitimate son in Philadelphia during the general's first winter's stay there. But Washington had become such a *"steel plate engraving"* in the public mind that the publisher destroyed the evidence, which he obtained at great expense, rather than risk a shock to public taste. "Philadelphia is an old city & is full of curious things," confided Swett. "I am enformed [sic] in a way I believe it to be true that there is an original autograph letter in existence there from George Washington from Mount Vernon that he (George) is saving up a very fine yellow girl which he proposes to send when ripe to his friend at Philadelphia. How would this story do to ornament the steel plate engraving?" [1]

Herndon was ready to give up. "I guess we had better bow to the semi-omnipotence of public opinion," he wrote to Weik. ". . . We can tell all necessary truths—all those truths which are necessary to show Lincoln's nature, etc., characteristics, etc. We need not, *nor must we, lie*. Let us be true as far as we go, but by all means let us with grace bow to the inevitable . . . Make things straight & rosy. Success is what we want. We want no failures. Do what is necessary to gain that end, short of lying—or fraud. Please Lincoln's friends—the Publishers—and all mankind, past present & the future."

No one would get angry if they suppressed Nancy Hanks' illegitimacy or unchastity, he explained in a later letter, "but thousands will go crazy—wrathy—furious—wild etc if

---

[1] These and other similar stories have enjoyed wide circulation, but students are convinced that they have no basis in fact.

we insert such a suggestion." "Jesse, get on the safe side," he admonished. Why could they not say simply that *"in law"* Lincoln was the son and heir of Thomas Lincoln and Nancy Hanks Lincoln? The general reader would not notice "the sharp point *in law,"* especially if they treated the whole question in general terms.

But Weik rejected his advice, and since Herndon read the proofs, he must have acceded. The Enloe story, as well as other stories concerning Lincoln's paternity, were alluded to in the book; and while they were represented to be gossip, their inclusion was predicative of doubt.

On other matters Herndon either mellowed or bowed to expedience. "Jesse," he wrote, as the book was nearing completion, "in one of my letters to you I stated that we wanted friends, defenders, etc., and to that end let us speak illy of no one. I said some hard things of Logan—wipe 'em out—So I said that Stuart pursued us, L and myself; wipe that out too—This is the prudent course, is it not?"

When Herndon lacked definitive information he turned to others for help. He knew Lincoln's methods at the bar; but he had seldom traveled with him on the circuit. Henry C. Whitney, who was a frequent circuit companion of Lincoln's, helped him with this phase and also revealed what he knew, or thought he knew, about Lincoln's feelings toward his colleagues at the bar. Lincoln "believed in" Herndon, Whitney assured him, and in Swett, "Archy" Williams, Browning, Norman Judd, Logan, and Stuart; but he "despised" Oliver L. Davis, of Danville, and Davis "hated" him. He "barely tolerated" Lawrence L. Weldon and C. H. Moore; but he liked Shelby Cullom and Lamon —"this he told me himself in 1856, when both wanted to be Pros. Atty." "I took to Lincoln on the Circuit from the start and happened to have gotten more intimate with him than ordinary," Whitney claimed. "[David] Davis and Swett were more intimate—Lamon, Weldon, Parks, Moore, Hogg, Voorhees & McWilliams less so."

Herndon confessed that he had never been sure of Lincoln's true feeling toward Judge David Davis who did more than anyone else to obtain the presidential nomination for Lincoln. Whitney proceeded to enlighten him, although the subject touched him "on a tender chord." Davis was dead, and had many virtues as well as some serious faults. He had treated Whitney kindly and did so much for Lincoln that he deserved every favor he received at his hands. Yet, Whitney doubted if Lincoln ever held him "very close to his heart." Davis "forced" Lincoln to appoint "Archy" Williams United States District Judge of Kansas and John A. Jones as superintendent of statistics in the State Department. "Lincoln felt very sore over this to *my certain knowledge*," Whitney declared; and he was also vexed at Davis' efforts in behalf of his cousin, Henry Winter Davis, of Maryland.

As for Davis' appointment to the United States Supreme Court, "the old man justly felt as if he should have been rewarded," Whitney declared, "and Lincoln couldn't see the exact place for him: I have no idea he intended to make him Supreme Judge." When Noah H. Swayne was appointed to the first vacancy on the court, Davis was angry; and when the second vacancy was filled by the appointment of Daniel F. Miller, he despaired. Going to work in his own behalf, he urged Swett, Lamon, W. P. Dole, Commissioner of Indian Affairs, and Caleb Smith, Secretary of the Interior, to "punch Lincoln up." He made no secret of his dudgeon, but was "very loud & noisy and would send for everybody he knew to come to him at their expense & pour out his sorrows." Whitney, himself, had listened to his woes for two whole days at the Planters House in St. Louis, where Davis "substantially" commissioned him to take a message to Lincoln, although Whitney never delivered it.

Davis told Whitney that Lincoln would undoubtedly elevate him to the Supreme Bench if he asked him to; but that he would never do. *"No sir*: he wasn't that kind of a man." "But he sent others on the hunt," Whitney remembered.

Yet Whitney thought Davis got no more than was coming to him, when Lincoln finally appointed him. But Lincoln was remiss in ignoring Leonard Swett, who aided him in many ways. Always poor, except for a few months during the war, Swett was never recompensed.

Whitney believed Herndon's book would be "the most graphic American biography of anyone"; for Herndon would be as forthright as Lamon while treating his subject with a respect which Lamon did not seem to feel.

Herndon sent Whitney's letter to Weik, and continued to write to Weik himself. In the summer of 1887 he spent a month with Weik in Greencastle, and later Weik visited him at the farm. Weik organized, compressed, and composed, while Herndon poured forth his soul. And Herndon was well pleased. "I am glad to see you careful & exact, substantially so all through the book," he wrote.

If Weik slipped occasionally, Herndon quickly caught him up. He must not call the pioneers around New Salem "ruffians," Herndon warned. This was not only incorrect, but it "would set loose ten thousand hornets on my head." The descendants of these people were among the leading citizens of Menard County, and they themselves were brave, generous and hospitable. Call them "wild," or "uncultured" or "untamed," but never "ruffians."

Thus, while Weik wrote the book, it was Herndon's

product in all other respects. Weik did some independent research but added little to what Herndon contributed in the form of memoranda, letters, and reminiscences. Herndon also read every line of proof, correcting carefully for factual accuracy while leaving literary niceties to Weik. Proofreading spurred Herndon's recollections, reminding him of things that should go in; and it must have been with some strain on his patience that Weik opened the voluminous letters that never stopped coming even after the book had gone to press.

Neither Herndon nor Weik had any acquaintance or experience with publishers and both feared they might fall among thieves. In September, 1886, Herndon received a letter from the Elder Publishing Company of Chicago, which had learned that the *Century* was about to publish a Lincoln biography by Nicolay and Hay. This would create a "new boom" in Lincoln literature and if Herndon would write a similar biography, to be published serially in their *Literary Life* and then as a subscription book, they were sure he would find himself "famous like Byron in a day."

They were a little evasive about money, and when they learned that Herndon was being assisted by Weik, they preferred—indeed, they insisted—that Weik's name should not appear. The fact of Herndon's partnership and long friendship with Lincoln was the thing. They would give Herndon all the help he wanted with the manuscript provided they could use his name. Competition with the *Century* would excite unprecedented interest, and both the magazine and book should have an enormous sale, perhaps one that would rival that of Grant's Memoirs. When finally pinned down on terms, they suggested a royalty of ten per cent on the book, the author to receive nothing from serial publication.

After consulting Weik, Herndon replied that he and his colleague were in no position to write articles gratis, and that $5,000 cash in hand or amply secured was the minimum offer they were prepared to consider; whereupon Mr. Elder suddenly discovered that he could not use their material under any circumstance.

Undaunted, Herndon suggested that they "push along somewhat" before talking to publishers. He was not worried about publication, for he had an acquaintance in New York, C. O. Poole, who had connections in the book business. A lawyer, agriculturalist and mill owner, Poole was attracted to Herndon by his "strong, emphatic and unmistakable way of using words." "Knowledge must be dogmatic," he asseverated. Both men were interested in psychoanalysis, although Poole leaned more toward spiritualism. Like Herndon, Poole had known the solace of strong drink, had used spirits and the weed "expressly & *knowingly* to make me more pliable, more sociable, and often to excite my mind into greater activity in reasoning or imagining something." But he had repented and forsworn; "And now my Brother," he implored, "let us shake hands to entire prohibition, as far as we are concerned in their personal use."

Poole, too, had been a fervent Abolitionist, "born under the drippings of the sanctuary of *Gerrit Smith*"; but he regarded his efforts in that line as puny when compared to Herndon's. Herndon was to Lincoln what "John the Baptist was to Christ," in so far as the abolition movement was concerned. "Indeed you were," he affirmed, "You little realize the ground work you did in Babtizing [sic] A. Lincoln."

Poole was delighted to learn what Herndon and Weik

were doing and believed he could help find a publisher;
but when his efforts were unavailing, Weik approached
Charles L. Webster & Company, of New York. But in their
opinion, Nicolay and Hay had pre-empted the field, and
competition with them would be too hazardous.

Weik then thought of Mrs. Gertrude Garrison, former
editor of the American Press Association, with whom he
had corresponded about publication of articles. She was
interested at once and believed the book would sell ex-
tensively if written with "vivacity and verve." Herndon's
name was a valuable asset, and as far as Nicolay and Hay
were concerned, the two books, coming out close together,
would excite mutually beneficial controversy. For a reasonable fee she would undertake to obtain a publisher and
would also see to it that the book was "well gossiped about
through the press."

Weik was inclined to accept her proposition; but Herndon was wary, and suggested that they seek advice from
Chauncey Black. Black could tell Weik a shocking story
about publishers and their ways. "We will have to keep
both eyes & ears open or we are gulped down—swallowed
up body, breeches & soul," Herndon warned.

So matters hung for eighteen months, when Weik, despairing of doing any better, reopened the correspondence
with Mrs. Garrison. She offered references and finally convinced the authors of her good faith, whereupon they gave
her power of attorney, constituting her their literary agent.

She went to work at once, presenting the manuscript to
Belford, Clarke & Company, and stipulating American
readers. Publishing houses often employed foreign readers,
many of whom were Englishmen, she explained to Weik,
but "I held, and the head of the house agreed with me,

that no foreigner, particularly no Englishman was fitted to pass judgment on the life and character of Lincoln, the most American of Americans."

The publisher's reader was immediately impressed with the "immense merit and untold interest" of the book, which he found as absorbing as a work of fiction. Its chief merits were its naturalness and simple truth. "We see in the man all that his early life would make of him; though in the after years the rough places in his character were more polished, yet they never could be eradicated, and Lincoln the man was also Lincoln the boy, till the sad and tragic end." He recommended immediate publication; and predicted an "immense sale" and "liberal abuse" from critics.

Belford, Clarke & Company did not fear abuse. According to Mrs. Garrison they rather prided themselves on having the courage to publish anything deserving—that was why she went to them. Mr. Belford told her he doubted if any other publisher in New York would touch the book because it told "so many plain and unpalatable truths about the republic's idol." But he foresaw a good sale resulting from the furor he anticipated. Mrs. Garrison agreed, although she knew "what a tremendous engine of wrath the public can become if one of its idols is broken."

After some haggling a contract was signed by Belford, Clarke & Company and Weik whereby the publishers would own the copyright, bear all costs, and retain all profits from the first 1500 copies; profits thereafter to be divided equally. Weik offered Mrs. Garrison $100 for her efforts, which she agreed to accept, if that was the best he could do. The raising of even that sum was difficult; but Weik obtained it, and paid her in full.

Herndon was not a party to this contract and seems to

have known little about what was taking place. "I am as ignorant as a horse about the book business and yet I do willingly adopt what you have done," he wrote to Weik. Above all things he wanted the matter pushed along, for he was in a desperate state financially. In June, 1887, he gave Weik a lien on his manuscripts as security for a loan of $100, which was soon increased to $200; and at one time he suggested that they accept $3,000 cash for the book if anyone would give them the money at once. From time to time Weik sent him money: ten dollars for groceries, twenty-five dollars for clothes, five dollars for this or that; and in September, 1888, Herndon offered to assign all his interest in the Lincoln records if Weik would give him fifteen or twenty dollars a month until he began to receive remuneration from the book. On Christmas, 1887, and again in 1888, Weik sent the Herndon family a big box of candy, oranges, peaches, sardines, and groceries; and Herndon was almost tearful in his thanks. "I hope it will be a success *in the money line,* particularly," he wrote to Weik in July, 1889. "The money line is my line & *not the glory line.* I need the dollars. Glory may go to thunder if I get the dimes & this you ought to know."

While Herndon was not a party to the contract with the publishers, he was protected by a written agreement with Weik. Sometime during the summer of 1888 Weik proposed a new agreement, stating his case, as Herndon thought, "admirably well—'lawyer like,'" and Herndon agreed to consider his proposal. "It has always been my purpose to give you the Lincoln records, letters—evidences, etc under conditions. Jesse, after our book is out and when I hear a statement of your case, accounts, etc I will do what is fair—honest—just, between man & man. I think I am a reasonable creature and easy to deal with. I think you can

risk my word on the question of justice—right—& equity.
So let the thing rest till the book . . . is . . . out . . . I
admit that you have been kind and clever to me and this
I willingly and gladly confess to you. You have done much
work and spent much money in and about our endeavors—
book. I hope that our book will compensate both of us
when out and some or all sold."

Throughout the autumn, Weik kept recurring to this
matter, until Herndon became peevish. For, in the meantime, he and Weik had had a tiff. Some time before they
had jointly written a preface for the book; but it did not
suit the publishers, and at their suggestion Weik wrote
another, which he sent to Herndon for approval. As Herndon read it, his indignation flamed; for it not only seemed
to give undue credit to Weik, but was also unflattering to
Herndon. What business was it of the publishers "to know
or wish to know who wrote this sentence or that—this paragraph or that—this chapter or that?" And why did Weik
permit himself to be "pumped" about it, Herndon demanded. "I shall never agree to it," he declared, "nor have
my name attached to it . . . I may not be familiar with
the technical terms or words of the mechanism of book
making, but I know shugar from salt. I do not know that I
am ill-adapted to carry on the undertaking. Erase 'and un-
familiar with literary details.' Erase 'ill-adapted to carry
out the undertaking' etc . . . You may subject to my approval put in any kind of a paragraph in the preface or
book which shows that you are entitled to great Honor, but
don't go into particulars—Say in substance that our book
is the joint product of Jesse W. Weik & myself and that
will be the truth, but don't go into particulars. Let the
future if it is fool enough discuss what you did and what I
did and the merits of each exactly in matter of composi-

tion etc. etc., but good Lord, Jesse, let you and I quit such
follies . . . In short Jesse your preface would ruin our
book. It would be said by critics and by the reading world
that I had nothing to do with the book."

Weik may have written the book; but it was Herndon's
Lincoln. Weik should read their contract, read it carefully,
every word of it, and he had better not assume that Herndon was unmindful of what it contained.

This letter, following a long and uniformly pleasant
correspondence, must have jolted Jesse; and he hastened
to explain that a critic at the publisher's had offered bad
advice. Herndon forgave Weik, except for having the bad
judgment to listen to an "arrant ass" who knew nothing
"of the great beating, pulsing & warm heart of the world
and what will suit it." Critics acted like fools when they
emerged from their closets. No matter what the publishers
or their critics said, "If the word authorship or author is
mentioned I desire that honor." But he also wanted Weik
to be mentioned "gratefully & honorably in the preface as
having assisted me greatly."

Although Weik rewrote the preface to Herndon's satisfaction, the old man was still a little jealous. He was about
to realize his life's ambition, and he wanted the world to
know the book as his. "In our contract you had the right to
be noticed in the preface," he wrote to Weik, June 22,
1889. "The mention of this right excluded all other right
of that kind, and yet I find your name scattered around—as
author—aider—assistant etc. etc. You took a kind of shot
gun idea of things."

But Herndon did not wish to quarrel. He was very fond
of Jesse. His concern was for the book's success; and if he
got "crabbed" once in a while, Jesse should overlook it—
"say damn and pass on."

Meanwhile the presses had begun to roll, and both Herndon and Weik braced for the shock of criticism. "You seem to think that we will catch . . . Hell because of our book," wrote Herndon. "Very well, let it come. Truth can stand it." If criticism was fair and honest, they would modify their future editions accordingly. Blackstone devoted his whole life to perfecting his great work; and they could do the same for their life of Lincoln. "Let us make it *the* life of Lincoln for some years to come," urged Herndon. He would continue to gather facts and seek truth, even after the book was out, always with perfection as a goal.

In the late summer of 1889 the forthcoming work began to be "gossiped about"; and the scribes of the cult of the sacrosanct awaited the unveiling, their pens deep-dipped to scratch or splatter.

No sooner had the book appeared than the Chicago *Evening Journal* hurled a mucky, baneful blob. "It is one of the most infamous books ever written and printed in the garb of a historical work to a great and illustrious man," it roared. "It vilely distorts the image of an ideal statesman, patriot and martyr. It clothes him in vulgarity and grossness. Its indecencies are spread like a curtain to hide the colossal proportions and the splendid purity of his character. It makes him the buffoon and jester which his enemies describe—that is, it makes his buffoonery the principal trait of his mind and the most conspicuous of his habits. It brings out all that should have been hidden—it reproduces shameless gossip and hearsay not authenticated by proof— it magnifies the idle and thoughtless antics of youth as main features of the man in his life and accomplishments— it degrades and belittles him. Where it aspires to be pathetic and eulogistic it is a failure. The pathos is maudlin, and the eulogy is tawdry . . .

"The obscenity of the work is surprising and shocking. Anthony Comstock·[1] should give it his attention. It is not fit for family reading. Its salacious narrative and implications, and its elaborate calumnies not only of Lincoln himself but of his mother, and in regard to morals generally of his mother's side of the family are simply outrageous . . .

"That portion of the narrative which relates to Lincoln's courtship of Ann Rutledge and his subsequent attentions to Mary S. Owens, with his final marriage to Mary Todd, is indelicate, in every way in bad taste, is insulting to the memory of the dead, and calculated to mortify and lacerate the hearts of the living. Equally shameful is the discussion of Lincoln's unripened religious, or rather irreligious, beliefs, which he abandoned when he came to feel and know that an overwhelming Providence was his guide. In all its parts and aspects—if we are a judge, and we think we are, of the proprieties of literature and of human life—we declare that this book is so bad it could hardly have been worse."

Herndon's home-town paper reprinted this tirade; and Springfield gossips of the idealistic school looked on the book as the festering of a resentment which had gnawed at Herndon's soul for twenty years. Lincoln had refused to gratify his ambition for office; this was his revenge.

Herndon's treatment of Thomas Lincoln and Nancy Hanks, the Ann Rutledge incident and its supposed enduring influence, the "fatal first of January," Lincoln's domestic troubles, and his alleged religious shortcomings

---

[1] A professional reformer who campaigned against obscene literature and vice.

were inviting points for attack. To *The Athenium,* such
stuff was "gossip," "scandal," "twaddle."

But it was the personal attacks that were most virulent.
The Decatur *Republican* did not wonder, in view of Herndon's past life, that he should give to the world "a salacious
bit of reading such as he and creatures of his class most
delight in . . . He will be remembered only as the one-
time law partner of his more famous associate who wrote a
filthy book about a great subject, in order to direct attention from his life-long failure to make even a faint mark on
the page of history."

The St. Paul *News* thought Herndon was overendowed
with vanity and deficient in common sense. His "holier-
than-thou" air was insufferable; and the reviewer shud-
dered when he remembered that this was a "friend"
describing Lincoln. But the "hideous conceit of this avari-
cious biographer can bring no harm to the great Emancipator. It is only the author that will suffer and the generation who knew and loved the greatest son of the republic,
and those that follow, will contemn the viper that has
warmed upon his hearthstone."

Herndon stood up to the blast. "We are catching the
very devil from the critics," he wrote to Weik; and there
were rumors that detectives had been set on Herndon's
trail to find what they could to smear him. But he defied
them. All they would find was that at one time in his life
he "drank rot gut" and perhaps that he couldn't pay his
debts, although he hoped to do so before he died. "When
men are driven to this it seems to me the furies have seized
them"; but at any rate the book was before the public and
would stay there for all time. He should not be blamed
for the wretchedness of Lincoln's background. "I would
clear Lincoln and his whole family from this state of facts

if I could do so," he protested, "and what I have said about him apparently disparagingly was to show the power of the man in overcoming or greatly modifying the terrible environment that surrounded him in youth or rather in bending or controlling them [sic] to his own purposes or ends." Here was the "dung-hill" theory again, except that Herndon described Lincoln as rising from "a stagnant, putrid pool."

Herndon believed he saw the hand of Robert Lincoln behind the Chicago *Journal* article; and he suspected that the English press was toadying to Robert. Its ferocious attacks were "due to the fact that Bob is minister to England and nothing else," he asserted. "A praise of the book, even a fair criticism, would be considered a slap at Bob in the minds of some. Abuse follows as a matter of course to tickle Bob. The English press abused Lincoln terribly when living, but now that he is dead and Bob minister to England," English hero worship begins. But this would not always be. Sober judgment would eventually be brought to bear.

On December 5, Herndon received a letter from his friend, T. H. Bartlett, an artist, who was living in France. Bartlett had been unable to buy a copy of the book, and a London bookseller, who was unable to fill his order, explained that Robert Lincoln had bought up every copy that was shipped to England. This confirmed Herndon's suspicions about the Chicago *Journal,* and he suggested that Weik investigate with Belford, Clarke & Company, to see if they had encountered any evidence of plots to suppress the book. "If Robt is able and willing to buy up whole Editions of our book we can supply him to his heart's content—can do so I suppose every month or so. If no one in London will sell the books we can land them on the wharf and notify the Minister of the fact. Weik, I always thought Bob a weak brother but never thought he was such a d—d fool. Why his acts in this matter are little—mean—malicious—He is a Todd and not a Lincoln—is a little bitter fellow of the pig headed kind, silly & cold and selfish. I do not think he will suppress the book in this way."

Belford, Clarke & Company thought Herndon must be misinformed about Robert Lincoln; in any event the supposed attempt at suppression would be difficult to prove. But Herndon was unconvinced. "I said to you a year ago that mere book sellers know nothing about human nature and the motives that move men. I say so now," he wrote to Weik.

Distressed by the harsh things said about the book, Weik despaired of its success; but Herndon never lost hope. "There is no such thing with it as fail," he declared. "If the thing is energetically pushed out it will go and there is no failure in it—failure, pshaw." Almost every day he received appreciative letters: Lyman Trumbull was complimentary; and Mrs. Leonard Swett—a widow now—hoped Herndon would edit her husband's recollections. Herndon's book confirmed her opinion that "my dear husband resembled Mr. Lincoln in many ways, in feature as well as traits of character." C. T. Hulburd, former congressman from New York, thought Nicolay and Hay's *Life* admirable in showing Lincoln "on dress parade as President," but Herndon's depicted the real man. Horace White, now editor of the New York *Evening Post,* considered it not only the best biography of Lincoln but the best biography in American literature. "It is certainly the only book that gives a picture of Lincoln that I recognize as true in all its lineaments. You know that I travelled with him throughout nearly the whole of the campaign of 1858 in all sorts of places & conveyances. You know also that I acquired an admiration and love for him exceeding that which I ever bestowed upon any public man in my life—or if you do not know it I now assure you of the fact. Yet I never could see any reason for deifying him, or, for painting him without his blemishes. It is because you have put in all his warts that I consider yours the best biography—this & the extraordinary industry & painstaking care you have bestowed in getting the facts together."

White had only two criticisms. He would have omitted the affair of the brothers Grigsby, in which Lincoln participated in the trickery of maneuvering the brothers' brides into the wrong bedchambers on their wedding night, even though such "horseplay" was not uncommon on the frontier, and the mistake was rectified in season; and he could not agree with Herndon's explanation of Lincoln's melancholy. He could understand how domestic unhappiness might intensify a disposition to sadness; but why should Lincoln's knowledge of his lowly origin have been a depressing influence. Weren't obscure and lowly origins considered rather as "titles to distinction to all Americans who, like himself, have achieved distinctions in spite of the same?" Unless, of course, Herndon meant to insinuate something worse than "lowly," as Lamon did.

Grateful for these tributes, Herndon refused to despond. The critics had better take care. The book was far from dead, and might "grow up to be a stout old man." And not all the criticism was unfavorable.

The St. Louis *Republic* thought Herndon would take top rank among Lincoln biographers and that the work of the others would be corrected by his. Other newspapers commended the book, and the leading periodicals were preponderantly well disposed. The *Literary World* considered it to be "the utmost that the plainest speaking in love has to deliver about the personal life of a strangely harassed and tortured man," exalting its subject to the status of "a noble man of Nature's making, a statesman who followed humbly the teaching of the Eternally Righteous Power, a scarred and suffering hero, forever dear to every true American heart."

The Atlantic Monthly thought the book was timely and valuable, even though the previous work of Lamon deprived it of much of its originality. Its very artlessness affirmed its honesty. Those who had envisaged Lincoln after their own imagination might be loath to give up the "shadow for the reality"; but truthseekers would profit. There was a growing disposition to regard Lincoln as a typical American, or at least a typical Western American. Without confuting this notion, Herndon also showed wherein he was unique.

The Nation thought Herndon's recollections would remain the most authentic and trustworthy source for Lincoln's pre-presidential years. The sincerity and honesty of the biographers were apparent on every page, and the narrative revealed what manner of man Lincoln was when he took over the presidency and how he attained to that estate. "We have much that is trivial, some things which are in bad taste, but we are made to feel, after all, that we are looking upon Lincoln's life as he actually lived it. It depends upon ourselves whether he is belittled by things ordinarily kept behind a curtain. We have the opportunity to know him as the valet would know him, and if we are of the valet's make-up, the proverbial result may happen, and he will be no hero to us. The judicious reader will know how to put things in their proper perspective, and will form a truer picture of the man by many little things which go to indicate character, though grotesque or even repulsive when taken by themselves."

Far more consequential to the fate of the book than the judgment of reviewers was the failure of the publishers just at the time it appeared. Within a few months they were able to rehabilitate their finances and renew operations, but their suspension was calamitous to the book. For it came just at that crucial period when reviews were appearing and interest was at its highest pitch. With printing and distribution suspended, many would-be purchasers were unable to buy the book; and by the time it was back in print curiosity was on the wane.

To aid in their rejuvenation, the publishers pressed Weik to accept a new contract specifying a royalty of twenty-five cents per copy in lieu of division of profits; and Weik finally agreed, with the proviso that if royalties did not amount to at least $500 a year, the copyright was to revert to him and he was to have an option to purchase the plates at cost.

As in the case of the first contract, Herndon was not a party to and seems to have had no prior knowledge of the change in terms. Nevertheless, he trusted Weik, and while he was suspicious of the publishers, he consented to what had been done.

But when no royalties came, and Weik stopped writing to him, he was petulant. "Jesse," he inquired, "are the women after you badly or have you the la grippe?" Desperately poor, he again appealed to Weik for money until royalties began to come. Twice a week he was taking his produce to Springfield and peddling it around, but he was getting too old to do that sort of work much longer.

One June 30, Belford, Clarke & Company reported that they were "out" something over $3,000 on the book to date. They were disappointed at the meager royalties the book had earned, but it was such a poor seller they could not keep an agent on the job. Perhaps a one-volume edition would sell better than the present three-volume work; and if Weik would come to Chicago, where their headquarters were now located, they would discuss the matter with him.

When Herndon studied the publishers' report he was indignant to learn that they had given away 416 copies of the book for review. Weik tried to explain that this was customary; but Herndon was adamant. What right had the publishers to give away their book? And why had Weik voided a contract under which they would have received forty cents per copy in favor of one that granted them only twenty-five cents? "There has been from 1887 to this day a kind of mystery hanging & hovering over this whole book affair," he complained. "You do not answer my letters nor the questions put to you in them. Human nature would teach you that your silence breeds suspicion . . . Why were the contracts with B C & Co made in your *name alone* & not in the name of H & W?" But when Weik replied, Herndon hastened to explain that his censure was directed at the publishers and not at Weik.

Meantime Weik had been corresponding with Horace White, who was concerned because the book was not reaching a wider circle. He was inclined to blame the publishers, and sounded out Charles Scribner's Sons as to the advisability of republication. When he found them interested, provided certain changes were made "in the direction of discretion," he suggested that Weik ask Belford, Clarke & Company if they would release the copyright and sell the plates. Weik consulted Herndon, who favored the idea; although he wanted any new contract to be in both names and also wanted to receive copies of the publisher's accounting statements.

Belford, Clarke & Company were willing to step out. Indeed, they had no choice, since the meagerness of the royalties made the contract voidable by Weik under its own terms. But they wanted $1,000 for the plates.

Scribner's thought $500 would be a fair price, and when Weik explained that even this was more than he could raise, they agreed to advance $300 against royalties. Weik then persuaded Belford, Clarke & Company to accept the reduced amount and to take Scribner's check and his own note for $200 in payment.

Scribner's recommended a change in the title page, a less aggressive tone to the preface so that it would not claim "uniqueness in a way invidious to other lives," the omission of anything alluding to the possibility of Lincoln's having been of illegitimate birth, and a more emollient treatment of Lincoln's domestic unhappiness, "although by no means failing to make the point." White advised acceptance of their terms; and both Weik and Herndon agreed, although the old man thought the title page was "plain English" and that "some hobby" must have seized them to make them want to change it.

Herndon was also displeased to learn that a rumor was going the rounds to the effect that Weik was the real author of the book; and while he did not attribute this to Weik, he was still piqued at Weik's reticence and at his exclusive handling of affairs. "The past transactions in your name was wrong," he insisted, "& yet, I impliedly agreed to what you did . . . You mean well, Jesse, I have no doubt, but you have a kind of kink in your ideas . . . Had you only answered my questions promptly as it was your duty to do, you would be a first rate fellow all through, but you see that that sticks in my craw and frets me till that craw is raw and sore."

Yet, things were looking up. Herndon felt that the prejudice against the book "among Christians" was wearing away. "I have been told this by several men who are our friends here—So might it be. Blind hero worshipers are beginning to speak well of the book."

But their optimism was short-lived. Another frustration impended.

Out of a clear sky, early in October, 1891, Weik received a letter from Scribner's informing him that the matter had "assumed a new phase" which made it impossible for them to consider themselves "the most advantageous publishers to co-operate with you in securing the greatest attainable success for the book." The revision they must insist on would be so drastic as to emasculate the book. Some other publisher might feel less compulsion in the matter, but Scribner's must withdraw.

Herndon was spared this final blow. On March 18, 1891, he had passed to his reward. To the end he continued to write long letters, attempting to clarify moot points and to put on paper everything he could recall about the man he reverenced. He almost seemed to grudge the words he sometimes found it necessary to write on other matters. "I must get back to Lincoln," he would scribble. His many tribulations never soured him. "Though poor I am a happy man," he wrote seven months before his death. "My life has been a happy one—saw much—learned some things of life; and now I enjoy myself as much as any person on the globe." Poverty-stricken, ill, approaching death, he still had faith in the book.

Upon receipt of Scribner's letter, Weik wrote immediately to Horace White. On October 6, White called on Mr.

Charles Scribner, the head of the house, who explained that regard for the feelings of Robert Lincoln had made him change his mind. He had just learned of Robert's buying up the copies of the first edition that were sent to England, and it was Scribner's policy not to be instrumental in publishing any book that was objectionable to the son of its subject. Scribner assured White that there had been no communication between Scribner's and Robert Lincoln, either direct or indirect, and that he knew of Robert's feelings only by hearsay. He had also learned that the book was objectionable to John Hay, but Hay's feelings had not influenced his decision.

When White assured Mr. Scribner that Weik would consent to any reasonable changes in the text, Scribner explained that "emendation to the extent of making the book satisfactory to Mr. Robert Lincoln would spoil it or seriously impair its selling qualities."

There is no reason to question Mr. Scribner's veracity in regard to communication between him and Robert Lincoln. And there is no doubt that he was correct concerning Robert's feelings. On September 14, 1891, White informed Weik that he had talked to George M. Pullman, of Chicago, the day before, and that Pullman had asked when the new edition of Herndon's book would be published. Robert Lincoln was closely associated with Pullman in business, as counsel for the company that bore the Pullman name, and would later succeed Mr. Pullman as its president; and it is possible that Pullman was seeking information for Robert. Robert was in Springfield about a year after the first edition of the book appeared, and when asked if he had seen it, he was reported to have replied with scorn, "No, nor do I wish to see it." Albert E. Pillsbury, writing to Weik in 1924, recalled the bitterness with which

Robert had spoken of Herndon and his work "in the only extended interview I ever had with him"; and in a letter to Henry C. Whitney, Robert referred to Lamon's and Herndon's "blackguardism."

In voiding their contract, Scribner's agreed to turn over the plates, without charge for the work they had done or reimbursement for the $300 they had advanced; but there remained Weik's note for $200 to Belford, Clarke & Company, which had been renewed on expiration and was about to come due again. Weik saw no possibility of paying it, so White offered to pay it himself "as a contribution to the memory of my dear, departed friend Herndon, & I will do so most cheerfully." Weik could repay him later, if he so desired, otherwise it could "stand to the credit of Mrs. Herndon with my best wishes."

Thus it was paid off, and White began negotiating with Appleton's. Their reader was "fascinated" with the biography, and they immediately communicated with Weik. At their suggestion White wrote a new introduction as well as a chapter on the Lincoln-Douglas debates. New matter on Lincoln's activities in New England in the campaign of 1848, which Herndon had obtained from Edward L. Pierce, a New England historian, was also added. White favored omission of the story of Nancy Hanks' illegitimate birth and especially Lincoln's revelation of it; but left the decision to Appleton's. After some hesitation they allowed it to remain, in modified form. But the insinuations about Lincoln's own paternity, the Grigsby incident, and the "Chronicles of Reuben" were deleted.

Appleton's published the book in two volumes and agreed to pay Weik a royalty of fifteen per cent after deducting the cost of altering the plates and the expense of setting up the additional material. White as well as Weik approved the proofs, and upon reading the book for the second time White was "more than ever impressed with its great value & its exceeding interest." "I don't think it will ever be superseded as regards Lincoln's ante Presidential life," he asserted. When this second edition came out, in 1892, White saw to its receiving a good review in the New York *Evening Post.*

Sales of the new edition were steady but unspectacular. For many years Appleton's kept it in print as a standard work. Weik wanted them to bring it out in one volume, but they could not be convinced that this would stimulate sales. At last the copyright expired, and other firms reprinted the book in inexpensive one-volume formats.

Harsh things were said of Herndon in his day, and even now there are those who regard him as primarily a mythmaker. Yet one cannot read his letters without recognizing his desire to tell the truth. Unlike Black, he loved and revered Lincoln, and his concern was that posterity should know him as he really was. Lincoln himself, after trying to read a life of Burke, had thrown it aside with the comment, "It's like all the others. Biographies as generally written are not only misleading, but false. The author of this life of Burke makes a wonderful hero of his subject. He magnifies his perfections—if he had any—and suppresses his imperfections. He is so faithful in his zeal and so lavish in his praise of his every act that one is almost driven to believe that Burke never made a mistake or a failure in his life . . . History is not history unless it is the truth."

In adopting a realistic attitude, Herndon sought to write as he believed Lincoln would have had him do. But this is not to say he never erred. He was not always capable of measuring up to the high standard he had set. Whenever he wrote from personal knowledge of facts and presented them solely as such, he is generally reliable, although even here his memory sometimes played him false. But when he depended upon statements of others his critical faculties were not sufficiently acute to winnow wheat from chaff. And when he tried to explain things through his supposed capacity for "intuitive seeing of human character," his conclusions were usually worthless.

But if he was imperfect as a draughtsman, he excelled in tone. To a portrait that might otherwise have been pallid he gave color, life, and personality.

Chapter Six

AN EPOCH ENDS

IN 1892 appeared *Life on the Circuit with Lincoln,* by Henry Clay Whitney, another of the six or seven men who could truthfully claim to have known Lincoln well.

A young man of twenty-three when he first met Lincoln, Whitney had close contact with him on the circuit for a period of seven years and knew him less intimately in Washington for four years more. Now Whitney was a man of fifty-one, with hollow chest, long overhanging nose, and dark-pouched eyes. Lush sideburns compensated for his thinning hair; the up-clutch of his shaven chin denoted dentures.

Never a man to underestimate his own powers, Whitney was held at a somewhat lower valuation by his colleagues. Born in Detroit, Maine, February 23, 1831, moving with his family to Poughkeepsie, New York, where, at the age of ten, he went to work, saving what money he could and studying in his spare time, he eventually entered Augusta College, at Augusta, Kentucky, later transferring to Farmers College, near Cincinnati. In 1854 he moved with his father to Urbana, Illinois, where he was licensed to practice law, and where he and Lincoln met. They were often associated in lawsuits, and eight personal letters from Lincoln, printed in facsimile in Whitney's book, attested Lincoln's trust and friendliness.

After Lincoln's election to the presidency, "I had no hesitation at all in asking Lincoln what place he thought I had better take under government," Whitney coolly observed. Lincoln had but to command and he would offer up his talents on the altar of public service. But Lincoln seemed to underrate his attributes. Writing to Lamon from Urbana under date of April 14, 1861, David Davis said, "Whitney is here & has got nothing & wants me to write to Mr. Lincoln for him. I told him I had written once & spoken to Mr. Lincoln 4 or 5 times & was not disposed to write again." Eventually Lincoln offered him a position in one of the land offices, which Whitney declined; and later —merely for the asking, according to Whitney—Lincoln appointed him a paymaster of volunteers.

With the coming of peace Whitney remained for a time in Kansas, whither his wartime duties had taken him, working as a lawyer and journalist. Then he moved to Chicago, where he got into a bad scrape. On March 1, 1886, Stephen W. Rawson, president of the Union Trust Company of Chicago, and Mrs. America Lucretia Lee were married, each for the second time. Three months later they separated, and Mrs. Rawson filed a bill for separate maintenance. Rawson, employing Whitney as counsel, countered with a charge of infidelity. Charges were met with countercharges, and public interest, already aroused by the social eminence of the contestants, was intensified when Mrs. Rawson's son by her first marriage tried to kill his stepfather. And worse was yet to come.

On June 1, 1888, Mrs. Rawson walked into the courtroom, advanced to where Whitney sat, whipped out a pistol, and fired five shots at him point-blank. Two bullets took effect and for weeks Whitney was in serious condition. Mrs. Rawson's lawyers—one of whom was John Barton Payne, a man whose word and character were irreproachable—justified her action by publicly accusing Whitney of driving her to desperation by manufacturing the most salacious kind of evidence against her character and hiring witnesses to swear to it.

Finding the courtroom atmosphere a bit torrid, Whitney retired temporarily to the sanctuary of his closet. For some time he had contemplated lecturing on Lincoln, designing "to work the business part of it for all it is worth." He had appealed to Herndon for suggestions, and especially for some of Lincoln's good stories; but Herndon could not recall any that would be appropriate to a mixed audience. "They would cut someone on some point."

Whitney's opinion of the published Lincoln books seemed somewhat muddled. He had criticized Lamon at length, yet he thought, "as I have always said," that his was "a first rate book" which was "unjustly treated." He thought Herndon went too far in his strictures on Lincoln's mother, in abuse of Thomas Lincoln, and in printing the "Chronicles of Reuben." Herndon had opportunity to get the truth, but could not always recognize it. Yet, when Ida Tarbell, who was just entering the Lincoln field, took occasion to attack Herndon's account of Lincoln's deserting Mary Todd at the altar and claimed that Herndon was excluded from the aristocratic circle of Springfield society to which Lincoln was readily admitted, Whitney sprang sturdily to Herndon's defence.

By what right did this "female," this "bluestocking," who was "hired" by *McClure's Magazine* to edit Lincoln's life, attack the memory of "one of the best men that ever lived," and in so doing "emphasize and spread far and

wide" that which she characterized as a "gross libel" on
Lincoln? "I know nothing of the truth or falsity of the
original story (and don't think it should have been told),"
Whitney admitted, "but I told Miss T. when she asked me
about it that it was doubtless true; nor do I doubt it now;
for Herndon, a man of the strictest honor, told me that he
verified every fact as if it was in a Court proceeding and
under oath. That a man like Herndon—a man recognized
by Lincoln for 25 years as a man of emphatic truth—should
now be held up to the scorn of mankind as a liar and the
slanderer of his cherished friend is a damned outrage and
infamy on the memory of the voiceless dead. The tribute
to the contemptible codfish aristocracy of the early days of
Springfield is equally contemptible. Billy Herndon was a
true aristocrat if there was any aristocracy in Springfield:
his honored father was in the legislature and senate, over
and over again: he was himself, Lincoln's confidant for a
$\frac{1}{4}$ of a century and his brother Eliot was a prominent lawyer for years. If he was not welcome—had not the *entree*
into the charmed codfish aristocracy circle it was because
he was too radical in his views about Slavery. But it is
absurd to talk about any genuine aristocracy existing in
Springfield anyway . . . Billy Herndon's standing as a
man ought not to suffer by such low flung talk." The old-
guard Lincoln men should close ranks against this Tarbell
upstart.

Whitney said he wrote his book by accident. Having
prepared several lectures, he discovered that his voice was
not equal to the strain of public speaking, so at the suggestion of newspaper and magazine editors he rewrote them
in the form of articles. The editors—according to Whitney
—then either declined the articles, "with a great profusion
of thanks," or "cribbed" them and ignored payment. So he

thought he would show "these one horse fellows" that he could "get before the public with no thanks to them." The book was three times as large as he had originally planned it, he told Weik, "but I have to talk about everything else as well as Lincoln."

This was no exaggeration. For in writing the book he not only attempted a full-length biography, instead of limiting himself to the period on which his knowledge was first-hand, but he also spiraled off at times in philosophic flights. Depending largely upon Herndon and Lamon for his account of Lincoln's earlier years, he avoided or trod softly on the controversial quicksands. Uncritical, he was sometimes led into error in discussing events of which his knowledge was second-hand; and his intimacy with Lincoln lost no luster in the telling.

But for the period from 1854 to 1861 the book was valuable. Rich in anecdote and vivid in its description of the joys, the tribulations, and the manner of circuit life, it not only appraised Lincoln the lawyer, but also described Lincoln the politician and campaigner. Whitney's admiration of Lincoln was unbounded; but he could see him as no more than a first-rate lawyer who was ordinarily successful —surely not as the knight-errant of the courtroom that some biographers depicted. In the gush of their enthusiasm, these men "incline to inculcate the idea that Lincoln was wont to retire from every case in which he found himself to be wrong," Whitney observed, "and to surrender up his fees, and to try both sides of his cases . . . such is by no means the case. In a clear case of dishonesty he would hedge in some way so as to not, himself, partake of the dishonesty. In a doubtful case of dishonesty, he would give his client the benefit of the doubt, and in an ordinary case he would try the case, so far as he could, like any other lawyer, except that he absolutely abjured technicality and went for justice and victory, denuded of every integument, and Lincoln's honesty was excellent stock-in-trade to him, and brought success and victory often."

Whitney's book contains at least one instance of deliberate falsification; for the supposed text of Lincoln's speech at Urbana on October 24, 1854, which Whitney printed as the original, was found on closer examination to be the Peoria address of October 16, 1854, with certain parts of the introduction and conclusion omitted.

Moreover, Whitney sold *McClure's Magazine* the alleged text of Lincoln's "Lost Speech" at the Bloomington Convention on May 29, 1856—that speech which so gripped and thrilled the audience that no one, it was supposed, had thought to write it down. But Whitney—so he told Miss Tarbell, who was editing *McClure's* Lincoln series—had made notes, wholly accurate so far as Lincoln's argument was concerned, and verbatim in part.

Joseph Medill, editor of the Chicago *Tribune,* who had heard Lincoln deliver the speech, vouched for the accuracy of Whitney's product. "I regard it as a close reproduction—literal in many parts of the original," he asserted. He recommended publication; and *McClure's* printed it, together with Medill's own account of the circumstances of its delivery, in their issue of September, 1896.

Soon afterward, Whitney offered four other unpublished Lincoln speeches as well as other "original" material to the *Century.* R. U. Johnson, the editor, sought advice from the *Century's* old standby, John G. Nicolay, who cautioned him to beware. True, Whitney was a personal friend of Lincoln's; but in Nicolay's opinion he had no qualification whatever as a historian. To confirm this Johnson needed only to examine Whitney's book, where

Henry Clay Whitney

enough in the way of reminiscences for a short magazine article was "diluted by rambling digression" into six hundred pages. This same "mess" would doubtless be "warmed up" for his magazine articles. And the "Lost Speech" was plainly spurious. Nicolay himself had heard it delivered, and he could no more restore a single paragraph than he could restore the text of the Sibylline Books. "Whitney pretends that he took notes," wrote Nicolay, "a statement I feel disposed to doubt, because in his book he devoted three pages and a half to describing the Convention and also quotes Scripps' description of the speech. He says not one word about his having made notes." Furthermore, Whitney's version was not only "devoid of Lincoln's style and phraseology," but it contained anachronisms which, in Nicolay's opinion, reduced the whole thing to absurdity.

But Whitney was proud of his handiwork. So excellent was his performance that he almost convinced himself that Lincoln had dictated it to him. "I don't think he could have written it out any more accurately than I did," he wrote to Weik. "After such a lapse of time: I think I had his aid in writing it out."

Miss Tarbell refused to doubt its accuracy, even when Isaac N. Phillips, and other Bloomington residents who heard the speech, denounced Whitney's version as "no more Lincoln's than sweet currant wine is champagne" and declared the speech "still lost." Arthur Brooks Lapsley printed it in his collection of Lincoln's *Works,* and Albert J. Beveridge defended it from the attacks of skeptics. But in 1930 there came to light a contemporary report of the speech, printed in the Alton *Courier* of June 5, 1856, which was so different from Whitney's version as utterly to discredit it.

Whitney thought to make a good income from his book.

"I would feel very cheap if I don't get more than $500 a year" from a book of such "literary merit & written so close to Lincoln," he confided to Weik.

But like Lamon and Black, and Herndon and Weik, he was too optimistic. In the first five months after publication only 428 copies were sold; and when, for the six months ending February 1, 1895, his publishers sold "all over the broad U. S.—14 Books," Whitney's cries were shrill. This was "not business"; and he would sue.

Whitney was the curmudgeon of the Lincolnites. Always he was contemplating or threatening suit against his own publishers for fraud, or against other publishers for plagiarism; and his characterizations of rival authors were uncommonly crusty and tart. Raymond's and Arnold's work was "trash." W. O. Stoddard's *The Table Talk of Abraham Lincoln* was a "most vapid thing . . . a cancer among letters." Miss Tarbell was an "obscure Bohemian," whose series in *McClure's* was "a weary & oft told and plagiarized narrative," "sponged" and "cribbed" from others and written in the style of a kindergarten teacher.

When Allen Thorndike Rice, gifted young editor of the *North American Review* brought out *Reminiscences of Abraham Lincoln by Distinguished Men of his Time,* Whitney thought his printing the recollections of such "codfish" as Ben Perley Poore, Dan Voorhees, and Walt Whitman, instead of going to men like Herndon, John T. Stuart and "Jim" Matheny, showed "how humbug rules the world." But worst of all was *Abraham Lincoln: The Man of the People,* by Norman Hapgood. Here was a "daisy," Whitney thought, gotten up in a garret with paste pot and shears, which pirated from Nicolay and Hay, Lamon, Tarbell, Herndon, "and largely from the words of Lincoln himself." "They stole entire pages from me," he averred, "without giving me even credit simply said 'An observer thus says etc.'" Whitney would sue, and in writing to Weik he urged him to do likewise.

Miss Tarbell pitied "poor Mr. Whitney." He didn't have enough to do. She thought well of Hapgood's book, and didn't think he pirated unduly. "I know that he used a lot of historical details which I dug up by the sweat of my brow . . . ," she wrote to Weik, "but . . . I feel complimented when any one finds anything good enough in any of the work that I have done to reincorporate it in his own."

Abqut 1895 Whitney moved to Salem, Massachusetts; and there he recurred to the idea of lecturing on Lincoln, although he anticipated it would be "uphill business" in the present state of American intellectuality, with such dramatists as Shakespeare, Knowles, Kotzebue, and Boucicault replaced on the theater boards by Lillie Langtry,[1] May Yohe,[2] "Gentleman Jim" Corbett, and Buffalo Bill, and philosophers and statesmen yielding the platform to blackface acts and the cancan. But he tried it anyway—with disappointing results. People would turn out to hear a preacher or an Englishman, he complained, but not a Lincoln man. They were interested in Thackeray, Catherine de Medici, orchids, sanitation, Buddhism, Guelphs and Ghibellines, the poets of the renaissance or Pompeian frescoes; but seemingly not in Lincoln. They would pay to see Mrs. Leslie Carter "undress 4 times each evening," but they thought Lincoln lectures should be free. That was the trouble with the Lincoln field—publishers, writers, speak-

---

[1] A British vaudevillian noted for her beauty, and a friend of Edward VII.

[2] Veteran vaudeville actress, married to Lord Francis Hope, and owner of the Hope Diamond which she sometimes wore upon the stage.

ers, magazine editors, all wanted something for nothing. Whitney wrote an article now and then, "a few dollars worth about Lincoln each year," but he was sorry he "ever invested in it." "It has been an unprofitable venture for me," he assured Weik, "and has done Lincoln no good."

On May 7, 1893, Ward Hill Lamon died, and two years later his daughter, Dorothy, edited certain notes and memoranda he had left and published them as her father's *Recollections of Abraham Lincoln*. This book gave an interesting account of Lincoln's trip to Washington in 1861 and a vivid description of Lamon's mission to Charleston, just before the war, to appraise the secession sentiment. Recounting many anecdotes illustrative of Lincoln's simplicity and tenderness, his dreams and presentiments, his humor and magnanimity, Miss Lamon also gave Lincoln's and Lamon's version of what really happened on the visit to Antietam where Lincoln was accused of asking Lamon to sing a comic song in the presence of the unburied dead. She showed that actually the occurrence took place several miles from the battlefield, sixteen days after the battle, when all the dead were buried, and that the song was sad, not comic.

Whitney thought the book was creditable to both Lincoln and Lamon, although Miss Lamon copied one of his letters without credit, and "a good deal of new stock is in for padding and much that he might have told omitted." "It will not pay you to buy it," Whitney told Weik, (the price was $1.00), "but it has some interest."

Whitney was interested in Lamon's appraisal of the public reception of Lincoln's Gettysburg address. "I had supposed that the whole world except me deemed the Gettysburg speech the *summum bonum* of eloquence: I always deemed it as *rot* . . . But I never found any support any-

where. Lamon conclusively shows that Lincoln was totally
dissatisfied with it before he delivered it & totally chagrined
about it after, that Seward & Everett were astonished at it
& the crowd utterly disappointed."

With publication of these books the giants of the Lincoln generation—those who cared to speak—had had their
say. The reminiscent epoch was passing as the Lincoln generation shuffled off. Already the modern point of view
impinged. Soon modern methods would be brought to
bear.

In the accumulation of reminiscent riches the groundwork of Lincoln biography had been laid. But there were
many interstices, where the documentary sources had been
ignored. It remained for the scholars of the modern school
to fill the gaps, to collate and resolve, to interpret and explain.

Although they would lack the first-hand knowledge the
men of the reminiscent school enjoyed, they could view
the portrait these men had drawn with the advantage of
detachment and perspective, noting where it needed to be
touched up, toned down, refashioned in the revealing light
of the documents.

Chapter Seven

AN IDEALISTIC REALIST

THE future would belong to the realists; but scholarship is evolutionary. From the middle nineties to the nineteen-twenties was a period of transition, with Ida Tarbell its prophet and exemplar.

A realist, in that she welcomed truth when it was demonstrated, she tried to keep her feet on the ground. But sometimes only her tip-toes touched, as she reached to grasp a star.

Taps for the Lincoln generation was her reveille. For in the memories of these oldsters must be stories yet untold; and in attics, basements, letter files, and desk drawers surely there were treasures unexhumed.

This idea suggested itself to Samuel Sidney McClure and his partner, John S. Phillips, as they took thought for the morrow of their magazine. McClure had long esteemed and studied Lincoln, and he now conceived the idea of setting up a sort of Lincoln bureau in his editorial rooms. Through this he would conduct an organized search for reminiscences, relics, pictures, and documents bearing on the Lincoln theme with a view to popularizing Lincoln in the magazine. And in Ida Tarbell he saw an ideal person for this work.

A career woman in an age when women did not often seek careers, she was now thirty-seven years old and ranked as one of McClure's editorial assistants. Tall and slim—slightly over six feet, in fact—she was attractive with her clear eyes and wistful smile. Like Lincoln she could look back upon a rural childhood, for she was born in a log house in Erie County, Pennsylvania, on November 5, 1857. But the parallel of their backgrounds ended there. She had graduated from Allegheny College at Meadville, served for eight years as an associate editor of *The Chautauquan,* and had then gone abroad to study at the Sorbonne and the Collège de France.

McClure first met her in France, and recognizing her potentialities, he brought her home to his staff.

Gracious, eager, apt, and dexterous with a pen, she had been a fortunate find. Already she had made her literary mark with biographies of Napoleon and Madame Roland. But why waste her talents on the figures of France, thought McClure, when a home-grown character like Lincoln needed explaining?

As the first assignment in her Lincoln work, McClure sent her to interview the Lincoln veteran, John G. Nicolay. But to her surprise, he was cool. He could offer her nothing. The collected works of Lincoln, that he and Hay had edited, were complete; and their ten-volume *Life* contained everything worth telling. He tried to dissuade her from her project, and when she persisted, and her articles began to appear, he called one evening to complain. "You are invading my field," he protested. "You write a popular Life of Lincoln and you do just so much to decrease the value of my property." She argued that her work would stimulate interest in all good Lincoln books; but he was unconvinced; and she thought he never forgave her.

Miss Tarbell was introduced to Robert T. Lincoln, now president of the Pullman Company, by Miss Emily Lyons, a mutual friend. In presenting her, Miss Lyons urged, "Now, Robert, I want you to give her something worthwhile." Good-naturedly, Robert agreed to oblige, although he doubted that he could be of any help. He intimated that Herndon had stolen all the papers from his father's office, and explained that the letters of the presidential period were packed away in Washington and had already been thoroughly explored by Nicolay and Hay. But he did give her an excellent daguerreotype, supposedly the first picture of his father ever taken, and one which had never been published. McClure used it as the frontispiece for her first article.

Thereafter, Robert was always kind and friendly, but would never grant access to his father's papers. "Impossible," he said. "They are in the safety vault of my bank. I won't allow anybody to see them. There is nothing of my father's there, that is of value—Nicolay and Hay have published everything; but there are many letters *to* him which if published now would pain, possibly discredit able and useful men still living. Bitter things are written when men are trying to guide a country through a war, particularly a Civil War. I fear misuse of those papers so much that I am thinking of destroying them. Besides, somebody is always worrying me about them, just as you are, and I must be ungenerous. I think I will burn them."

Miss Tarbell would have liked to ask Robert his opinion of many things pertaining to his father, but she feared it would be indecorous.

Miss Tarbell also sought advice and help from Jesse Weik. If he caught her "tripping," she would regard it as a "great kindness" to be shown wherein she erred. More

Ida Tarbell

obliging than Nicolay and Robert Lincoln, Weik supplied her with pictures and offered suggestions. Never blessed with abundance of worldly goods, he was glad to get the checks she sent in payment. He hoped to break into the series with articles of his own, but she explained that this would not be possible, although *McClure's* might be able to use them at a later date. Whenever she needed amplifying material, Weik was usually able to furnish it from Herndon's manuscripts. She planned to visit Weik in Greencastle, admitting that she hoped to "be able to get something out of you which will be valuable in my work. You don't know what a dreadful sponge I have become."

But Weik did know; and so did others. In her zeal Miss Tarbell sometimes pumped out of others things they had planned to use themselves; and without realizing that she might be harming them—wittingly she would never hurt anyone—she slipped their findings into print before the unwilling donors realized what had happened. Fond of her personally, other writers did not always welcome her visits; and at her approach they figuratively secreted their Lincoln treasures in mattresses or cubbyholes. When Katherine Helm was working on her life of Mrs. Lincoln, she was appalled to learn that Miss Tarbell planned to visit Lexington. She tried to discourage her from coming. "But," she wrote to William E. Barton, "here she is combing the town and the old newspaper files—Do you wonder that I feel like the poor little scared rabbit? Of course there is only one way she could get my *original stuff* and that would be by reading my M.S. and that . . . I will take good care she will not do."

The public response to McClure's published appeal for Lincoln material was staggeringly gratifying, and Miss Tarbell wrote hundreds of letters to track down the clues that came to light. But the material was too fragmentary and disconnected for publication; so, in lieu of the original idea, it was decided that Miss Tarbell should write a series of articles covering Lincoln's life to 1858. These were published during 1895 and 1896; and so enthusiastic was their welcome that the printers were unable to turn out copies fast enough. Within ten days *McClure's* gained ten thousand new subscribers and within three months one hundred thousand new readers were on their list. Popularly written and profusely illustrated with pictures of Lincoln and associated people and places, the articles stirred interest country-wide.

Miss Tarbell's discoveries were important and substantial. J. McCan Davis, a young Springfield attorney, searched the Springfield newspapers for her and came up with Lincoln's first speech as well as important letters bearing on his early law practice and political activities. Through interviews and search of public records he disclosed new facts on Lincoln's life in New Salem and his early years in Springfield—the record of his first vote, several maps and surveys made by him, his marriage certificate.

When the public showed no signs of weariness, McClure brought out a new series, dealing with the presidential period, which ran from November, 1898 to September, 1899.

Out of these articles grew Miss Tarbell's *The Early Life of Abraham Lincoln,* published in 1896 to meet a demand the magazine could not supply, and her two-volume *The Life of Abraham Lincoln,* published in 1900, and containing an appendix of some two hundred pages of new documents. Then came a respite while she wrote her *History of the Standard Oil Company,* during which time Weik asked her if she was through with Lincoln. "Of course, I

have not dropped Lincoln," she replied; "I intend to keep
hold of him as long as I live." And her interest did continue through her life. Her books ran to many printings
and editions and from time to time new books and articles
came from her prolific pen. She was adept at writing children's books and her *Boy Scout's Life of Lincoln* has long
been popular with boys. She was especially interested in
the physical setting of events, and her work is replete with
photographs, many of which she took with her own camera
on trips through the Lincoln country. She was ghost writer
for "Recollections of the Civil War," by Charles A. Dana,
Stanton's assistant in the War Department and later editor
of the New York *Sun,* which were published in *McClure's*
in 1897 and 1898; and she worked with Carl Schurz as an
"editorial representative" while he wrote his reminiscences.
In 1924 appeared *In the Footsteps of the Lincolns,* which
some consider her best book.

"I wanted to go over the story again," she explained regarding this book, "and find out whether on closer examination, with all the new material which had come out since
my first study, I would feel as strongly about his work as I
did before. Not only did this going over the story re-
enforce my judgment but it kindled a satisfaction in the
man greater than I had ever had."

Aside from the new material she unearthed, Miss Tarbell's most significant contribution to the Lincoln story
was her appreciation of the stimulus of frontier life, which
had been regarded hitherto as immoderately squalid and
unhappy. Previous biographers had tried to glorify Lincoln by magnifying the unattractive aspects of his early
life, picturing it as hard, dull, enervating, practically devoid of inspiration. In their view this background contributed little or nothing to the making of the later Lincoln.

He became what he did in spite of it. His surmounting such a handicap was proof in itself of innate greatness.

But Miss Tarbell begged to differ. Yes, frontier life was raw and rude; but it was also buoyant and adventurous. "I have never had any sympathy with the half-pitying, half-contemptuous attitude towards Abraham Lincoln's early life or the habit that biographers had fallen into of caricaturing him," she declared. "It seemed to me high time that somebody put emphasis on the other side." To her, Thomas Lincoln—the whole family, in fact—seemed to have been purposely written down to make Lincoln greater by contrast. She saw Lincoln as a typical pioneer child of typical pioneer parents. His family and his surroundings were no better and no worse than those of thousands of pioneer boys. There was poverty, to be sure, but it was offset by the endless "delights and interests the country offers a child." The journey from Kentucky to Indiana "must have been a long delight and wonder." And while life in Indiana was rough and hard, it did not lack amusement, fun, and frolics. The nearby Ohio River and the majestic Mississippi were the American "Appian Way," teeming with lusty life, swelling with the surge of a mighty civilization. Such a background was inspiring and uplifting.

Here Lincoln "saw labor as the foundation of all that might come after it," came to know the emotions and ambitions that moved men's minds. His very speech took flavor from this elemental life. "The horse, the dog, the ox, the chin fly, the plow, the hog, these companions of his youth became interpreters of his meaning, solvers of his problems in his great necessity, of making men understand and follow him."

Thus she flung her challenge at Lamon's "dung-hill"

thesis and Herndon's assertion of Lincoln's having risen from "a stagnant, putrid pool"; and if she did not succeed entirely in dispelling these misconceptions, others, following her lead, would do so later.

Miss Tarbell felt the puissance of American rural life. To Chic Sale, who enjoyed depicting her "Man Who Knew Lincoln" in one of his vaudeville skits, she wrote: "I know of no one on our stage that interprets with so much sympathy, humor, and understanding the honest-to-God American of our country towns and corners. You catch his shrewdness, independence of spirit, his love of fun and its practice. I always laugh at your characters and love them because they are so entirely themselves." And she might have added that every characteristic she enumerated was typified in Lincoln.

From Miss Tarbell's books came new appreciation of the power of the American West and what it could do in the way of fashioning a man. American historians, working in a broader field, were submitting the thesis that the influence of the frontier was a major determining factor of American national life; and Miss Tarbell, studying one man, was deducing a similar thesis about him.

Few persons realize Miss Tarbell's influence upon Carl Sandburg. She was his prime mover. Sending her page proof for his *Prairie Years*, Sandburg wrote: "Yourself and Oliver R. Barrett [the Lincoln collector] are the only persons receiving advance sheets, as you are the two who have helped me most." In his preface Sandburg credited her with putting fresh color into what had heretofore been pictured as "drab and miserable beyond the fact"; and her influence is manifest when he wrote: "In the short and simple annals of the poor, it seems there are people who breathe with the earth and take into their lungs and blood some of the hard and dark strength of its mystery. During six and seven months each year in the twelve fiercest formative years of his life, Abraham Lincoln had the pads of his foot-soles bare against clay of the earth. It may be the earth told him in her own tough gypsy slang one or two knacks of living worth keeping."

As a college student Miss Tarbell aspired to be a microscopist; later she studied some phases of Lincoln's life as with a microscope. She questioned Herndon's account of Lincoln's reaction to the slave auction at New Orleans, where he was supposed to have vowed, "If I ever get a chance to hit that thing, I'll hit it hard." Herndon gave John Hanks as authority for this statement; and Miss Tarbell pointed out that according to Lincoln's own assertion Hanks did not accompany the party to New Orleans but left it at St. Louis. But she questioned only the details of the story, never doubting that Lincoln was impressed by what he saw.

She also showed that William Cullen Bryant was wrong in supposing that Lincoln was the "raw youth" of "quaint and pleasant mien" whom he saw in command of a company of volunteers when traveling in the West during the Black Hawk War; because Lincoln's captaincy ended in May, and Bryant arrived in June, and he never got within fifty miles of where Lincoln was.

Miss Tarbell did not doubt that liquor was sold at the Lincoln-Berry store in New Salem—a point which had been argued since the time Douglas alluded to it in one of the great debates. It was sold at every frontier store, she explained; and when Lincoln and Berry obtained a tavern license, they were permitted to sell it by the drink, on the premises, whereas, without a license, they could sell it only in bulk for consumption off the premises.

On March 6, 1896, she warned Weik that she was going to try to "explode" Herndon's story of the wedding at which Lincoln failed to appear. Possibly Weik would be inclined to "explode" her in retaliation. If so, well and good. All she wanted was the truth, "and if we can bring out any new authority, why so much the better for both of us." She did bring out new authority averse to Herndon's statements; and while her hoped-for explosion merely fizzled, later investigators proved her suspicions to be correct by finishing the job of demolition.

Thus she was instrumental in clarifying doubtful points; although, on the other hand, her ardor sometimes led her astray as in the case of Whitney and Lincoln's "Lost Speech." Fervently devoted to Lincoln, when the scales were nearly balanced, she would let her hand rest—ever so lightly, and probably unconsciously—on the side that favored him. Thus she was tempted into endorsing Mrs. Caroline Hanks Hitchcock's supposed exculpation of Nancy Hanks' mother.

Near the end of the century, Mrs. Hitchcock, studying her own genealogy, discovered in Nelson County, Kentucky, the will of a Joseph Hanks, who died in 1793, leaving five sons and three daughters—Elizabeth, Polly, and Nancy; and to Nancy he bequeathed a heifer calf. Here was a Nancy Hanks of legitimate birth! Might she not be the mother of the president?

Convinced that she had made a great discovery, Mrs. Hitchcock sought corroborating evidence. From collateral data she concluded that Joseph was a son of William Hanks, who settled in Amelia County, Virginia, in the latter part of the eighteenth century and left a large family of Hankses scattered about in that vicinity. William, in turn, traced back to Benjamin Hanks, who came to Massachusetts from England in 1699. According to Mrs. Hitch-cock, Joseph Hanks married Mary Shipley, and their youngest daughter, Nancy, was born on February 5, 1774, and later went to live with her uncle, Richard Berry.

And now, behold the missing link that identified this Nancy as the mother of the president! Richard Berry witnessed the marriage bond of Nancy Hanks and Thomas Lincoln!

When Mrs. Hitchcock published her findings in 1899 in a book entitled *Nancy Hanks, The Story of Abraham Lincoln's Mother,* Miss Tarbell wrote an enthusiastic introduction and became her stanch supporter.

When Weik warned her to beware, and confided that he had discovered new material supporting Herndon's conclusions, she urged him to publish it. Now was the appointed time to settle the matter once and for all. And if he would not publish his findings, would he not at least reveal them to her in confidence? "I have absolutely no interest except knowing the truth," she avowed. "But for the life of me I do not understand why this will should not be considered about as good proof as can be produced. I have consulted lawyers on this and they have cited me authorities . . . saying that the recognition of a child in a will is accepted always legally as sufficient evidence of legitimacy. I beg of you to let me know your view of the case, the evidence which you say would 'control the courts.' I should be the first one to use it if I could get control of it."

But Weik knew the power of public wrath and decided to hold his peace, although in replying to Miss Tarbell he made a virtue of his reticence. "I have always been opposed to the publication of the details of Mr. Lincoln's ancestry," he moralized. "I never could see any good to result from it and I am sure Mr. Lincoln felt the same way himself. Mr. Herndon . . . said more than I would and more than I wanted him to tell. Whether Nancy Hanks was illegitimate or not cannot, in the least degree, affect the greatness of Abraham Lincoln. His place in history is fixed 'beyond our power to add or detract' and his fame is imperishable. I do not therefore agree with you that 'now is an excellent time to settle the question.' In the first edition of *Herndon's Lincoln* Herndon was given free rein to say what he knew about Lincoln's mother; but in the next or Appleton edition which was published after his death and which underwent some amendment at my hands you will find that the unpleasant reference to Lincoln's mother, Nancy Hanks, has been eliminated. That represents my notion as to the propriety of continuing the controversy. In my opinion no good can come of it and therefore the sooner it ceases the better."

Thus Weik blamed Herndon for what he now considered a mistake, and smugly took credit for trying to rectify it. Daniel Fish, the Lincoln collector saw through the subterfuge. "Since that dastardly slur . . . was inserted in the book with the concurrence of Judge Weik," he explained to Miss Tarbell, "his desire to 'make good' may well account for his present attitude."

With Weik committed to silence, it seemed that Mrs. Hitchcock's thesis would win by default. Joseph H. Barrett, writing in 1904, characterized Herndon's story as an "unfortunate hallucination" in the light of Mrs. Hitchcock's evidence; and Isaac N. Phillips felt "a little vehement" at Herndon's perfidy. When James Henry Lea and J. R. Hutchinson published *The Ancestry of Abraham Lincoln,* in 1909, they too accepted Mrs. Hitchcock's conclusions regarding Nancy Hanks, although they rejected her belief that the Hankses traced to a Massachusetts family in favor of a line of descent from John Hanks of Gwynedd, Pennsylvania.

Miss Tarbell herself decided to disregard Weik's warning. She was always somewhat sentimental about Lincoln, and thought he merited an honorable ancestry. But she never put sentiment above evidence. Here, happily, was a case where truth seemed in accord with sentiment. "The only theory advanced which has any documentary proof to support it is that of Mrs. Hitchcock," she wrote to Joseph H. Barrett. "Mr. Herndon certainly never repeated anything more than hearsay . . . I think him rather too quick to accept a sensational explanation of certain points . . . I want to be perfectly fair to everybody concerned, but I decidedly object to keeping up this old tradition . . . simply for the sake of adding more mystery to the origin of Abraham Lincoln."

So she became a leading promulgator of Mrs. Hitchcock's thesis.

But she realized how hard it was to change a preconception. For the public mind had undergone a change. True or false, anything tending to put Lincoln in a proper light would have had easy acceptance not so long before. Now people seemed more skeptical, more willing to look on him as a man like other men. They no longer seemed to feel he must be perfect. They were willing to accept him for what he was. "I have no hope of convincing anybody," wrote Miss Tarbell in regard to her championship of Mrs. Hitchcock's discovery. "I simply hope to give the only account of Nancy Hanks which has any sort of documentary support." Later, adverting again to the reluctance with which people gave up fixed ideas, she recalled the tenacity with which they clung to the story of Lincoln's leaving Mary

Todd waiting at the altar. "In spite of all the documents and evidence I collected demolishing the episode, I reaped only sour looks and dubious headshakes," she lamented. "I had spoiled a good story or tried to. It still remains a good story. Every now and then somebody tells it to me. A biographer who tries to break down a belittling legend meets with far less sympathy than he who strengthens or creates one."

Lamon or Herndon could have told her this was not always so. There must have come a change in public feeling.

The biographers before Miss Tarbell were a stubborn lot. It was a new departure to have a Lincoln author with an open mind. For Miss Tarbell had no false pride and no illusions of infallibility. Always and sincerely she expressed thanks when anyone exposed an error in her work. When Paul Angle, who was winning scholarly recognition as secretary of the Abraham Lincoln Association, informed her that he was about to publish evidence which would discredit Whitney's alleged restoration of Lincoln's "Lost Speech," she told him to go ahead. "I think you are rendering the Lincoln public a real service in this case as you have in so many others," she asserted. "It is a consolation to have a watch dog, like yourself, at the door in Springfield." As her wisdom ripened with age, she knew she was too uncritically laudatory by modern standards. "I am afraid I am over-lenient towards mistakes, having made so many myself," she admitted. When her conclusions were attacked, she could say with all sincerity, "It is a deep satisfaction to me that the work has become gradually so thorough and so scientific." "As one of the old guard, about the oldest, I think, I am never very sure of my standing with the younger Lincoln students, but I am thankful for them," she asserted at the age of eighty-four. "They are constantly unearthing things that I never found and enabling me to correct what are supposed to be facts."

She welcomed newcomers to the Lincoln field, anticipating that their point of view might be refreshing. When it was arranged that she should be a sort of counsellor to the German biographer Emil Ludwig while he wrote his *Life of Lincoln,* she immediately sent him encouragement. "I know you are going to give us something provocative and stimulating," she assured him; "and we need something of that kind over here on Lincoln. You see, we are so close that we are not yet able to appraise. We have been dealing in the raw materials, getting him into shape for future estimates, squabbling over controverted facts—all necessary, I suppose, but it is good to get an outside view, and I am eager to see yours."

She was suspicious of Herndon; yet she appreciated what he had done. "Where we would be without him I don't know," she wrote to Weik. "Though I have in certain cases disagreed with his interpretation of documents, I held in highest regard—and never failed to express it —not only his remarkable contribution of personal recollections but his equally remarkable collection of the recollections of others." There were rumors that Herndon's collection contained many things that even he had not seen fit to reveal; and Miss Tarbell's zeal for truth is attested by her appeal to Weik to annotate and publish the Herndon manuscripts. Weik never chose to follow her advice; but years later after Weik's death, Emanuel Hertz brought out a collection of Herndon letters, some of which seemed indiscreet. But Miss Tarbell was not one to protest. "I am glad you published these papers," she wrote to Hertz. "There has been a mystery about what was in them for so long, there have been so many hints that there were dark and sinister revelations in them concerning Lincoln's private life and his ancestry that every serious student of Lincoln's life will be grateful to you for publishing the material showing the worst. Certainly nothing is there that impairs Lincoln for intelligent people, but I am afraid, dear Mr. Hertz, that there is considerable that impairs Herndon as a careful student, an honest and patient searcher for facts.

"Nobody is more grateful to Herndon than I am for the tremendous amount of vital, human material he gathered on Lincoln," she continued, "but his early theory explaining Lincoln's melancholy so obsessed him that he was not willing to give the careful research the ancestry required nor was he willing to give up his notions about Tom Lincoln and Nancy Lincoln. That it was an obsession these letters and documents seem to me to prove and the tragedy of it is that it cost him the rewards that he ought to have had in his life time for a tremendous amount of valuable work."

Herndon sponsored one questionable story which Miss Tarbell was reluctant to give up. She hoped the romance of Lincoln and Ann Rutledge would never be proved untrue. "I have always been a believer in this romance," she wrote after it had come under skeptical scrutiny, "have believed it was the only time romance touched Abraham Lincoln. It seems to me that the definite proofs outside of tradition, which is of course a strong support, are sufficient to establish the fact of the love between them."

Denied romance herself—at least so far as we know—it seemed to her that a man whose life was so full of sadness and tragedy should be allowed this moment of happiness. "Frankly, I am probably influenced by my desire that the man should have had such an affair in his early life," she confessed. "How could you expect that a young man of a strong emotional nature such as Lincoln's, and his was strong if unusually well controlled, should live side by side with a girl whom everybody reported charming and not fall in love. It was a natural thing to do. I sometimes think people who dispute early romances have lived so long that they have forgotten their youth."

Miss Tarbell had idealistic tendencies; but she must be classed as a realist. She was no idolater. Her Lincoln was "altogether a man." "It is a mistake to think of him as a hero—a demigod," she declared. "It is a fine thing that he shows what a man can do with himself in spite of all handicaps, all the temptations of human beings—none of which I take it he escaped. It is the way he came through at the end that is so fine."

A young lady, an American, who was lecturing at the University of Manchester in England, once asked Miss Tarbell to explain Lincoln's ever-increasing popular appeal. To survivors of the Civil War, she replied, Lincoln was a warrior's hero, and somewhat mythical. But the contemporary feeling of admiration and respect was more soundly based. It was not due to Republican oratory, as her correspondent suggested, although the party had overlooked no opportunity to exploit him. Republican oratory of recent years was far removed from Lincoln's ideas and spirit. "They have denied him at every point," she asserted.

The problems of the World War had undoubtedly turned the country's thoughts to the man who had guided it through its last great military struggle. "His ideas of what democracy means, of the necessity of going through even a civil war to protect a great experiment in popular government, his arguments and his decisions—all these have been a subject of new study through this period," she admitted. And they went far to explain the growing Lincoln cult in England. But in America the roots were deeper.

Here, she believed, Lincoln's appeal came from the fact that he epitomized American characteristics. "Our people are much devoted to what they consider the American type," she explained, "with its characteristics of common sense, directness, humor, and a bull-dog grip—and Lincoln had all of these things." Then, too, Americans had always been attracted to the diamond-in-the-rough; so many of them, especially in the West, were diamonds-in-the-rough themselves.

This young lady correspondent wondered if Lincoln had not become too much the superman, and if his true greatness might be lost in over-adulation. But Miss Tarbell did not think so. "The people, on the whole, have him about right," she thought. "His place with us depends upon the conviction of the people that he was a man, and not that he was a superman. It is likeness to themselves, the fact that they understand the words he uses and the arguments—they understand, too, the struggle that he went through, it is so like their own. This is what binds the mass of the people to Lincoln."

Miss Tarbell had a rare appreciation of Lincoln. To a member of a discussion club who inquired whether Lincoln was interested in the "finer traits," such as art, music, color, or flowers, she explained that during the greater part of his life he lived in a community where music and art were not readily available. Yet, no man who was as passionately fond of the best in literature and so eager to acquaint himself with everything that had contributed to man's cultural advancement could have been insensible to art and music when they came his way. He was a student of the drama in that he never missed an opportunity to see anything that was presented on the stage, even such poor repertory as was available on his circuit travels; and after he went to Washington he not only attended the theater regularly; he could also discuss Shakespeare intelligently with some of the best actors of his day. Few men were more familiar with Shakespeare, Burns, or the Bible.

As a woodsman, he must have known trees, and perhaps flowers; but this was not the place to look for his interest in "finer things." "It is in his devotion to high literature and his own power of expression," Miss Tarbell pointed out. "You must not forget Abraham Lincoln wrote more than one piece of prose which is universally held to be as perfect as anything that has been produced in English." That alone should be proof of his interest in "finer things."

To a superficial observer he may have seemed smirched by a touch of grossness, she admitted. Perhaps his stories, for example, were not always in good taste. But they often helped elucidate a point and sometimes he used them for protection. "He had to push people away, and he often offended deeply by the habit."

With publication of Miss Tarbell's *History of the Standard Oil Company* in 1904, she came to be identified with the group comprising Lincoln Steffens, Charles Edward Russell, Gustavus Myers, and Upton Sinclair, who were called "muckrakers" by Theodore Roosevelt. The more sympathetic estimate of Vernon Louis Parrington depicted them as a part of the "host of heavy armed troops which moved forward on the strongholds of the new plutocracy" that had emerged in America as a result of the industrial revolution, and which, in alliance with venal politicians, was using the political machinery of democracy "to drive toward an objective which was the negation of democracy."

One is tempted to try to establish a connection between Miss Tarbell's alignment with these embattled democratic journalists and her interest in Lincoln; and to ascribe her trust-busting activities to the inspiration derived from study of the great exemplar of democracy. And while such a conclusion might be difficult to prove, the compatibility of her literary interests may not have been altogether fortuitous.

Miss Tarbell enjoyed her Lincoln studies. "I am working away at my story of the migrations of the Lincolns," she wrote in 1923, referring to *In the Footsteps of the Lincolns*, ". . . I don't know that I shall add much to the knowledge of the specialists, but I am trying to put a little flesh on the bones of Samuel and Mordecai and the rest of them. Whether the results of my work please others or not, I have gotten a great deal of interest and satisfaction out of it." Her story was built around a pilgrimage along the Lincoln route; and she was just as enthusiastic as when she traversed the same ground a quarter of a century before. At an old cemetery near Harrisonburg, Virginia, she climbed an iron picket fence to study the inscriptions on some Lincoln tombstones; and it gave her no small satisfaction that when William E. Barton, another Lincoln student, visited the same cemetery two years later, he stood outside the fence and took notes while the inscriptions were read to him. And he was only sixty-five, while she was sixty-seven!

Miss Tarbell stuck to the resolution she had expressed in her early years to Weik. At the age of eighty-four she wrote: "Anyone who really takes up seriously the study of . . . [Lincoln's] life is never willing to lay it down. He is companionable as no public mind that I've ever known anything about, you feel at home with him, he never high hats you and he never bores you which is more than I can say of any public man living or dead with whom I have tried to get well acquainted . . . An impressive part of this acquaintance with him as a man is watching him grow, expand. Nothing was ever finished for Lincoln."

People were continually asking Miss Tarbell what Lincoln would do about problems of the present day; but she always advised that speculation of this sort was futile. This was not to say that Lincoln could offer nothing to the modern world. It could profit immeasurably by studying and following his methods. "While others talked Lincoln listened—weighed. He came slowly to his decisions. But when he arrived at them, he defended them sturdily, though never so obstinately he was not ready to consider new facts." He was "steady in storms," uncowed by criticism, unwavering when sure that he was right. He was impersonal in handling public matters, knowing neither vanity nor malice. In pressing for his goal, he took no thought for himself; and in dealing with men, he asked no more than they could give. His appeal was to the intellect; but he could stir the moral forces, too.

"It is not his opinion on a particular subject, not his wit and wisdom as expressed in his letters and speeches which are his great contribution," she explained in another letter; "it is from the temper with which he approached his problems, the methods by which he handled them that we can learn most. His life was a call to self-training—of training of the mind until it can form sound—workmanlike, trustworthy conclusions, training of the moral nature to justice and rightness—training of the will until it can be counted on to back up the conclusions of the mind and heart. It is a call to openness of mind, willingness to learn.

"His method is a constant lesson in liberality towards others, to a recognition that there may be something to be said of the other man's point of view as well as of yours, that you no more see all the truth than he does, and that if what each of you see can be fused, a larger amount of truth will result. Above all, his method is a revelation of what a man can make out of himself if he will. Indeed, I am sometimes inclined to feel that the greatest service Lincoln has done this country was to demonstrate what could be made of a mind by passionate, persistent effort. What moral heights the nature would rise to if dealt with in perfect candor.

"Taking him all in all, it is doubtful if this country or any country has produced a man so worthy of studying and following as is Abraham Lincoln."

This was her conception of our Lincoln heritage; and comprehension of Lincoln was her own most precious literary legacy. Small wonder that on January 7, 1944, the day after Miss Tarbell's death, the New York *Times* predicted that "her work in the field will be on any small shelf of Lincoln books for countless years to come. She was as honest, as kindly, as thoroughly American in the loftiest sense as he was. He would have loved and understood her as she did him."

Primarily Miss Tarbell was a popularizer, and with the passing years her books have been outmoded. But if she is not read as much as she once was, she should continue to be appreciated. She was the pioneer scientific investigator whose work foretold the revelation of Lincoln as he really was. "I cannot say enough for the wonderful contribution you have made in the field of Lincolniana," a Wisconsin educator told her. "In fact, you blazed the way for research work in this field." Carl Sandburg wrote to tell her how he and Oliver Barrett "talked long this evening about how much less of *fresh glint* there would be on the Lincoln legend without your work"; and when his *War Years* was published, he sent her a copy "not merely with my compliments, but with respect and affection—and something like reverence for a wisdom and integrity that have lasted so well across the years."

Chapter Eight

AN INTERLUDE OF ASSIMILATION

For seventeen years after publication of Miss Tarbell's *Life* few significant contributions were made to Lincolniana. The generous effusion inspired by the Lincoln Centennial, in 1909, was disappointing; and the Lincoln Centennial Association, organized to commemorate that event, gave no indication of the importance it was to assume at a later date under a different name. Professional historians still shunned the Lincoln field, leaving it to the amateurs. The emphasis of the graduate schools, where the foremost teachers were European-trained, was upon European history and the bringing of Old World influence and institutions to America during the Colonial period to the neglect of native phenomena; and the index of *The American Historical Review*, vehicle of American historical erudition, contains few references to Lincoln. Were historians just not interested in Lincoln; or did they cower before the thought of offering themselves, a living sacrifice? For this seemed to be the lot of those who deviated from the popular ideal.

But there were signs that times had changed. Speaking

before the Century Club, in New York City, Horace White told the facts of Cameron's appointment to Lincoln's cabinet and of his ejection from it, and concluded that "there was an admixture of human clay in the make-up of Father Abraham." "Hitherto the prevailing cult has been mythological as regards Lincoln," he observed to Weik in telling him of this experience. "People have believed that he was a demigod who issued out of a cloud in order to deliver mankind from dragons and was then withdrawn' into a cloud. No other conception of him would be tolerated. I was myself doubtful whether even the Century Club—the most highly cultivated group in New York—would tolerate what I found it necessary to say about the taking of Cameron into the Cabinet in the way we know about. I was therefore considerably surprised when I found that they were quite disposed to applaud what I said, & really wanted all the facts about Lincoln without abatement & without varnish . . . It is needless to say that my judgment of Lincoln & my affection for him have undergone no change. They are still the same that they were when I wrote the introduction to the second edition of Herndon-Weik, in which I said that the tendency in the public mind toward apotheosis of Lincoln was entirely natural but that it would not last forever."

Confirmation of this change of view came to Weik in a letter from James R. B. Van Cleave of Springfield. He and "some members of our Assn" (the Lincoln Centennial Association) wanted the real facts on the Enloe story. Weik replied that he was considering publishing what he knew; and when he procrastinated, Van Cleave encouraged him. He did not believe the truth would stir up any "whirlwind," as it once might have done.

This access of tolerance worked to the benefit of Hern-

Horace White

don's reputation. Worthington C. Ford, Chief of the Division of Manuscripts of the Library of Congress and in the first rank of historians, told Weik he had become very much interested in Herndon's personality as revealed in his letters to Lyman Trumbull. Evidently he was a man who was "controlled by a moral idea, and who was not afraid to carry it to the extreme. Such men seem to have been so much more numerous in that day than at present, and they are of the men whom I admire."

Yet Weik and White both hesitated to speak out. Weik said he had proved Lincoln's legitimacy to his satisfaction, but was equally satisfied that Nancy Hanks was born out of wedlock. White advised Weik not to "rake over the dust" unless it became necessary to vindicate Herndon; and others advised him to lay away what he had "for the action of those who come afterward." Daniel Fish, the Lincoln collector, suggested that a small group of those who were interested and had open minds should get together "to try privately to resolve the conflicting theories. As the matter now stands the biographers and genealogists seem to have substantially agreed upon the Joseph Hanks parentage of Nancy Lincoln and upon the regular birth of Abraham . . . It would afford me great satisfaction to know all the facts bearing upon the subject, whithersoever they might lead. I could never see any profit in being mistaken about anything important enough to excite my curiosity."

White had always thought Lincoln had a sort of "moral obtuseness as manifested in his association with and tolerance of low & dishonest characters like Simon Cameron, Ward Lamon & M. W. Delahay." Cameron's appointment was "the most colossal blunder of Lincoln's public life — if it is proper to call it a blunder," White declared to Weik.

"It may have a worse name in history one hundred years hence. I think he sinned against light." And White might lengthen his list of rogues to include William H. Seward and Thurlow Weed. The word "low" might not be applicable to them, but "dishonest" was—to Weed, at least. Weed was a "grafter" and Seward, while he did not share in his loot, aided and abetted him.

White felt strongly on this point of Lincoln's obtuseness; yet when Weik urged him to publish an article on the subject, he did not feel inclined to "go out of my way to pick flaws in Lincoln's record." It would not be expedient to add anything to what he had already said in his life of Trumbull. Some people thought that book disparaged Lincoln; and White had no desire to appear before the public in the role of a detractor.

White was probably right, thought Weik; but there was certainly a broadminded curiosity developing. The inquiries he was getting about Lincoln! "Did he sweat easily?" "Was he good at chess?" "Did he have piles or hemorrhoids?"

Thus matters rested till the First World War brought a resurgence of the democratic spirit. It was a war to save democracy, and the time was opportune to reappraise the man whose name had come to symbolize democracy. So it was not strange that 1917 should witness the appearance of the best one-volume life of Lincoln ever written; but it was astonishing to have it come from the pen of an English peer. Thirty years before, when the New England scholar John T. Morse, Jr. was editing the American Statesmen series, no English house would publish it. "American statesmen?" "Really, old chap, there aren't any," was the essence of the British response. But now there was at least one Englishman who disagreed.

Godfrey Rathbone Benson, first baron Charnwood, was born on November 6, 1864, and was educated at Winchester and Balliol College, Oxford, where he later lectured. He served as a Liberal member of parliament and as mayor of Litchfield, where he was also councillor and alderman. Although he was always studiously inclined, the life of Lincoln was his first major literary venture.

Charnwood unearthed no new facts—he relied on the writings of others—and he changed no major conclusions. His originality consisted in the detached and balanced judgment he brought to bear, in his delineation of Lincoln as a towering native growth rather than an unintelligible prodigy, and in his appreciation not merely of Lincoln's determination to save the Union but of his larger purpose of demonstrating democracy to the world as a workable political philosophy.

Charnwood's knowledge of American political history was penetrating and complete; and while sketching the portrait of Lincoln he kept his brush constantly flicking at the background, never allowing himself to become absorbed in the man to the exclusion of his setting. Thus he achieved a lucid entity. Nor did he seek to hide the wens and wrinkles. He acknowledged Lincoln's faults, particularly in early life, and while recognizing the rigorous mental discipline to which he subjected himself from 1849 to 1860, he brought him to the presidency somewhat less prepared than had the other biographers. Charnwood's own experience in public life made him sensible of Lincoln's feeling for public opinion and of the way he delegated responsibility to subordinates while yet retaining a checkrein against excessive zeal or petty despotism. While appreciating Lincoln's ability to understand people in the mass, he agreed with Herndon, Arnold, Weik, and White that inability to judge an individual man was perhaps his greatest fault. He was the first biographer to credit Lincoln with a major part in planning war strategy, an activity that had been revealed in the latest studies of the Civil War, most of which were also written by Englishmen. He elucidated the slow but natural flowering of Lincoln's religion under stress of war, a development that Herndon was never able to understand.

John T. Morse thought it almost incredible that a European with the traditions and prejudices of the Old World could do such an excellent job. There was no idolatry, but a deep, sincere appreciation. Allowing military events to run through the volume "like a river," Charnwood never permitted them to spread "like an inundation." He focussed interest on the actors with "keen insight into character," and "vivid portrayals couched in the happiest expressive phrases."

A product of thorough reading and painstaking thought, the book displayed such keen analysis and literary facility that Carl Russell Fish, appraising it for *The American Historical Review,* predicted with rare prescience that it might well become a classic.

Since the publication of *Herndon's Lincoln,* Jesse Weik had been living quietly at Greencastle, corresponding with Lincoln students, writing Lincoln articles for the magazines, and browsing through the Herndon manuscripts. In 1894 Wilbur B. Ralston, administrator of Herndon's estate, wrote to Weik in evident suspicion, demanding a full accounting to date; but when Weik explained how matters stood between him and Herndon, Ralston seemed completely satisfied. Weik tried to buy out whatever interest the Herndon family still had in the manuscripts, and while the course of the negotiations is not clear, Weik retained the manuscripts and seems ultimately to have come into undisputed possession. A memorandum by Weik shows how things stood between him and Herndon in 1897:

"Herndon owes me		$650.00
Royalties to date	$892.46	
Herndon's half	446.23	
		446.23
H. owes me		203.77
Royalties Feb 94		$335.86
" 95		176.85
" 96		125.35
" 97		72.45"

In 1917, finding that Herndon's grave was still unmarked, Weik wrote to friends and acquaintances soliciting contributions for a monument which was erected in the summer of 1918. Whatever suspicions the Herndon family may have had about his dealings with their father seem to have been allayed.

In 1910 Weik felt constrained to sell the Herndon collection and sounded out prospective purchasers. None of the Lincoln collectors seemed to have sufficient funds, and Andrew Carnegie and John Pierpont Morgan were not interested. Senator Albert Beveridge and Horace White tried to rouse interest in support of an appropriation by means of which the Library of Congress might acquire it. But there was little interest; and Weik, unable to dispose of the collection, gave it a re-working.

In 1922 he published *The Real Lincoln,* the third book based on Herndon's materials.

Except for the question of Lincoln's paternity, in which he gave Nancy Lincoln a clean bill, Weik reasserted Herndon's conclusions on controverted points, buttressing them at times with minor supporting evidence. Strangely enough, not one reviewer seemed shocked at the reassertion of Nancy Hanks' illegitimacy (which he dealt with at length in spite of his assertions of distaste to Miss Tarbell), the "fatal first of January," Lincoln's unhappy home life, or his pre-marital affairs of the heart, all of which Weik reaffirmed just as Herndon had told them. Most reviewers regarded the book as a supplement to Herndon. The New York *Call* thought it "exhaustive" and "vivid," and the New York *World* considered it "profound." But the New York *Herald* sized it up as essentially gossip and hearsay, while the Boston *Herald* hinted that it got a little dull. The New York *Tribune* thought it put Lincoln's so-called admirers to the test in that if they did not like the book, they probably would not have liked Lincoln himself, but only his legendary mask.

William H. Townsend of Lexington, Kentucky, who would make his own mark in the Lincoln field, congratulated Weik on preserving the "personal, intimate, real Lincoln" to the world. Reading in his study, far into the night, it seemed to him, as he closed the book and relaxed, that "the Volk Life Mask of Lincoln on my library mantelpiece ought to smile and say 'Goodnight' and that Volk's Cast of the Hands, beside the Mask, would grip mine in a warm, living grasp at the close of an evening's confidential chat." How poor Herndon would have relished a compliment like that!

Albert J. Beveridge, who had already gained fame as a historian with his life of Chief Justice Marshall, and who was now beginning a similar study of Lincoln, acted as an intermediary between Weik and his publishers, and also wrote a complimentary review of the book for *The Inter-*

national Book Review. Looking forward to using Herndon's materials himself, he seems to have been buttering up Weik. His letters were interlarded with "dear Jesse," and he told Weik the book would have a steady growth "in spite of the Tarbells and Rankins." [1] Never backward about coming forward, Beveridge believed his review "had boosted your volume considerably"; whether this was so or not, the book sold well.

Except for Charnwood's contribution, however, the writings of these twenty years were undistinguished. It was a period of settling and assimilation, a pause before the robust fare about to come.

---

[1] Henry B. Rankin had been an office-boy in the Lincoln-Herndon office and was author of *Personal Recollections of Abraham Lincoln* and *Intimate Character Sketches of Abraham Lincoln.* Strongly romantic in point of view and hostile to Herndon, he was instrumental in spreading the idea that Herndon was a drunkard and drug addict. Dec. 6, 1916, he wrote to Lord Charnwood: "I would not consent to tell all the story for history, about his shadowy decadence and incapacity for serious historical work while preparing with and for others the manuscripts for the "Lives of Lincoln" with which his name was associated. His brain all through those lamentable years had been inflamed by alcoholic stimulants and his imagination distorted and made unreliable by his habitual use of opium." In a letter to F. W. Ruckstuhl, editor of *Art World,* Rankin referred to Herndon's "later and sad years that were so clouded with alcohol and morphine." Actually Herndon had given up drinking in his later years and there is no reason to believe he ever took drugs.

Chapter Nine

A PROLIFIC PREACHER

THE years following the first World War saw a revival of interest in American biographical studies, with new emphasis upon the use of documentary material rather than reminiscences. The disillusionments of the war and the peace made people skeptical, and brought a questioning attitude toward men and things. Our cultural, economic, and political heritage was reappraised, and our national heroes were subjected to fresh scrutiny. With a few exceptions where "debunking" was the aim, the attitude was not iconoclastic or irreverent, but it was one which looked at men as men. The new spirit in biographical writing was inspired by Lytton Strachey, who recognized no obligation to be complimentary. The business of the biographer, as he saw it, was to lay bare the facts.

First of the "new biographers" in the Lincoln field was William Eleazer Barton, who dominated the period of the 'twenties.

Born in Sublette, Illinois, on June 28, 1861, Barton worked his way through Berea College by teaching a mountain school during summer vacations, and working as a book agent in central and southeastern Kentucky. After graduation he worked for the American Missionary Association, traveling through the Kentucky mountains on horseback, organizing Sunday Schools, and conducting evangelistic services. Attaining ordination as a Congregational minister, he was pastor at Robbins, Tennessee, from 1885 to 1887, when, aspiring to a larger service, he entered Oberlin Theological Seminary.

His arrival was sensational; for he strode down the main street of the town adorned with a flowing beard, while his wife, with their baby in her arms, followed behind on horseback. Behind her walked a negro boy driving the Bartons' two cows, and bringing up the rear was a negro girl, laden with household goods.

A student pastorate at Litchfield, Ohio, eased their financial burdens to the extent of enabling Barton to complete his course and graduate at the head of his class in 1890.

Then, after preaching for three years at Wellington, Ohio, he was called to the Shawmut Congregational Church in Boston. His six years there resulted in a call to the First Congregational Church of Oak Park, Illinois, a "state of mind" at that time, rather than a town, but a place that was destined to grow rapidly while Barton grew with it. While at Oak Park he lectured at the Chicago Theological Seminary, and in 1928 went to Nashville to lecture at Vanderbilt University. In Nashville he organized and became the first pastor of the Collegeside Congregational Church.

Barton became interested in Lincoln through study of his religion. Over a period of years he took notes for use in sermons until he realized he had enough material for a book. "Everybody else has written a book about Abraham Lincoln," he wrote to Robert Lincoln, "and I have written a book about everything else. So I am writing one about him—a small book."

"I know what kind of preaching Abraham Lincoln heard in his boyhood from very ignorant Baptists, very noisy Methodists, and very dogmatic Southern Presbyterians," he continued. "When he mimicked preachers, I know what he mimicked, and when he doubted and rebelled, I know what he was rejecting. I can therefore better understand some things that Herndon and Lamon have told with very bad taste and some bias. And I have read with what I think is a fair allowance for the personal equation what Drs. Reed and Smith said of his Springfield attitude, and so on."

Barton would welcome any information Robert Lincoln might wish to give; but if he preferred "to keep out of a stream already darkened by overmuch of ink," he would understand.

Barton's *The Soul of Abraham Lincoln* appeared in 1920 and was immediately acclaimed as the most perceptive study of Lincoln's religion. *Bookman* correctly predicted it would be the standard work; and *Booklist* considered it essential for all libraries, although "lacking in charm for general reading." But like all other books dealing with this theme, it had to make its way against the reviewers' personal predilections. The Springfield *Republican* thought it left one unconvinced; while the Boston *Transcript* regarded it as "utterly futile." At the last page its critic had "no clearer idea of Lincoln's religious belief than in its first. Despite the mass of material he assembles, Dr. Barton proves nothing."

Lyman Abbott, reviewing it for the *Outlook*, agreed essentially with Barton that there was no reason to think Lincoln "either believed or disbelieved in the current theology of the evangelical churches . . . These are parts of a system of philosophy, and philosophy never interested

William Eleazer Barton

Abraham Lincoln; but he was profoundly interested in life. Justice, mercy, humility, and reverence were his life. That the American Nation should be just and merciful was his supreme desire; to make it just and merciful he devoted himself with an inexhaustible patient courage. In his lonely life of service he was sustained by the reverent faith in an unseen companion. To do justly, love mercy, and walk humbly with God was Abraham Lincoln's religion."

To aid him in his work, Barton bought books; and as his interest in Lincoln widened, his purchases increased until he owned one of the finest private Lincoln collections. His ambition was naively modest at first, for he aspired to write a new biography of Lincoln "as accurate as Morse (more so in some few instances) and not cold and scholastic as his is, and as bright and readable as Miss Tarbell's book." But as his reading expanded, he came to realize how many areas remained uncharted, and the superficiality of much of the earlier work. Soon he was going to the sources to check, reject, or confirm, often traveling many miles to study them.

While living in Boston he bought a cottage at Foxboro, Massachusetts. It nestled beside a brook, between two lakes. Back in the seclusion of the nearby woods he built a study with fireplace and book shelves. Later he added a "Lincoln Room"; and here, in his "Wigwam," he wrote scores of articles and books. No phase of Lincoln's life was too vast, no doubtful point too trivial, for his incisive intellect. His Lincoln studies, together with his theological writings, made him the proud possessor of the longest citation in the American *Who's Who;* and the volume of his Lincoln output is the more remarkable in that it was all done in the last ten years of his life.

He aspired to be the final authority on Lincoln; and for a time—in the public mind, at least—he was; although professional historians and the "inside" Lincoln group were only languidly approbative. Of his abundant procreation *The American Historical Review* saw fit to appraise only one book, and that in its "Minor Notices."

Despite this academic unconcern, Barton was not bashful of his eminence. One time, on a trip to New Salem, he alighted from the train at Petersburg and engaged a hackman for the day. The mud on New Salem hill was axle deep, the air was raw and penetrating, but the driver, proud to be of service to the great, was undeterred. All day he and Doctor Barton drove about. What must have been his surprise, however, when the doctor, taking leave of him at the station that night, shook hands warmly; and then, scorning to offer the usual mundane recompense, promised the worthy fellow a copy of his projected book as his reward.

It would have been strange if he was not a little spoiled. Nature had endowed him with a tall and, supple frame and a visage whose natural distinction was enhanced by the Vandyke beard that he affected. His mien was at once benign and forceful. Ida Tarbell described him as "a big, splendid looking person, very fierce and authoritative—knows he is somebody, as he is." Elderly library ladies welcomed his beck and call. Clubwomen twittered when it was announced that he would speak; and when he appeared they welcomed him—figuratively, of course—with open arms. Spinsters in Kentucky gladly left their household duties to search the records for him, often discovering important documents. His profession was one which has ever commanded deference.

Stylistically, Barton's writings are discursive and prolix,

and sometimes offer overmuch about the author. "You indulge in a good deal of obiter dicta," Luther E. Robinson, author of *Abraham Lincoln as a Man of Letters* and at that time a research student at the Library of Congress, told him, "but for me, and for future judgment, this feature of your style gives the element of the writer's personality, lacking which so many biographies are sterile . . . For personal atmosphere (or color, as we have grown to say) makes against the feeling of what we at one time pedantically called *detachment,* when we wanted to say something smart without meaning very much. But I cannot give you my 'detached' impression of your work better than to say . . . that its Boswellian *veracity and effect* puts it thus far into a permanent and distinguished position among the multitude of books on its great and perennially interesting subject."

Joseph B. Oakleaf, the Lincoln collector, was less complimentary. Barton's work reminded him of the sausages made of horse meat and rabbit meat that the man guaranteed to be fifty-fifty; and they were—one horse and one rabbit.

Barton was coldly impartial. When Katherine Helm, a niece and biographer of Mrs. Lincoln and one of Barton's faithful correspondents and friends, was aggrieved at things he wrote about her aunt, he consoled her for what he felt constrained to say but explained that he could not forego truth even to spare the feelings of a friend.

Nor did he allow his high calling to prejudice his judgment when dealing with so-called moral issues; for when a prohibitionist objected to his conclusion that Lincoln was no prohibitionist and claimed that Barton was contradicted by other and better historians, Barton was moved to scorn. "Some men procure books and read them to learn the truth," he replied. "Others dip into them in the hope of confirming their prejudices . . . As for 'other historians' who make up their books out of gossip, as some of them do, I am not contradicted by them. My books are written out of long study and earnest search for truth. You will not like them."

Having clarified the matter of Lincoln's religion, Barton undertook to establish his paternity. There was no longer any doubt of Lincoln's being born in wedlock; but it did not necessarily follow that Thomas Lincoln was his father, and stories to the contrary abounded, especially in the South. "The woods there are full of them," Barton wrote to a friend. Even Lincoln's admirers were responsible for some, for they thought he merited an illustrious ancestry. Others were the product of partisan or sectional viciousness.

Moving into this labyrinth, Barton flushed out seven reputed sires, each of whom he skilfully despatched by showing how and why it was impossible for him to have fathered Lincoln. Carl Sandburg admired the way he did it. "Toward the end one has the feeling it's like a bowling game," he wrote. "You set 'em up and knock 'em down with a short-arm, sure shooting logic." The book was not only a "tough woven piece of Lincolniana that will last," Sandburg affirmed. "It is a classic study of gossip and credulity."

The Nation thought Barton left "not a square inch of ground for the scandal to stand on"; and historians agreed. By dragging out and refuting every scandalous story, Barton showed that the paternity of Lincoln was as certain as that of any man can be.

Before writing this book Barton consulted Jesse Weik at Greencastle, and was surprised to learn that Weik had already rejected Herndon's Enloe story and had concluded that Lincoln was legitimate. Weik read Barton's book in proof and was astonished at the "herculean" labor that went into it. And Barton felt kindly toward Herndon despite the misconception he had done so much to foster. "If Herndon had been able to go as deeply into this matter as I subsequently went into it," he explained to John T. Richards, another Lincoln writer, "I am confident his last doubt would have been removed." "Herndon was a lawyer of considerable ability and while he was much to blame in this matter, it is important that he should be treated fairly," he insisted.

In 1925 Barton brought out a two-volume *Life of Abraham Lincoln* which he hoped would be his greatest book. Albert J. Beveridge, who was at work on his own life of Lincoln, read the manuscript and thought Barton had "achieved a big thing." "Do not fail to stand fearlessly on whatever you find the facts to be," he advised. "If you do, I think you can depend upon it that American scholarship will back you up, and, of course, I, too, will do so for whatever little it will amount to." Beveridge thought it would be especially felicitous if Barton was "so lucky as to be able to say that you find that you, yourself, have made mistakes and wish to correct them. Nothing has such appeal to that Brahman caste called scholars as much as frank forthrightness."

After reading the book in proof Beveridge congratulated Barton on the new material he adduced and hoped and believed the book would sell. "The manner in which you handle Nancy Hanks' mother Lucy, and annihilate the outrageous fiction heretofore published is most pleasing and refreshing," he declared; "your revelation as to Lincoln's ownership of the German paper in Springfield is new

and striking;[1] and your demolition of Mervin's [sic] prohibition propaganda tale[2] is as fine from the point of
scholarship as it is courageous from the point of authorship. These three points alone will cause your book to be
talked about a great deal; and that, dear Barton, is just
what you want." Beveridge intended to cite Barton "a great
deal" in his own book. "I expect to back you up in most
things—practically everything," he promised.

The "outrageous fiction" about Nancy Hanks to which
Beveridge alluded was Mrs. Hitchcock's contention that
Nancy Hanks was a legitimate child and not the offspring
of illicit love as Lamon and Herndon had it. January 10,
1924, Barton had written to Professor William L. Burdette
of the University of Kansas: "I am sorry to tell you that
I am unable any longer to follow Mrs. Hitchcock's view.
When I wrote my book, 'The Paternity of Abraham Lincoln,' I regarded the question of the maternal side of his
ancestry as purely incidental and I was disposed to accept
Mrs. Hitchcock's view if I could do so. Before the book was
published, however, my confidence was considerably shaken
and my subsequent investigations are such as to surprise
me that I was ever deceived by it. It has no place in
serious historical literature. Mrs. Hitchcock loaned her
papers to Lea and Hutchinson[3] and they accepted her con-

---

[1] On May 30, 1859 Lincoln bought the *Illinois Staats Anzeiger* to be sure
the Republican Party would have a German paper it could depend upon
and in order that he himself might be assured of German newspaper support in case of need.

[2] Charles T. White's *Lincoln and Prohibition* had presented the testimony of the Rev. James B. Merwin to the effect that he and Lincoln
stumped the state of Illinois in 1855 in behalf of a proposed law prohibit-
ing the sale of liquor. Barton contended that if Lincoln, between his two
campaigns for United States Senator, had given six months to such lectures, the Illinois newspapers would have been full of it. Actually, not a
single notice of any such lecture could be found.

[3] Authors of *The Ancestry of Abraham Lincoln*.

clusion. Of their beautifully printed book it is high praise to say that it is not always wrong."

Mrs. Hitchcock had said that Joseph Hanks had three daughters, Polly, Betty, and Nancy, who married Jesse Friend, Levi Hall, and Thomas Lincoln, respectively. But Dennis Hanks had avowed that Nancy Hanks, sister to Polly and Betty, was his mother, not Lincoln's, and that she married Levi Hall—after she had borne Dennis out of wedlock, however.

This aroused Barton's suspicions; for to credit Mrs. Hitchcock was to deny that Dennis knew who his own mother was or the name of the man she married. Furthermore, Dennis said Betty married Thomas Sparrow, not Levi Hall, as Mrs. Hitchcock averred; and according to Dennis there was a fourth sister, Lucy, who married Henry Sparrow; and it was their daughter, also named Nancy, who was the mother of the president.

Mrs. Hitchcock ignored Lucy, but to satisfy his suspicions Barton resolved to track her down. Joseph Hanks' will did not mention her, but to Barton it seemed that until she could be produced and placed in her proper position on the Hanks family tree, Dennis Hanks' and Herndon's contention that she was Lincoln's grandmother could neither be denied nor confirmed.

And a Lucy Hanks finally was discovered—in a rather unsavory situation—when Louis A. Warren, a young minister residing in Kentucky, found a clue which led to the finding of a court summons against a woman of that name who was accused of fornication! Finally, Barton ran down Lucy's marriage records; and they proved that she did marry Henry Sparrow. But the date was April 30, 1790, and Nancy Hanks was born in 1783, seven years before this marriage. How could this be reconciled with Dennis

Hanks' insistence that she was the legitimate child of this marriage and went by the name of Hanks only because she was "deep in Stalk of the Hankses"—that is, she resembled the Hankses rather than the Sparrows?

Years before Herndon had decided that the crafty Dennis Hanks had lied to protect Nancy Hanks' good name and the reputation of her mother when he insisted that Henry Sparrow was Nancy's father; and Barton concluded that Herndon had the answer. If so, the whole thing squared with Herndon's claim that Lincoln told him his mother was the natural child of Lucy Hanks, born before her mother's marriage to Henry Sparrow.

To nail down his conclusions, Barton went to Amelia County, Virginia, where Mrs. Hitchcock had found the records of the Hankses; and here, lo and behold, was a real surprise! For examination of these records convinced Barton that these people were not named Hanks at all, but Hawks. Where did Joseph Hanks live before moving to Kentucky? In desperation Barton searched the records of the Bureau of the Census and compiled a Who's Who of Hankses in the United States from 1782 to 1790. And at last his labor was repaid; for he found a Joseph Hanks— supposedly the one he sought—not in Amelia County, but in far-off Hampshire County, in what had since been set off from Virginia as West Virginia. Moreover, he had nine children—one more than was mentioned in his will. To Barton this was proof positive. The additional child must be Lucy, who, for some reason, possibly her waywardness, was cut out of her father's will. This seemed to clinch his case, although Daniel Fish, the Lincoln collector, warned him that "the public will not take kindly to your thesis . . . it isn't too much to say, even to one of your profession, that you will have a heluva time with it."

Subsequent events were to prove that Fish knew whereof he spoke; but Barton was undeterred.

Barton knew that Waldo Lincoln, a Massachusetts genealogist, was preparing *A History of the Lincoln Family;* and to save him from error, Barton warned him not to credit Mrs. Hitchcock's theory, because he was prepared to disprove it. Lincoln, not only incredulous, but somewhat scornful as well, asked Barton for his proof. Barton was not ready to divulge it; and he replied with some asperity that he was not accustomed to having his word doubted. Lincoln considered this pure impudence and demanded an apology; and when Barton wrote again, without offering amends, Lincoln discontinued the correspondence by ignoring his letter.

Nevertheless, Waldo Lincoln's apprehension was aroused, and he informed Miss Tarbell that he had decided to modify those parts of his book where he had depended on Mrs. Hitchcock. He doubted if Barton had conclusive evidence, but he could take no chances. "To tell the truth," he confided, "I have not formed a very high opinion of the reverend gentleman, not so high, I fear, as his own. He impresses me as desirous of advertising himself and not caring how much he does it. I may, however, be doing him an injustice, and he has certainly been of some assistance to me for which I am duly grateful, though I may not seem so in thus expressing myself about him."

Miss Tarbell was as surprised as Waldo Lincoln. Barton must be relying on hearsay evidence picked up in Kentucky, and she would never accept that in preference to a bona fide document. "I trust pretty soon to be able to take a whack at it," she wrote to Lincoln, ". . . as strong as I can make it."

To fortify herself, she asked Mrs. Hitchcock how she was progressing with the Hanks genealogy upon which she had been working, and informed her of the "dark revelations" hinted at by Barton. Mrs. Hitchcock was scornful. "That man Weik," son, she supposed, of "the wretched liar Jesse Weik," had come out with the same sort of thing in his book, and she had not deigned to notice it. "Parson" Barton had already written her "threatening letters"; but she thought it best to keep silent "until he exposed his tricks and then hash him up a bit."

Miss Tarbell was also confident that they could handle Barton, and was going to "take a fling" at him and Weik in a series of magazine articles. "They have got to produce better testimony than they have if they are going to upset the will and the testimony of Joseph Hanks," she assured Mrs. Hitchcock.

But an article by Barton made Miss Tarbell pause. She found that he and the young minister, Warren, really had turned up a good deal of new data in Kentucky, and while she was still unconvinced, she thought it best to play safe. If there were only a reliable Hanks genealogy, she could write with more assurance.

Meantime, Mrs. Hitchcock, wishing to know more about Barton and his works, had read *The Paternity of Lincoln.* Her modesty was shocked! She had never read such scandalous stories in her life! "How could any man say such vile things about women?" she asked Miss Tarbell. "I never heard such vulgar language as he uses constantly throughout the book. And he is a minister of a big church of God. The same church my father was," she gasped.

In her hysteria Mrs. Hitchcock wrote to Barton himself, denouncing him for propagating filth and declaring that no true man of God would write as he did. Some day, she warned, the "crucifixion" he had inflicted upon Nancy Lincoln by publishing these stories would be visited upon him. In her extremity she implored the commander of the Grand Army of the Republic at Chicago "in the name of Honor and Justice" to choke off the man who dared publish these "terrible insinuations," suggesting that Barton's book would make good fuel for a bonfire at the encampment's next patriotic celebration. But the commander was Barton's friend; and he forwarded her letter to the doctor with a Christmas greeting, suggesting jokingly that the next time Barton went to Foxboro (Mrs. Hitchcock lived in Massachusetts) he had better seek out this woman and make peace with her.

But Barton's mood was not pacific. Plain talk was what this woman needed. Not only had her careless work involved him in much unnecessary labor, but here was fine thanks for proving the chastity of one of her kinfolk. He was sorry she was so disturbed by what he had done, he informed her, but he felt absolutely justified in doing it. If she doubted his spirituality, there were thousands who did not; and she was not the person to judge him. The time was coming when he must expose her own shortcomings. "You do not possess the facts to support your conclusions," he declared. "You have never published the Hanks genealogy you promised so long ago. If you ever publish it, and it tells the truth, it will have to deny what your little book already published has given toward the confusion of a problem already sufficiently complex."

Mrs. Hitchcock poured out her troubles to Miss Tarbell. Unless something were done, Barton would "repeat those terrible things about the Hanks girls 'and the scandalous doubts' about Nancy Hanks to a greater extent in the next book—on the plea of proving the chastity of the lady." Miss

Tarbell should don armor and to horse, for she was the only person with the authority to silence him.

With her usual levelheadedness, Miss Tarbell tried to soothe the irate lady. "Now, don't get excited about Brother Barton's book," she admonished. She did not like these salacious tales herself; but after all, Barton had retold them only to refute them. "What he has put down here is something that is on men's tongues and what those who love and honor Mr. Lincoln and his mother must contend with . . . Every now and then I get a letter from some distressed person who has for the first time heard one or another of these tales, and I can say today, Now, go and read Mr. Barton's book and you will find he has utterly disproved this yarn . . . Don't worry over it, dear Mrs. Hitchcock."

When Barton wrote to Miss Tarbell, regretting that Mrs. Hitchcock was so irritated, Miss Tarbell explained how she had tried to soothe her. But Mrs. Hitchcock would not be comforted. "Please dear Miss Tarbell," she implored, "do *not* stand up for him! It hurts you . . . The whole family & all of Lincoln's admirers are rising against Barton and his wicked insinuations."

Miss Tarbell was more concerned about Barton's forthcoming book than with those already in print; and she thought Mrs. Hitchcock should be thinking about it too; for, having demonstrated Nancy Hanks' chastity, Barton was now preparing to put Mrs. Hitchcock's thesis of her legitimacy to the test. "What you ought to do," Miss Tarbell advised Mrs. Hitchcock, ". . . is to get all the Hanks documents that you have together for publication . . . That is the only thing that is going to settle this matter. We cannot do it by berating Barton however much we may dislike his work and however undefensible we may consider it to be."

But Mrs. Hitchcock was too upset to do more than wring her hands. "That horrible Barton," she groaned, ". . . Why the very words he used would never pass the lips of an honorable or even a decent minded man . . . He is trying to frighten all the historians by his insinuations about Little Nancy." Nevertheless, she would get to work, and Barton would "not escape with a whole skin again." If he did, it would be only for a season. He must be over eighty years old, and "will soon be mercifully gathered to his fathers where justice will be gloriously given."

Barton's findings were revealed when his *Life* appeared in 1925. Miss Tarbell reviewed it in *The Christian Science Monitor*. Naturally, she dealt most fully with his ideas about Lucy Hanks, refusing to concede that he had proved his case. All he showed, she contended, was that there was *a* Lucy Hanks who was indicted for misbehaviour and that *a* Lucy Hanks had taken out a marriage license and later married Henry Sparrow. He did not prove that the two Lucys were the same or that either was the mother of Nancy; nor that Lucy was a daughter of Joseph Hanks.

Waldo Lincoln agreed that this was all Barton had done. The rest was pure conjecture. "Of course," he wrote, "he may be right, as a matter of fact, he probably is, but the modern genealogist asks for more than family tradition; and Mr. Barton, although not a genealogist, should know this since he tries to be one in these early chapters."

Joseph B. Oakleaf thought Miss Tarbell's review was "excellent and scholarly," but too charitable to Barton. One man, whose opinion Oakleaf valued, thought: "All that Barton has that is interesting can be found in the first hundred pages of Volume One—the balance is just preaching." Barton was unsparing of Mrs. Hitchcock; and Oakleaf felt sorry for her "because she feels the hammering she got from our mutual friend, William 'Ego' Barton. Really and truly, Barton's book would have been much better if he had not used the hammer."

Miss Tarbell was glad to know that Oakleaf approved her review. She considered the first third of Volume One "an unusual contribution," and there were "scattered bits through the rest"; but the second volume showed too many marks of haste and was "poor stuff." "I am particularly glad that you think I was not too hard on Dr. Barton," she wrote. "I do not want to be unappreciative of what I think he has really done, but I do not see how an honest reviewer could pass over what he has not done and yet what he claims so loudly to have done."

Like Oakleaf, Miss Tarbell pitied Mrs. Hitchcock and tried to offer consolation. "As I told you before," she advised, "don't worry about Barton. Whatever he has found that is true will stand, but as far as his probabilities and likelies etc. etc., are concerned, they are not worth a sou . . . Don't worry your head about them."

Barton bore Miss Tarbell no resentment. He was sorry, he told a mutual friend, that she had said in her review that the story of Lincoln's illegitimacy was buried until "Barton took the pains to dig it up, and repeat it to the world." This was not so, as she would have known if she had recently visited Kentucky. And Miss Tarbell did pose one pertinent question: Might there not be another Lucy Hanks? Yes, there might be, he admitted; but he was sure he had the right one.

When Barton invited Miss Tarbell to the formal opening of his "Lincoln Room" at Foxboro, she was sorry she had to decline. She supposed they would never cease "squabbling about Nancy and Lucy and the rest of those Hankses"; but as long as they did it good-naturedly, no one would be harmed and eventually she might drive him to produce a genealogy which she could accept. "I consider that sufficient justification for any saucy comment that I may make on your productions. Am I right?"

She was, Barton replied. After all, their differences were few compared to the points they agreed on; and "no difference of opinion shall mar our friendship or my sincere regard for you."

In lieu of more conclusive evidence, it seemed that Barton's view would prevail; but even while his work was being appraised, another investigator, Louis A. Warren, was adducing a new theory to restore Lucy Hanks' good name.

Warren became interested in Lincoln genealogy while he was pastor, and editor of a weekly newspaper, in a small town in Kentucky. Impressed by the contradictory nature of the numerous Lincoln and Hanks traditions, he determined to see what could be proved by public records. His removal to Elizabethtown in 1921 gave him easy access to the Hardin County courthouse, and here and in other courthouses he found a wealth of virgin documents. Before long he had supplemented the known records by 550 additional court entries bearing the name of Lincoln or Hanks. Eventually his investigations brought him to the same paths Barton was pursuing.

Warren's work revealed that Thomas Lincoln was not the shiftless ne'er-do-well so many had supposed him to be, for he had worked as a laborer at good pay and later as a carpenter and farmer, had served in the militia, on juries, as a guard of county prisoners, as appraiser of an estate, as a "road surveyor" or what we should call a supervisor, and that after reaching maturity he always owned one or more horses, paid his taxes regularly, could sign his name, and was a church member. Warren also clarified his ownership of three Kentucky farms, showed that he was always sober and law-abiding, and that as he migrated, he left behind no unpaid debts.

For some time Barton and Warren worked along parallel lines and gave mutual assistance to each other. After a trip through Kentucky together, Barton wrote to Warren: "Our journey was a very interesting one to me and a very profitable one. A man can write a Life of Abraham Lincoln just as readable and quite as salable without taking any of this trouble, but it is my ambition to write a biography that shall add materially to the world's knowledge of Abraham Lincoln."

Barton and Warren agreed that Mrs. Hitchcock was in error in thinking Joseph Hanks was Abraham Lincoln's maternal grandfather. But beyond this they differed and eventually came to controversy. Warren was unwilling to credit Dennis Hanks or to reject Mrs. Hitchcock's theory in its entirety. She had said that in Amelia County there were five Shipley sisters who married into the Hanks, Lincoln, Berry, Sparrow, and Mitchell families; and following this lead Warren evolved the idea that Lucy Hanks' maiden name was Shipley, that she married a Hanks, by whom she had the child, Nancy, and that she was a widow at the time she married Henry Sparrow.

Warren's argument rested on a document bearing Lucy's name and, preceding it, certain undecipherable letters which he thought spelled "widow" or "widoy," but which Barton insisted spelled "day."

To substantiate his theory, it was necessary for Warren

to refute Barton's conclusion that the Amelia County people were Hawkses rather than Hankses and that the Hankses never lived in Amelia County at all. Repeated scrutiny of the records convinced Warren that they did read Hanks; while Barton was just as positive they read Hawks. Thus the controversy passed the bounds of reason and resolved itself into a question of eyesight.

Walter Beals, a Seattle attorney, asked Miss Tarbell what she thought of this latest development, and she replied that she would withhold judgment until she had an opportunity to see the original of the document which indicated that Lucy was a widow. "Dr. Barton hoots at it," she said, "and the facsimile published is not convincing." Five years later she had the opportunity to look at the original, and after close scrutiny could see no sign of any "w" or "i" before the "day"—or "doy"; nor was there any evidence that anyone had tampered with the document. She confessed her disappointment, for she would have liked to believe Warren right.

Barton published all his genealogical material in *The Lineage of Lincoln* in 1929; and Warren, who had become Director of the Lincoln National Life Foundation at Fort Wayne, Indiana, continued his research after Barton's death in 1930, publishing many of his later findings in the *Lincoln Kinsman*, a pamphlet which appeared monthly from August 1938 until discontinued because of the war in December, 1942. This was a valuable supplement to his *Lincoln's Parentage & Childhood*, which was published in 1926.

Without being able to clinch his own case, Warren weakened Barton's by showing that he had not been able to adduce documentary proof of the actual relationship between any two of the five generations of Hankses he

purported to trace. So, as matters rest, neither the legiti-
mists nor the illegitimists—if we may so designate them—
have made a clear-cut case. The consensus of opinion
among Lincoln specialists is illustrated by an exchange of
letters between Miss Tarbell and Judge James W. Bollinger of Davenport. He asked for her personal opinion
about Lincoln's maternal grandmother; and she replied
that further documentary evidence might turn up at any
time. Until it did, she was not going to answer yes or no.
The mistake on both sides was in insisting on a flat yes or
no. "The best answer I can give," she said, "is that I am
not sure though I think the weight of evidence at the
moment is on the side of illegitimacy . . . Not very satisfactory, is it, my dear Mr. Bollinger."

"Yes, your letter *is* satisfactory," the judge replied.
"All we can do is say on which side we think there lies
what lawyers call the preponderance of evidence. Personally, I feel Lincoln is the best witness and that he told
Herndon as Herndon says he did."

Barton was glad Miss Tarbell was "unregenerate," he
banteringly wrote her. One of his life's ambitions was to
"convert" her to his thesis, "and when that is accomplished
and you come to the mourners' bench, I shall feel that my
occupation is gone."

Even *The American Historical Review* conceded that
The Lineage of Lincoln was "for the most part, a solid
piece of work," although the reviewer thought Barton
strained a point to link the Lincoln family with the Lees.
Barton thought the establishment of this connection was
one of his most noteworthy accomplishments, but the reviewer thought he missed it by one link. And "one link, as
in the case of the famous gentleman who did not marry the

lady because she refused him, is sometimes important," he was at pains to point out.

Lyon G. Tyler, son of President John Tyler, former president of William and Mary College, editor of *Tyler's Quarterly Historical and Genealogical Magazine,* southern gentleman of the old school, and self-appointed defender of Southern chivalry, honor, blood, culture, or anything else Southern, rushed to repel Barton's insult to Virginia aristocracy. "Your book has excited universal indignation among the Lees," he protested, "who do not wish to own any relationship with the blackguard Lincoln." Tyler tried to refute Barton with a pamphlet in which he contended that if there was any possible connection between the Lincolns and the Lees, which he was not willing to grant, it stemmed from a servant, an undistinguished William Lee, rather than the hallowed Colonel Richard.

Tyler's letters became so vituperative that Barton protested that his correspondents "mainly use the language which gentlemen employ in addressing each other. I am at a disadvantage in addressing a man whose abuse is so virulent and unprovoked. I implore you, sir, in sheer self-respect, to exercise some degree of self-control." Tyler was a very old man, soon to meet his Maker, Barton pleaded; "do not saturate your soul in intemperate language and thereby harm yourself." But neither the soft answer nor apprehension of the world to come could turn away Tyler's wrath.

Worthington C. Ford also wrote a carping review in the Chicago *Tribune,* which moved Barton to reply. "Now you can't say that it is on the basis of meager and fragmentary records I base my positive statements," he complained, "for if you do, you can't go to heaven when you

die. You ought not to have published that statement."
"And why did you think you had to be so nasty about it,
anyway? You might at least have been civil!"

But Barton really knew why. The same day the review
appeared he wrote to the literary editor of the *Tribune*
defending his conclusions and pointing out that he was
at a loss to understand Mr. Ford's asperity. He did recall
that he had recently written a fourteen-page review of
Beveridge's *Life of Lincoln* for the *Mississippi Valley Historical Review* in which he had occasion to "call attention
to a considerable number of significant errors on the part
of the editor," who prepared the manuscript for publication after Beveridge's death. "The editor," he concluded
his letter, "was Worthington C. Ford."

Most critics of *The Lineage of Lincoln* thought Barton
overreached himself in the matter of the Lees, and some
thought he would have done better to confine his work
in closer bounds. The critic for *The American Historical
Review* commented ironically that he "has contributed a
considerable number of new documents to his already
large collection of the archives of everybody related to
Lincoln"; and the *New Republic's* critic thought Barton
indulged in "unlimited draughts of minutiae, large mouth-
fuls of carefully prepared and discreetly served nothing."
After all, he wondered, what possible value was there in
knowing just what part of England the Lincolns and
Hankses came from?

But the *Mississippi Valley Historical Review* marveled
that Barton made so many bricks with so little straw; and
the New York *Times* thought he followed the scent like a
bloodhound.

Long before he finished his genealogical studies, Barton

cast a dubious eye on Ann Rutledge. He reluctantly accepted the story at first, even though he thought it "detestable" of Herndon to tell it. But the more he thought
about it, the more it seemed "vulnerable at certain points";
and in *The Women Lincoln Loved* he pointed out that
John McNamar, from whom Herndon got most of his information about it, was away from New Salem from the
autumn of 1832 until many weeks after Ann's death in
August, 1835, just the period when the affair supposedly
took place.

Barton adduced a letter from Mathew S. Marsh, a New
Salem resident, written less than a month after Ann's
death, in which Lincoln was referred to as being normal
and well; and he emphasized the fact that in less than a
year Lincoln had another love affair with Mary Owens.
Surely his grief was evanescent.

Barton did not doubt that Lincoln and Ann may have
cared for each other, but he regarded the affair as nothing
more than a youthful attachment. Herndon, he believed,
had deliberately embellished the tale because of his bitterness toward Mrs. Lincoln.

Mrs. Lincoln perplexed Barton. "I have spent so much
labor digging out the facts about Mrs. Lincoln," he complained to Gamaliel Bradford, ". . . There are people
living in Springfield who believe that Lincoln and his
wife hated each other, and others who tell you that they
lived a totally blissful life. I think they quarreled and yet
respected each other, and in a very real way loved each
other and were mutually helpful. I do not know of any
one who has put in more hard work in impartial investigation of the matter than I have had to put in."

Barton's skepticism about the Ann Rutledge affair was

confirmed by a study made by Paul M. Angle, then executive secretary of the Abraham Lincoln Association, and published in the Association's *Bulletin*.

On the basis of these studies historians had just about relegated the story to the realm of mythology, when, fourteen years after Barton and Angle attacked it, Jay Monaghan, then editor of the Illinois State Historical Library, now Illinois State Historian, discovered in the *Menard Axis,* a newspaper published at Petersburg, Illinois, an article under the date of February 15, 1862, written by John Hill, editor of the paper and a son of Samuel Hill, the New Salem storekeeper. This described Lincoln's hardships in New Salem and, without mentioning Ann's name, told of Lincoln's love for a young girl of the village, of her death, and of Lincoln's nearly insane grief. Antedating Herndon's lecture by almost five years, this article proved he did not fabricate the story. The clipping containing the article was found among his notes and was undoubtedly the clue which induced him to try to track the story down.

The "fatal first of January" also came under Barton's view. He concluded that Lincoln did not desert Miss Todd at the altar, but that there was no question that something having to do with the courtship had put him in mental turmoil. Further than this he was unable to penetrate. "What started the trouble, no one knows," he said, "and it is not likely that anyone will ever learn much more than is here recorded."

No facet was too small or rough for Barton to polish. Studying Lincoln's famous letter of condolence to Lydia Bixby, the widow who was supposed to have lost five sons in the war, Barton concluded that the original had probably been destroyed and that the numerous facsimiles which had been circulated were prepared from a forgery.

The text was genuine; but the facts of the case did not warrant such a letter, because Barton's examination of the records of the War Department and the Massachusetts Adjutant General's office revealed that Mrs. Bixby had only two sons killed, and of the other three, two were deserters and one was honorably discharged. But the fact that Lincoln wrote the letter under a misconception detracted in no wise from the nobility of his motives or the beauty of his language. So Barton entitled his book *A Beautiful Blunder*.

Since Lincoln's day a multitude of articles and books had discussed the Gettysburg address; but all they proved was the existence of disagreement and uncertainty about where and how the speech was prepared, the manner in which it was delivered, the effect upon the audience, and the actual content of the speech itself. Anything so unfinished was grist for Barton to grind. "And now I am trying to put salt on the tail of everything I can learn about the Gettysburg Address," he wrote to Emily Mitchell of the Library of Congress staff. *Lincoln at Gettysburg* was published in 1930.

Barton died on December 7 of that year, and his *President Lincoln,* an undistinguished book, was published posthumously in 1933.

Barton was a prodigious contributor, but his standing suffered in the estimation of professional historians by his readiness to rush into print and by the discursiveness of everything he wrote. In more than one instance he expanded what should have been a monograph into a book; a chapter was often written where a paragraph would suffice. One of his books was described as a "pot-boiler" by a competent reviewer, and another was called "an excessively padded footnote." Even his publishers thought *Lin-*

coln at Gettysburg "a pretty long book about a very short speech, important as that speech is"; and Barton confessed to a correspondent: "I am accustomed to peddling out my stuff to the magazines before it appears in book form. This has two or three advantages. It brings me letters of correction, protest, confirmation, and added fact. It brings me a little money in advance of royalties . . . And I shall have that much cash whether the book pays or not." But it also brought frowns from scholars who disapproved of publishing anything short of one's best.

Yet there can be no doubt about the permanence of Barton's mark. On Lincoln's paternity and on much of his lineage he said what seems to be the final word. Little can be added about the Gettysburg Address; and he went far toward clearing up the facts of the Bixby letter. If he fell short of being a great historian, he was a great historical detective. The first of the modern, thoroughgoing realists, his work foretold and helped make possible the triumph of the realistic school; for his calling gave a certain sanctity to his pronouncements even when they were at variance with what the public preferred to hear.

Chapter Ten

THE ROUT OF THE
ROMANTICISTS

ALBERT J. BEVERIDGE was born in an isolated farmhouse in Highland County, Ohio, on October 6, 1862. Son of a Union soldier, one of his earliest recollections was "of the blue-clad soldiers marching home after the war was over, to the strange wild music of the fife and drum." Overtaken by financial adversity, the Beveridge family moved to Moultrie County, Illinois; and here, at the age of twelve, Albert assumed a man's burden in helping operate their farm. At fourteen he was working with a section gang, and at fifteen was in charge of a rough, tough logging camp at Buffalo Hart, a few miles east of Springfield.

Despite poverty he obtained what education the country schools afforded and at sixteen entered Asbury College, now DePauw University, at Greencastle, Indiana, the home of Jesse Weik. Forced to make up the deficiencies of his secondary education, carry a full college schedule, and work his way besides, he lived almost without sleep during his freshman year. Oratorical prizes and summer work enabled him to graduate, and after a brief respite in Kansas for his health, he went to Indianapolis to study law. A dozen years of law practice were followed by election to the United States Senate in 1899. Here he served two terms, moving in the vanguard of the progressivism of the Theodore Roosevelt era and becoming a leader of the insurgency against the reactionism of Taft.

A prodigious and tireless student, widely traveled and enjoying a wide acquaintance in literary as well as political circles, his reputation for erudition was well deserved.

Defeated for reelection in 1910, he turned naturally to scholarly pursuits and began his *Life of John Marshall*. He interrupted his labors to fight for Roosevelt and the Progressive Republican ticket in 1912, and suspended them again in 1914–15 to visit Europe as a war correspondent. Never entirely divorcing himself from political activity, nevertheless he finished the *Marshall* in 1919. Three years later he was persuaded to run for the Senate again. Unsuccessful, the bitterness of defeat was assuaged by the pleasurable anticipation with which he took up the biography of Lincoln.

Beveridge believed "that in reality the story of a public man, to mean anything, to be truthful, or even to be entertaining, is part of the epic of the nation into which that man's deeds and words are woven during the period in which he wrought." Thus his *Marshall,* more than a biography, was also a history of the nation during Marshall's lifetime; and the chief justice being the character he was, it became an interpretation of the development of American nationalism. This interpretation Beveridge proposed to continue in his *Lincoln.* "I plan to make it a companion piece of the *Marshall,*" he wrote to Jesse Weik, "continuing the constitutional interpretation of America, weaving it about the life of Abraham Lincoln as I tried to weave the first part about the life of John Marshall."

Having cut his eyeteeth on the *Marshall,* Beveridge was well equipped to venture in the Lincoln field. Starting with only vague ideas of historical method, he had evolved a technique calculated to satisfy the most rigorous canons of scholarship. Eschewing secondary works, he went to the contemporary documents which he read exhaustively, making copious notes in pencil. Usually he worked on a chapter at a time. Having completed the research, he studied, collated, and absorbed his material, and then began to write. His first draft was typed by a secretary, then rewritten—sometimes two or three times—then re-typed. When it was in fairly good shape mimeographed copies were prepared and sent to historical scholars, specialists in particular fields, for marginal suggestions and criticism. When these were returned another revision was made, incorporating such new ideas as Beveridge believed worth while and eliminating any errors brought to light. Then came condensation—"I have cut . . . until it bleeds, and still it is too long," he wrote—refinement, and the final polishing. "Herewith I send you a very rough draft of chapter one," he wrote to Weik after he had been at work for many months. "It is of course, crude in the extreme, and requires months of artistry, etc."

Beveridge believed in taking time, but in working "like the devil" when he worked. "That is the only way to get out good stuff," he told Weik. "You know my methods," he wrote to William Connelley, secretary of the Kansas State Historical Society, "I was able to do my Marshall and have been able thus far to make progress (although very slow) on my Lincoln only by giving every minute of my time and every atom of my strength to it to the exclusion of all other activities and well-nigh to all other thought." He became so full of his subject he exuded it. Once when he was working in Springfield, Mr. and Mrs. Logan Hay entertained him at their home. All evening he monopolized the conversation, pacing back and forth before the fireplace, holding forth on Lincoln as though he were delivering a lecture. Next day Mrs. Hay received a beautiful bouquet. Attached was a card referring her to a passage in the *Diary of Orville Hickman Browning* which read: "Had a wonderful time—I spoke."

Ten to twelve hours was Beveridge's daily stint, with a long walk in the early morning and another in the afternoon. Facts, facts, facts were his passion. Just facts, all the facts, unembellished by interpretation, but so arranged that the reader could make his own deductions. "Historical interpretation" was synonymous with "indolence, ignorance and egotism. It means," he affirmed, "that certain facts are missing: that the author does not have the humility and industry to search for these facts and keep on searching until he finds them; but that, instead, he tells the reader what he thinks these facts would have meant if they had been as he imagines them to have been." Facts, properly arranged, interpret themselves, he claimed, although Professor Charles A. Beard pointed out that "The moment you say arrangement, you say interpretation."

And facts about the hero alone were not enough; they were merely the beginning. The words and acts of others were essential to the interplay of the plot, and full study of the times gave proper setting. To neglect these things was like presenting Hamlet on a bare and unlighted stage with no Polonius, no Laertes, no Ophelia, no King, no Queen Mother.

At the very outset Beveridge suffered a grievous disappointment. He had hoped to obtain access to the Lincoln manuscripts in Robert Lincoln's possession; but despite his

Albert J. Beveridge

entreaties and the intercession of mutual friends, Robert Lincoln was adamant, as he had always been, and finally locked the documents away in the Library of Congress with the stipulation that they remain sealed for twenty-one years, well beyond Beveridge's life expectancy.

It was a blow; but Beveridge went on, investigating newspaper files, official documents, letters, court records, every conceivable contemporaneous source. Before he had been at it very long, the elusiveness of Lincoln drove him to despair. "I become more and more puzzled about Lincoln," he wrote to Worthington C. Ford. "Sometimes I feel like throwing it up altogether. I am doubtful whether the Mid-Victorians will permit any truthful and scholarly life of Lincoln to be written." After a year's study he wrote to Professor Edward Channing: "I have not yet gone over the data sufficiently to form a sound judgment, or any judgment at all; but it is already fairly clear that the Lincoln of youth, early and middle manhood showed few signs of the Lincoln of the second inaugural." Two months later he complained to Ford, "the farther I go into this morass, the deeper and more confused it appears to me." No wonder he was discouraged when, after eighteen months, he had written only three chapters, reaching the point where Lincoln was elected to the Illinois Legislature.

He had thought to pass over these early years rather quickly. The material had been re-worked so many times that he would need only to review it. But with his usual thoroughness he would take nothing for granted. He did not suppose there was much more to be had in the Herndon manuscripts, but perhaps he had better give them at least a hasty look. His political activities had made him acquainted with Jesse Weik, who worked as a precinct committeeman when Beveridge campaigned for the senate.

He helped Weik obtain a publisher for *The Real Lincoln*
for which he wrote a favorable review. Now he and his
publishers asked Weik to reciprocate by permitting him
to use the Herndon manuscripts. His book would inter-
fere in no wise with the sale of Weik's, he said; in fact
his references to the Herndon-Weik collection would re-
invigorate the interest in Weik's book.

Weik was willing to oblige; Beveridge could use anything he wanted. For the fourth time the Herndon collection was re-worked.

Beveridge had considered Herndon an unreliable biographer; but as he read the records his admiration grew.
"About Herndon," he wrote to Professor Frank H. Hod-
der, on December 15, 1925, "do not get me wrong about
that old man. I have gone into his credibility as if I were a
lawyer trying a murder case. There is absolutely no doubt
whatever about his entire truthfulness and trustworthiness
general When Herndon states a fact as a fact, you can
depend upon it. It is only when he gets to analyzing the
souls of others . . . that he is not to be relied upon." "In
all my investigation, his character shines out clear and
stainless," he wrote to Weik, ". . . he was almost a fanatic
in his devotion to the truth. Wherever he states a fact as
such, I accept it, unless other indisputable and documentary proof shows that his memory was a little bit defective.
On the contrary, I do not care at all for his speculations
and imaginings." Beveridge was glad to learn that Weik
was writing a life of Herndon. "What a rotten deal that
dear old man has had at the hands of the historical propagandists and the preachers and women of the Mid-Victorian period of the eighties and nineties." Weik owed it to
the world to rescue him from "the morass of misrepresenta-

tion and even slander into which interested and prejudiced persons threw him."

Beveridge based his whole narrative of Lincoln's early years on Herndon's manuscripts, checking them by other available evidence. William E. Barton thought it was "a rather muddy stream which flows from his fourth treading of this already thrice-trodden wine press," and Professor James G. Randall, one of the most competent latter-day Lincoln students, thought that in these early Lincoln years Herndon often led Beveridge astray. Beveridge himself admitted that the material was baffling. The amount of it was "perfectly appalling"; and being almost wholly reminiscent and obtained after a lapse of years, naturally it was sometimes unreliable and often contradictory. Over against Nathaniel Grigsby's assertion that Lincoln read the Bible "a great deal" was the conflicting testimony of Dennis Hanks and Sarah Bush Lincoln that he didn't read it "half as much as had been said." Opposing William G. Greene's description of Thomas Lincoln's cynical hostility to Abraham's efforts to acquire an education was Wesley Hall's claim that Tom was proud that Abe could read and write and would "brag about how smart Abe wuz to the folks around about." Testimony that the imbroglio recounted in the "Chronicles of Reuben"—as well as the "chronicles" themselves—were inspired by malice, was contradicted by statements—some by members of the Grigsby family, themselves the victims of this wit—to the effect that the whole thing was conceived in a spirit of fun.

Beveridge accepted Lincoln's reputation for laziness as proof of his studiousness, for the frontier was not sympathetic toward mental as opposed to physical exertion. Yet Lincoln's own statement that "there was absolutely noth-

ing to excite ambition for education. Of course, when I
came of age I did not know much," could be reconciled
with the many stories of his omnivorous reading and thirst
for knowledge only by making generous allowance for his
modesty.

Beveridge solved the problem by presenting all the evidence; some in the text, the rest in footnotes. "I have purposely over-annotated," he explained to Connelley, "because this is the controverted period of Lincoln's life and
the part which the ancient surviving remnants of the Mid-
Victorians have been trying to Tarbellize." "You are quite
right about the bigness and complexity of my task," he
wrote to Weik. "The magnitude and perplexity of it sometimes all but discourage me . . . However, I am plugging
right along, night and day."

The farther he went the more he was amazed at the
superficiality of previous investigations. While studying
the Springfield newspapers he wrote to Ford: "I had not
been at work a single day until it was plain to me that nobody else had made a careful and scientific search through
the dim columns of those thousands of musty old pages.
What a task it is! What drudgery! Still it has to be done, of
course. I am finding out things all the time."

And the reaction of the scholars was encouraging. Connelley thought it was "a wonderful piece of work." He
was reared in Kentucky "in exactly the condition of society
which you describe as that of Lincoln's early years," and
he believed he knew "the feelings of that class of people to
which Abraham Lincoln belonged as well as any man now
living." While Lincoln had to contend with poverty, it
was an independent poverty; and it never threatened star-
vation or want. Beveridge's description of the wilderness
of the Ohio Valley was the best Connelley had ever seen.

"The great forests, the rivers, the wild animals, the insufficient dwellings—you have painted them all beautifully." Connelley's own family had spent one winter in a half-faced camp, just like the one the Lincolns occupied. And Beveridge's description of the early mills called to mind one he had known as a boy. He supposed it would grind about two bushels in a day. Corn was put into the hopper in the morning and the miller then went off to do other work until noon. One day as he was returning with a friend, they heard a hound dog howling in the mill. He was sitting in the meal chest, licking up the little wisps of meal as they came out, howling for more in his intervals of waiting. And the miller supposed that if they had left him there he might have starved to death, "which was not saying much for the amount of meal his mill would grind."

Connelley remembered all the pioneer superstitions that Beveridge described. His uncle nearly thrashed him once for killing a snake and leaving it with its belly up. It would never stop raining while a snake was thus disposed. And how vividly he remembered the frequent frontier fights. "On the frontier courage was an absolute necessity. To brand a man as a coward was equal to ostracism . . . It was necessary for him to fight if he was challenged or if the occasion arose. The fact that he was defeated in a personal combat did not detract from his courage if he fought well. But a lack of physical courage was a degradation from which none could recover in a frontier town or community."

When Beveridge received this letter he was "dogging Lincoln's footsteps through the Legislature." He had expected to cover this in a few pages. It was all a matter of record and had probably been thoroughly investigated; but as he checked the facts he found rich fruit, unharvested. Apparently the sources had never even been consulted; and small wonder, for they consisted primarily of eight large volumes of the *Journal of the Illinois Legislature,* badly printed in small type, on poor paper, and with an index so inaccurate and incomplete as to be worse than no index at all.

Working with a magnifying glass, Beveridge read it page by page. "Work so huge and complicated," he complained to Mrs. Beveridge. "It really never has been done . . . I'm disgusted and tired and blue and I'd seize ary excuse to drop Lincoln—politics or anything. I am pouring out my life and more than my money on it."

"It was some job," he told Connelley; "but the whole dramatic story is there, albeit hidden in mountains of print." Instead of a few pages, he wrote two long chapters, and even then had to "cut out at least five times as much as remains."

And what a disillusionment! Apparently he had expected to find a record of moral leadership; but instead he found that Lincoln voted both for and against abolition measures, made speeches against and in condonement of slavery, and was opposed both to prohibition and to "putting more teeth into liquor legislation." Yet it was here that Beveridge did his most original work. "A revolutionary piece of historical writing," revealing the early Lincoln "in a blinding light," wrote Charles A. Beard in returning Beveridge's manuscript.

"I now understand as I never did before, how he learned the fundamentals of economics and state craft," wrote William L. Patton, Springfield attorney, who helped Beveridge check some of the Springfield court records, "for you make it very clear that the Illinois Legislature of 1834–1841 was a wonderful academy of political science, with a most competent staff." "The people of America owe you a debt of gratitude," wrote Connelley, ". . . Instead of finding two uninteresting chapters as you suggested I have found two of the most valuable chapters you will write of Lincoln's life. I realize that you will write many chapters which will be more eagerly read but few of them will be more important to the right understanding of the character of Abraham Lincoln."

Other scholars confirmed what Connelley said about these chapters; and Beveridge was glad to know they liked them. He had been "pretty blue" about them himself; for Lincoln did not measure up to what he had been led to expect.

Beveridge found that Lincoln, after keeping in the background during his apprenticeship, forged rapidly ahead thereafter. Floor leader of his party during his second term, during that whole session he "subordinated everything to Springfield's interest." Acting with unity throughout the session, the Sangamon County delegation, known as the "Long Nine," threw their support to local improvement projects of every sort and description in exchange for votes for Springfield as the state capital. "The session became one of barter and deal, a debauch of log-rolling," Beveridge deplored, with Lincoln right in the thick of it, helping to push a program that was destined to bankrupt the state.

Lincoln's steadfast opposition to all measures designed to harass or embarrass the State Bank at Springfield not only evinced innate conservatism, but also ingratiated him with the state's financial and business interests. Throughout his legislative career the State Bank was a controversial issue. "Lincoln's whole attitude and conduct in the Bank controversy," said Beveridge, "were strongly conservative and in firm support of vested interests and the conduct of business, unmolested as far as possible, by legislative or any kind of governmental interference."

Giving the full background and a detailed discussion of the protest of Lincoln and Daniel Stone against a resolution denouncing abolitionist propaganda, Beveridge concluded: "Thus when Lincoln was scarcely twenty-eight years old, the entire subject of slavery came directly before him, and was debated thoroughly by men of high standing. He studied the Southern view as presented by memorials and resolutions drawn with utmost care by the ablest men in various slave-holding States . . . He pored over the well-written reply of Connecticut, the evasive answer of New York, the curious response of Illinois . . . and he finally stated his conclusions, from which he did not vary for more than a quarter of a century." Yet even here Beveridge found him bowing to the expediency of practical politics. For the protest was not voiced until six weeks after the passage of the slavery resolution, by which time Springfield had obtained the capital.

During his whole legislative course Beveridge found Lincoln shifty, evasive, constant only in his devotion to party welfare. "I wish to the Lord he could have gone straight-forward about something or other," he wrote to Ford. "Of all uncertain, halting and hesitating conduct, his takes the prize."

Beveridge told the whole story of Lincoln's narrowly averted duel with Shields, making Shields look much less the swaggering fop that Nicolay and Hay had depicted and Lincoln more the blameworthy wiseacre. But he thought Lincoln learned a lesson from the affair in that he gave up anonymous letter writing—which had been the cause of the quarrel—and became considerate of people's feelings.

Beveridge re-told the story of the Ann Rutledge romance much as Herndon had given it; but he also quoted contradictory testimony, and intimated that the whole thing had been overdrawn. The nature and course of the courtship were "misty" and neither Ann nor Abraham "displayed any precipitancy of passion." Connelley liked the way Beveridge handled it. He never took much stock in the story, and he did not believe Lincoln ever would have married Ann, in any event. Connelley had known Stephen Perkins, who knew Ann and was Lincoln's bedfellow for a time at New Salem. Perkins thought there was very little truth in the romantic part of the tale; and Lincoln's sadness at Ann's death was merely a manifestation of his usual sympathy for anyone in distress.

While Beveridge had reservations about this story, he accepted Herndon's version of the "fatal first of January." He checked carefully with Weik, and was not convinced that Miss Tarbell or Barton had refuted it; and while he obtruded no personal opinion, he arranged the evidence so "craftily" as to "produce the effect of an assertion." It was a striking demonstration that "when you say arrangement, you say interpretation." Beveridge did not doubt that Lincoln actually contemplated suicide on this occasion; and Connelley agreed. "Lincoln's mental breakdown was a catastrophe which is liable to overtake any man with a delicate nervous organization who had ambition and high aspirations, but who mistrusts his culture, his polish, his manner of appearance in the higher social circles," Connelley thought.

Meantime, Beveridge plodded on. "I have now dogged Lincoln's foot-steps into Congress," he wrote to Connelley, "and it is almost a worse muddle than the Legislature. I am appalled, dear Connelley, to find that writers have not so much as looked at even the Journal of the House of Representatives—I mean the National House. Is not that astounding? It is the most obvious and conspicuous as it is the most trustworthy of all sources. Why should anybody fail to examine that carefully the very first thing?

"I repeat to you that if I had so much as suspected that none of this work had been done, I should never have undertaken to wade through this boundless and uncharted morass. But now that I am on my way, I suppose I shall have to go through to the end."

So he worked on—through newspapers, the Congressional Globe, the Journals of Congress, the literature of the Mexican War, letters, more newspapers. "Senator Beveridge is here today," wrote William L. Patton from Springfield, "He is up to his ears in the newspapers running from 1845 to 1860." "The work is so heavy and the material so voluminous that I would throw up the sponge if my friends among the scholars did not write me such charming letters," Beveridge wrote to Weik.

And all the while Lincoln's development seemed so slow. "I shall of course, find my hero on the highest peak of Mt. Everest," Beveridge said, "but I shall have to go through many a bog, gully, and chasm in the painful ascent before I at last reach him on the heights of glory."

In Congress, as in the Illinois Legislature, Lincoln held to the party line unswervingly, opposing the Mexican War, even at the risk of his political future, repudiating his personal loyalty to Henry Clay to work for the nomination of Zachary Taylor for the presidency in 1848 in obedience to the politician's plea of availability. A fervid nationalist, Beveridge had no sympathy with the Whig position; and he was convinced that Lincoln had no thought of opposing the war until he came to Washington and fell under the dominance of the national Whig leaders. Beveridge may even have had some sympathy with Connelley's view that if slavery caused the war and brought the great access of territory which resulted, then it was to slavery's credit. Connelley thought: "Our debt to slavery is large, for without it we would not have acquired those vast stretches of land from sea to sea which put us in control of the world . . . We abolished slavery too soon. If we had but let it alone another quarter-century we would now be at Panama . . . I hope someone with the time at his disposal will write us a fine volume on the benefits slavery gave America—and the calamity we have suffered from abolishing it before it had worked to a beneficent end—when it would have disappeared of itself in any detrimental form . . . Nations are not ultimately governed in attaining their ends by what we term justice and righteousness. Nations advance or decline. They cannot remain stationary. The example of every fallen power in the world proves that internal development of a country will not take the place of expansion. People are the blood of the world and must circulate. Most of the present nations of the world must perish that the world may have progress."

From Beveridge's conclusion that Lincoln was wrong in his opposition to the Mexican War, it followed that Herndon was right; for he consistently tried to dissuade Lincoln from his oppositionist course. "I have nearly finished the very long chapter dealing with Lincoln in Congress," wrote Beveridge to Weik, "and Herndon looms up big.

"He was right about the Mexican war just as Lincoln was wrong; and I wouldn't be surprised to find that he was the pushing force behind Lincoln on the slavery question. Neither would I be surprised if I should find that he is the carburetor in the great man's career." Later, when he came to examine the slavery struggle he wrote: "I am just revising Chapter VIII—the nomination of Lincoln for Senator, his 'house-divided' speech, and all that sort of thing—and I can tell you that Herndon looms up bigger than ever as the most active—if, indeed, not the most effective—of Lincoln's friends . . . Your life of Herndon will be a great hit. *Take plenty of time* to it—it must be your masterpiece."

Thus Beveridge brought Lincoln to his fortieth year, still a small town lawyer and politician. Yet there was no disparagement and there was evidence of latent qualities which later would become more manifest—inflexible personal honesty, ambition, firmness, understanding, caution, clarity of expression, moral courage, capacity for mental and moral growth.

And Beveridge had reached a turning point. Lincoln, at the end of his congressional term, would have liked to remain in Washington in some appointive job. But the party powers ruled otherwise. Disillusioned, disappointed, chastened, Lincoln had no alternative but to return home, turn his back on politics, and go to work. Five years of "waiting, thought and growth" ensued, and when he re-entered politics with the repeal of the Missouri Compromise, he was purged of "narrow partisanship and small purposes, with the foundations of greatness firmly established and visible even to hostile eyes." Beveridge had passed the disillusioning period and could now begin to appreciate Lincoln's emerging greatness.

Still there was so much work to do; and instead of its getting easier, "the thicket grows denser and the morass deeper," he complained. He had never worked so hard in his life. He felt "chained to the oar." How had so many people attempted to write history and biography without examining the sources? "The only explanation I can give is that it is so easy to write a lot of language, and so hard to dig out the facts." "It is a slow and long pull and a very, very hard pull," he asserted.

Now he was in the maze of the Kansas struggle, and he found that "a lot of lies were told on both sides." Channing had discovered the same thing and those "our people" told had well-nigh driven this New Englander crazy. And the voluminous data that must be absorbed and organized! "I have slaughtered regiments, divisions, Army Corps of details and dates, yet I fear there are still too many incidents," Beveridge wrote to Connelley.

He was relying on Connelley to keep him straight in the matter of the Kansas conflict, and he hoped Connelley would go through these chapters as thoroughly as "a dose of salts." Connelley would; for he believed "no other man alive can do this work. To write this work as you have commenced it, is greater than to have been president of the United States or to have had any other office or title or honor." It would be the greatest biography ever written.

Connelley warned him about the work of some of the historians. They were fine fellows, but what they didn't know about Kansas history "would make an immense book." Above all, Beveridge should be careful not to give undue credit to the Emigrant Aid Society for the final outcome in Kansas. Most of the people it sent there came from the workshops of New England, and were wholly unfitted for pioneer life. It was the people of the Ohio Valley who made Kansas free. "They did all that was accomplished, and the Yankee did the writing and took the credit," Connelley asserted.

Beveridge's work was one long series of surprises and awakenings, not the least of which came with his investigation of the repeal of the Missouri Compromise. From his youth he had believed it resulted from a slave-holders' conspiracy to open new territory to slavery. But he confessed to Weik, "as was the case with the other chapters, examination of source materials has well-nigh dazed me, since they revealed the truth to be exactly the contrary to the teachings of my youth." In his reaction from these teachings Beveridge sometimes swung too far the other way. In his scrutiny of the events that led to war he often leaned to the South. Shocked by the malignity of the abolitionist attack, he sometimes presented extreme examples of Northern fanaticism, and while letting the facts speak for themselves, he was not always judicious in his choice of facts.

With revision of his ideas came new appreciation and respect for Stephen A. Douglas, who forced the repeal of the Missouri Compromise through Congress and evolved the theory of popular sovereignty as the answer to the slavery problem. As Beveridge probed the records, Douglas loomed ever larger in his theme until it seemed to him that the really significant conspiracy was not that of the slave power but that of the post-bellum historians against Douglas. When Professor Channing suggested that Douglas was a great man, Beveridge replied: "Douglas! You bet Douglas was a great man, and he grows bigger all the time . . . It becomes clearer and clearer to me . . . that the literary Lincolnites had almost a hijacker conspiracy against Douglas—and against any other man of power who for any cause happened to run counter to their hero; and especially is this true of Douglas."

Delving further, Beveridge again wrote to Channing: "What an incredible quantity of 'bunc' has been written about Douglas! How shamefully he has been written down —and written down in order to write Lincoln up. That is

neither history nor art. Against all the teachings of my boyhood and young manhood, and in opposition to every
prejudice, my admiration for Douglas grows all the time—
and it grows solely from what he said and did."

And again: "How Douglas does loom up! And what rotten treatment he has had at the hands of the so-called 'historians'! I am beginning to think that, after all, writers of
history in former, and even in recent years are not above
being propagandists."

Against the broad backdrop of contemporary events,
Beveridge placed both Lincoln and Douglas in proper perspective, integrating them with their era. With this it was
apparent that Lincoln's great Peoria speech of October 16,
1854, was neither original nor inspired but primarily a
masterly re-statement of the ideas of those who were opposed to the expansion of slavery as those ideas had already
been threshed out in Congressional debate. The propositions of the Lincoln-Douglas debates were no new thoughts
struck off almost extemporaneously, but powerful reca-
pitulations of Republican and Democratic arguments with
which both men were thoroughly familiar and which they
had expounded in many previous forensic combats under
less spectacular auspices.

All these things that were surprising Beveridge were not
unknown to historians. They had been investigating them,
and they were changing and modifying many misconceptions. In proving them to his own satisfaction, bringing
them to bear upon the Lincoln story, and bringing that
story into accord with them, Beveridge brought Lincoln
scholarship out of the sheltered eddy, where it had been
circling, back into the full current of the historical stream.

Connelley did not know how to express his appreciation
of the chapters dealing with Douglas. They constituted

one of the greatest pieces of historical writing he had ever
read. They were profound; and they had stirred him as
nothing ever did before. "I see Douglas now in his true
magnificence for the first time," he wrote. "I had taken the
Abolition view of Douglas and had always believed that he
sold himself for the presidency, but now see that he was a
true patriot and that the presidency would not have purchased him. The people can never thank you enough for
doing justice to Judge Douglas and his memory. I never
did admire Chase much but had believed Sumner a true,
patriotic man. I see now that they were only d—d scoun-
drels, to be held up to ridicule by all honest and patriotic
men in the future."

In an article on "The Making of a Book," Beveridge
told how in the unfolding of a story "other characters,
some of them hardly less important than the hero himself
—in certain acts more prominent than the hero himself—
also play their parts . . . At the end comes the climax
with the hero, who from the first has been slowly but surely
coming to the front, holding the center of the stage as the
curtain falls."

Thus, throughout the period of the fifties he gave Douglas the center of the stage, with Lincoln in a supporting
role. Then, just as Lincoln was about to take the lead for
those great, final, stirring scenes, Beveridge was forced to
put the work aside. A few weeks later, on April 27, 1927,
the curtain fell prematurely, when he died. Worthington
C. Ford gathered up the loose ends and the two volumes
were published in 1928.

Here, done by a layman, was a work even the historians
could applaud. It was so heavily documented that some
pages were like "a rivulet of text flowing through a
meadow of footnotes." The bibliography contained 350

published titles, not to mention newspapers and manuscripts. And despite its prolific documentation, it had smoothness and verve. The treatment of controversial issues was unusually impartial, and Lincoln moved among events and men a living, breathing man. The politics of the day were treated with a skill and understanding to be derived only from personal participation in practical politics. Complete objectivity was lacking, as Beard said it would be, nor was definitiveness achieved. Yet—a history of the period as well as of the man—the book was truly monumental.

Here was a portrait painted large, with no embellishment; although, being unfinished, it lacked something of final luster.

Critics were lavish in praise. It was "a vivid picture, full of stir and life," showing the "workings of American democracy during this critical period of its growth"; "learned," "masterful," "mercilessly dispassionate," "stupendous," "scholarly in the extreme but none the less the record of a human being." There would have been "something of epic grandeur when Beveridge reached the years of storm and stress."

The New York *Times* observed that "he makes nobody great or small; he shows them to you, that is all, but when he has shown them to you, you see them, and you do not forget the way they look."

Literary critics considered it definitive as far as it went, but those who were more familiar with the Lincoln story knew that it was not. A student of Beveridge's methods thought that if anything, his judgment of Lincoln was too harsh. He subjected him to an ordeal such as few men ever had to undergo.

Historians rejoiced that Beveridge had put the romanticists to rout. The critic for *The American Historical Review* was relieved when he did not have to sniff the usual "roseate vapors." Claude Bowers, who would later write a biography of Beveridge, thought those "who love their myths and cherish the illusion of perfect men may resent the realistic method which for so many pages depicts a Lincoln not so admirable and certainly not so great; but most, we trust, will rejoice in a method which permits us to witness the growth, inch by inch, of a self-seeking country politician into a figure of such moral grandeur and greatness that it must command the admiration of all future years."

A lay critic thought that if Beveridge had lived he would have "shattered the Lincoln myth." But historians had little to crow about. That this "should need to be done more than sixty years after Lincoln's death is an illustration of the large fields that American scholarship has still to conquer."

Chapter Eleven

THE ACADEMIC
PROCESSION

About the time Beveridge began his Lincoln studies, a man in Springfield, Illinois, evolved a fertile idea.

In 1909 a group of citizens in Springfield had organized the Lincoln Centennial Association to take part in the commemoration of the one-hundredth anniversary of Lincoln's birth. Arranging a magnificent patriotic meeting with speakers of international renown and a panoply of guests of national repute, they planned a sumptuous banquet with tickets at twenty-five dollars a plate and wine to savor every course. As such affairs sometimes do, the banquet took an unanticipated bacchanalian turn; and the ladies, barred from the board, but admitted to the balcony, watched with awe, or pride, or trepidation, each gauging the staying powers of her helpmeet, as viands and potations were laid by.

It was a memorable occasion; and it was repeated from year to year on Lincoln's birthday, although the subsequent celebrations were restrained.

The first World War brought suspension of these exercises; and while the organization was maintained and an-

nual exercises were resumed after the war, the old fervor
could not be recaptured.

In 1924, however, Logan Hay became the Association's
president; and by giving this moribund society new purpose, he revitalized it, gave it national scope, and made it
the medium of durable historical contributions.

A member of Yale's venerated "Skull and Bones" and
an honor student in college, Mr. Hay had become a small-
town lawyer who was nationally known. He could have
quadrupled his income had he chosen to practice law in
Chicago, New York, or Washington, for few metropolitan
legal lights excelled him in competence. But, like Lincoln,
he loved Springfield and chose to make it his home.

He was all intellect. Day, night, and Sunday found him
at his office desk, or in his library at home, either working,
or reading in his favorite fields. Primarily a student, he had
greatest relish for those of his cases which posed legal or
human problems, regardless of the fees that were involved.
He had that type of mind in which everything he ever read
or learned was pigeonholed, to be recalled when needed.

Absorbed in thought, he would often pass his closest
friends on the street without a sign of recognition; and
some who did not know him thought him gruff and un-
approachable. But really he was kindly, friendly, generous
—and when time permitted—gregarious.

A rotund man, with large head crowned with brown
curly hair, and legs somewhat disproportionately short for
his big body, he had many oddities. Careless but not sloppy
in his dress, his battered hat was out of keeping with the
cane he carried when he had not forgotten and abandoned
it somewhere. To see him answer his office telephone was
an experience. The phone was placed at a far point on his
desk, and when his buzzer sounded he had to flip one of

Logan Hay

three keys to establish the proper connection. Totally inept in things mechanical, he invariably had to fumble with all three before he found the one desired; and then, instead of pulling the whole instrument to him, he would put the receiver to his ear, take a deep breath, and leaning in the general direction of the upright mouthpiece would bellow at it with a deep, long-drawn-out "HULLOOO" that reverberated to the farthest reaches of his spacious office suite.

This man's roots were deep in Lincoln ground. His grandfather, Stephen T. Logan, was Lincoln's second law partner. His father, Milton Hay, studied in Lincoln's office and was one of his personal friends. John Hay was a first cousin; and his law firm traced back to the partnership of Stuart and Lincoln.

Widely read in Illinois and American history, he had made the study of Lincoln his hobby; and with his avid, questioning turn of mind, he recognized the need for further study. To his personal knowledge there were Lincoln records in Springfield and other nearby places in Illinois, in public repositories and in private hands, which had never been investigated and which might be lost forever unless speedily utilized. Why could the Association not undertake their recovery and thus fulfill a more useful purpose?

Calling the directors of the organization together, Mr. Hay presented a plan which resulted in changing the name of the society to the Abraham Lincoln Association and in adoption of a program destined to reduce materially the unexploited areas of Lincolniana.

Having followed with appreciation the results achieved by professionally trained historians in other fields of American history, Mr. Hay wished to apply their technique to the Lincoln theme; so, at his suggestion, Paul M. Angle, a young man who had pursued postgraduate studies in history at the University of Illinois, was employed as the Association's first secretary. The choice was fortunate; for when Angle resigned, after serving for seven years, the Association had won recognition in the world of scholarship and Angle himself had developed into a finished research technician, a facile writer, and a dauntless critic who would increase his stature as a Lincoln authority after turning his talents to broader fields.

Like Beveridge, Mr. Hay had a passion for facts. A sincere admirer of Lincoln, his purpose was not to eulogize. And the thoroughness he proposed to apply to the work is exemplified in his ambition to publish a record of Lincoln's activities day-by-day from his birth to his accession to the presidency. He sensed a story in the record of Lincoln's personal finances; studying the entries of deposits and withdrawals in Lincoln's bank account, he must know whence the money came and where it went.

It is a tribute to his tenacity that the day-by-day project was carried through, and that Lincoln's whereabouts and doings were determined on a surprisingly large percentage of those days.

It involved an enormous amount of tedious, dirty work in newspaper collections, court files, legislative and congressional records, and a multiplicity of miscellaneous sources; but it did not lack thrills and satisfactions. The present writer, who succeeded Angle as secretary, well remembers the days he spent in dingy courthouses, usually in the basement, turning the interminable pages of dusty ledgers, poring through grimy files long undisturbed. Invariably the clerks declared it was a waste of time—no Lincoln documents had been found for years. Yet, in every single instance documents were found, and in more than one courthouse they numbered a hundred or more. True, very few bore Lincoln's signature; almost all these had disappeared. But they were in Lincoln's unmistakable handwriting, either unsigned or signed by him with the name of the local attorney with whom he was associated in each particular case. In each instance permission was obtained to remove the documents for photostating. This done, they were returned to their incredulous custodians. The secretaries always hoped these keepers of the records were men of integrity, conscious of their duty, devoted to the public weal, and that the documents went back to their proper resting place. But this was not their affair.

Questing for facts, Mr. Hay did not overlook the interpretative function. He conceived of Lincoln as a man of continuous growth who profited from every experience. He recalled how Emerson had said: "How slowly, and yet by happily prepared steps, he came to his place"; and this squared with his own conclusions. He was always alert for clues to explain this process of self-teaching, and knowing that it derived in only small measure from book learning, he sought the explanation in the influence of environment. The result was books giving the history of New Salem and Springfield and their influence in developing Lincoln's character. And many other publications bearing on the Lincoln theme have appeared with the Abraham Lincoln Association's imprint.

Although Mr. Hay always insisted that the various Association secretaries should have full credit for the books that bore their names as author, a great deal of him went into everything they wrote. Constantly peering over their shoulders as they worked were his kindly but questioning eyes. As a critic he was unexcelled; with loose writing or

loose thinking he was merciless. When one made a statement or offered a conjecture in his presence, he had better
be prepared to back it up.

As the Association's scope widened and its reputation
grew, he became so absorbed in the work that Lincoln
study, instead of being a hobby, became an avocation
which threatened at times to force his profession into the
background. Each year, from about the first of February
until after Lincoln's birthday, he became increasingly un-
available to clients as he prepared the address with which
he would introduce the speaker at the Association's exercises. Invariably this speech was in the nature of a sum-
mary—the secretaries thought a rather lengthy one—of Lincoln's activities of the hundredth year preceding; and
when delivered, it was followed without pause by the brief-
est presentation of the speaker. Normally Mr. Hay was
preoccupied, but during these periods of preparation he
became increasingly absent-minded, often with disastrous
results; for on one occasion Mrs. Hay discovered, just in
the nick of time, that he had arrived at the Association's
banquet impeccably dressed in his evening clothes except
that he had forgotten both collar and tie.

With his death in 1942 the Association suffered a grievous loss; but he had built well; and the work goes forward
under leadership whose inspiration derives from him.

Logan Hay brought professionally trained historians
into the Lincoln field in the persons of the Association's
secretaries; but other professionals—and by the term we
mean those trained in graduate schools and earning their
livelihood as scholars—still passed Lincoln by. They were
working around Lincoln, turning out articles and books
that touched him at many points, but scarcely any of them
were making him the focus of their work. Yet there were

encouraging signs. At a meeting of the Mississippi Valley Historical Association in 1930, a Northern professor and a Southern professor debated the question "Lincoln's Election an Immediate Menace to Slavery in the States?" and at the 1933 meeting of the American Historical Association there was a round-table discussion of Lincoln's policy in respect of slavery and the South.

Then, at a joint session of the two associations held in Washington in December, 1934, Professor James G. Randall of the University of Illinois read a paper that posed the query "Has the Lincoln Theme Been Exhausted?"

Randall was one of the few professionals who had studied Lincoln closely; and after giving due credit for work already done, he pointed out vast stores of source material still untouched, many topics still untreated, and collateral studies which must be made before Lincoln's acts and motives could be fully comprehended. Lincoln as president had hardly been studied at all; and so far as the academicians were concerned, Lincoln authorship was in danger of passing from bud to decay without ever coming to full flower.

After all these years the true full-length portrait of Lincoln was still far from realization. In certain features the detail was worked out; but other portions, smudged by unskilled hands, needed correction and finishing; and over large areas of the canvas glaring blank spots bore witness to the spotty nature of the work.

Beveridge, Barton, and Hay showed what could be done. Randall sounded a bugle call.

Responding to the challenge, the schoolmen went to work. Soon scholarly monographs began to issue from the academic cloisters. Bringing the technique of the graduate schools to bear, the academicians dug deep for new pay dirt; and finding it, especially in the presidential period, they mined exhaustively, seeking out the documents, doubting everything that was not contemporaneous, questioning the accuracy of reminiscences, often rejecting them when they could not be validated. Using what is called "historical method," they weighed and balanced, tested old conclusions, sought truth and impartiality.

Once in the Lincoln field, the academicians evinced a disposition to preempt it. When Otto Eisenschiml suggested a new theory about Lincoln's assassination, they derided him because he was a chemist. Astounded by the personal invective of some of his reviewers, Eisenschiml took the historians to task for being unscientific. He had not expected to encounter such bitterness "among people who brush their teeth." "New chemical thoughts always find a respectful and serious, if skeptical reception," he declared. ". . . An author's thesis is checked and tested; and eventually it is either accepted or discarded, as results warrant. Never is the proponent's name unduly emphasized, nor are personal attacks made on him." When he and a colleague proposed a new chemical process, some years before, "No one cared whether we were university graduates or sewer diggers."

Eisenschiml should have realized that intolerance is no new thing among Lincoln biographers. The whole effort to get at the truth about this most tolerant of men has been marked by singular intolerance.

There was probably merit in Eisenschiml's complaint, for Professor Randall saw fit to warn his colleagues against professional smugness. "It must never be overlooked," he said, "that there are informed collectors and there are distinguished amateurs. Scholarship need not be tenacious of its hallmarks. The high degree of expertness in the Lincoln field exhibited by men occupied with the business or professional world who modestly consider the subject of Lincoln a hobby or a side issue, is a matter worthy of every specialist's consideration . . . The Lincoln world is best regarded as an open world."

Even to enumerate the contributions of the schoolmen would require an extensive bibliography. For despite their relatively recent interest, they have written scores of articles and numerous books dealing with many phases of Lincoln, his times and his contemporaries. Yet, of them all, only Professor Randall has written anything approaching a full-length biography, and he disclaims any purpose to do so. The two published volumes of his projected four-volume work are entitled *Lincoln the President: Springfield to Gettysburg*. Nevertheless, he devotes a considerable part of his first volume to Lincoln's pre-presidential years in order to show what sort of man Lincoln was when he entered the White House; and since Randall has not only given us his own views but has also synthesized the conclusions of his fellow professionals, his work may be said to depict Lincoln as academic scholars see him.

Now to our mind's eye comes the familiar figure of a lank, tough-framed Kentuckian with bony visage and ambling gait, but with new emphasis on his never shaking off —never wishing to shake off—Kentucky.

Moving to Indiana, he acquires some Hoosier traits. Settling finally in back-country Illinois, this son of undistinguished parents goes on to develop there, while a civilized society, of which he is a part, unfolds around him. Of rural origin, he never loses his earthiness. Humor, self-sufficiency, caution, patience, respect for fundamental forms are qualities early acquired. As a boy he seeks to learn; and thirst for understanding characterizes his life.

Ambition lifts him from common labor into the professional class; and ambition drives him on with its demands.

A practical man, when he enters politics he learns and practices political maneuver, learning that to get results, one must give as well as take.

In the Declaration of Independence he finds a political creed; in Thomas Jefferson a man who voiced his feelings about human rights.

Although popular fancy is reluctant to give up the idea of Lincoln the railsplitter and country lawyer, Randall showed that before Lincoln had lived in Springfield very long, he was moving among cultured people in the higher social strata. Indeed, he found his social eminence a political handicap, for he was put down as the candidate of "pride, wealth, and family distinction." Before he became president, in a day when many people never journeyed far from home, he had been all over Illinois and had traveled from the Atlantic seaboard states to Kansas and from Chicago and Niagara Falls to New Orleans. At home and in far places, refined and educated audiences had listened respectfully while he spoke, impressed by his close-woven logic, pulled by the power of his words. Much more than a country lawyer, he had become an outstanding practitioner in a populous and flourishing state that boasted many competent attorneys. He might even have been termed a corporation lawyer by reason of the many cases he handled for large business interests, although the bulk of his practice was still humdrum circuit work. And the law had made investiture in his growth; giving him knowledge of American institutions, of democratic traditions, of civil rights and duties, and teaching him to solve complicated problems by searching out their essential elements.

Randall saw Lincoln as a politician of higher caliber

than the party liegeman Beveridge depicted. He was "made of better stuff than that of politicians reaching out for the spoils of office," as was shown by his refusal to truckle to racial or religious intolerance at the time the Know-Nothing party, with its antiforeign, anti-Catholic rant, was tipping the political beam.

Yet Lincoln knew and used political wiles. In his contests with Douglas both he and Douglas "dragged red herrings over the trail, indulged in misrepresentations, hurled taunts, introduced extraneous matter, repeated the same statements from place to place with little regard by one debater for what the other had said, and seemed often more interested in casting reproach upon party opponents than in clarifying the issues." Lincoln tried to make Douglas seem a conspirator in a plot to extend slavery when no such plot existed. He assailed Douglas as repealing the Missouri Compromise with a purpose to promote the proslavery cause in the territories at the very time when Douglas was risking his political life in opposing the Buchanan administration's efforts to organize Kansas as a slave state. He gave Douglas no credit for resisting policies in respect to Kansas that he himself was resisting.

Looking back, the scholars take the position that the policy of either Lincoln or Douglas would have made Kansas free and would have stopped the spread of slavery in the territories. The two men did not differ fundamentally in their views of racial relations or in their antagonism to sectionalism, although each claimed that the other's policy fostered sectionalism.

Randall intimates that a more conciliatory attitude on Lincoln's part between the time of his election and his inauguration might have kept the middle slave states in the Union; and these retained, the deep South might have been brought back peaceably. Yet he concedes that Lincoln was conciliatory on all questions except slavery extension, and that his fault lay perhaps in failure to "effectively dramatize" his conservative position.

Faced with secession as an accomplished fact, Lincoln did not fumble about without a policy, as has been supposed. Citing the researches of a colleague, Randall shows that Lincoln's formula was to suspend the Federal authority in those places where it was challenged while refusing to yield where it was still effective. In practice this meant non-interference in the interior regions of the Confederacy and retention of Fort Sumter and Fort Pickens. Thus, as Lincoln stated in his inaugural address, there would be no resort to force unless the seceders chose to be the aggressors.

In the ensuing crisis at Fort Sumter, Randall concedes that the Lincoln administration was guilty of bad faith in breaking pledges to the South; but he places the responsibility on Seward, who took it upon himself to direct affairs in the early stages before Lincoln had had opportunity to bring about administrative unity. This effected, Lincoln was straightforward and aboveboard, not maneuvering the South into firing the first shot, as Southern historians would have it, but keeping his non-aggressive record clean in a determination that if a shot was fired, it would be the South that fired it.

Randall sees the "leitmotif" of Lincoln's presidency as a problem of reconciling moderate and radical elements. "A fateful dualism it was to be, and as time went on it showed increasing power to pester and harass. It was the dualism of Kentucky on the one side and Frémont on the other, of border-state moderation against crusading zeal, of opportunist realism against impatient reform, of limited objectives, with emphasis on the Union, *versus* an all-out abolitionist program of virulent anti-Southernism. On the one hand were moderate men who wished the South to be satisfied when the Union was remade, meantime sparing Southern civilians the worst horrors of war; on the other hand were unctuous rebel-haters to whom suffering on the part of slaveholders and 'traitors' seemed a kind of Divine vengeance."

To understand Lincoln's background and personality was to foresee where his own sympathies would lie. To him the Union would be paramount and he would move cautiously toward limited objectives, holding the border states at all costs, taking a legalistic attitude toward slavery until toleration of slavery and salvation of the Union became incompatible, and even then seeking constitutional justification of his acts.

Randall is at pains to destroy the stock picture of Lincoln the Great Emancipator "sitting in the White House and suddenly striking the shackles from millions of bondsmen at a stroke of the presidential pen." Lincoln's preferred policy was compensated emancipation with colonization of the negroes on some foreign shore; but this being rejected by Congress and the loyal slave states as well, he finally took action on the ground of war necessity, freeing only those slaves in areas still in rebellion, confessing his lack of authority to touch the institution where the constitution still controlled. Thus his proclamation touched only those regions where he exercised no power and exempted those states and parts of states where his authority was effectual.

In Randall's view the most unlovely phenomenon of our Civil War was the Northern Radical group, which sought to assume control of affairs and bend Lincoln to their will.

Cloaking their real designs of sectional supremacy, social revolution, economic exploitation, and party aggrandizement behind the comely façade of crusading antislavery zeal, in Randall's view no trick, intrigue, lie, subterfuge, or rascality was too mean to serve their purpose. They were far worse in his estimate than the Democrats, whose fault lay in failure to distinguish between salutary opposition to unconstitutional or unwise measures on the one hand and exploitation of national misfortunes for party advantage on the other.

As one might expect, this "revisionist" thesis did not escape challenge. Lloyd Lewis, Civil War student, book critic, and sleuth of Lincoln myths, reviewing Randall's book for the New York *Herald Tribune,* thought the professor showed a most "un-Lincolnian impatience" with the Radicals and that he went too far afield in his treatment of General McClellan, whom the Radicals hated because of his failure to get results and because he was a Democrat, and whom Randall defended as a competent commander who was sacrificed to hold the Radicals in line. Lewis thought Randall looked upon the Radicals "as little better than a pack of wolves whose pursuit, through the snows of '62 is so hot that Lincoln has to keep throwing General McClellan, that 'Little Napoleon,' out of the sleigh," and that Randall seemed to feel so sorry for the general that "he picks the little victim up in his arms and parades him as a mistreated man."

Like Lewis, the majority of Randall's colleagues refused to accept his attempted rehabilitation of McClellan. Nevertheless, Randall did make it evident that Lincoln, in his relations with McClellan, and in other aspects of his job as commander-in-chief, left much to be desired. Yet, despite failures and mistakes, Lincoln emerged from the scrutiny of Randall and the other professionals as essentially the same towering, compelling figure the people had come to know. His faith in democracy, his high moral character and courage, his great common sense, his sympathy, his moderation and self-effacement, his keen feeling for popular opinion, his sane, conservative approach to the manifold aspects of the slavery problem stood out more strikingly than ever.

Herndon did not fare so well at Randall's hands. Throughout the book, details in which he erred are pointed out and the "fatal first of January" is re-examined and rejected. In an appendix Randall applied the technique of historical method to an analysis of the evidence of the Ann Rutledge romance, excluding the story from the text on the ground that it is *un*proved rather than *dis*proved, and in consequence "does not belong in a recital of those episodes which one presents as unquestioned reality."

Thus the professionals, bringing their precise technique to bear, are enduing the Lincoln portrait with an incisiveness of line that has been lacking. Yet, in their failure to agree on some moot points they leave some features of the man as obscure as they were before.

Moreover, in so far as the Lincoln theme is concerned, the very strength of their technique is also weakness. Their method venerates the document; and while study of documents is essential to fact-finding, there is reason to doubt that we can really get to know Lincoln solely through "prosaic documentation." Lloyd Lewis thinks historians may have recognized this inadequacy in their technique and that they avoided the Lincoln field because they "suspected that Lincoln is only to be recreated by literary artists whose imagination can grasp the magic and the mystery which the public, either by instinct or by absorbing sustained propaganda, has come to feel inherent in the life of the prairie president. They may have doubted if realism alone could explain the man."

Here is a discouraging conjecture!

Our theme has been the gradual triumph of realism with the implication that when realism prevailed the true Lincoln would stand forth. Yet, if Lewis' hypothesis is correct, this may not be the case. And that it is correct was attested by William E. Barton, one of the most forthright realists, when he confessed to a feeling of futility. "I am working very hard to make a real contribution to the world's knowledge of Lincoln," he asserted. "I think I know the facts; but does anyone know Lincoln? . . . I feel that somehow Lincoln has eluded the biographers. I wish I might hope that I could interpret him. I have been so occupied with gathering facts, I sometimes think I am farther from my real goal than I thought I was when I began."

Similarly, Miss Tarbell admitted: "I am such a slave to facts, dates and things, I mean, that I fail to see the greater facts often."

Can it be that all our supposed progress has been futile? Does the triumph of realism bring us only to frustration?

Chapter Twelve

AN IMPRESSIONIST TRIES HIS HAND

IF WE adhere to the purist historian's definition of history, the next book should not merit our attention; for Milo Quaife, reviewing it for the *Mississippi Valley Historical Review*, declared that "whatever else it may be, it is not history as the reviewer understands the term." Yet how can we ignore the work of a man whose ability to sense the meaning of his material and get the feel of his subject amounts to genius, and whose portrayal of Lincoln is in many respects the most vivid, real and stimulating of all? How, in short, can we appraise the work of Carl Sandburg?

Can we accept as a Lincoln authority a poet, an author of fairy tales, a singer of folk songs, a man who thumbed his nose at the precepts of the historical profession, broke rules of literary composition with impunity and gloried in his unconventionality? Shall we characterize his work merely as "imaginative poetry and historical fiction," "a literary grab bag into which one may reach and draw out almost anything," as Mr. Quaife did; or shall we look deeper for the reason for its undoubted popular appeal?

For there can be no doubt that *Abraham Lincoln: The Prairie Years* is entitled to high rank in Lincoln literature.

Nor can it be dismissed as purely literature. It has meaning for historians as well. For if Sandburg was not the first to discover the wellsprings of Lincoln's growth, he was a masterful interpreter of the concept that these wellsprings were peculiarly American. He realized that Lincoln was an indigenous growth, the product of that multiplicity of influences and impulsions which make America what it is. Others had sensed this before him; but Sandburg, with the vision of the poet, excelled in talent to translate it. He saw Lincoln as "keenly sensitive to the words and ways of people around him. Therefore those people, their homes, occupations, songs, proverbs, schools, churches, politics, should be set forth with the incessant suggestion of change that went always with pioneer life. They were the backgrounds on which the life of Lincoln moved, had its rise and flow, and was moulder and moulded." A book seeking to depict these things might seem to be diffuse—"a literary grab bag"—as Mr. Quaife complained; but with the author's purpose understood, its diffuseness becomes meaningful.

Sandburg was born in Galesburg, Illinois, on January 6, 1878, of Swedish immigrant stock. His father, August Johnson, changed his name to Sandburg because there were so many Johnsons in the railroad construction gang with which he worked that some other Johnson was always getting his pay envelope. As a boy young Sandburg worked as driver of a milk wagon, porter in a barber shop, scene shifter, truck driver, and in a brick kiln. At seventeen he "rode the rails" to the West, where he worked in the wheat fields, washed dishes in cheap hotels, and served as a car-

Carl Sandburg

penter's apprentice. Returning to Galesburg, he became helper to a house painter until he enlisted for the Spanish-American War. Returning from Puerto Rico, he entered Lombard College, where he earned his way as tutor and janitor until he graduated in 1902. Then came years of journalistic work, interrupted by two years as secretary to the mayor of Milwaukee. Beginning in his college days, he wrote poetry, and by 1914 had established a reputation as a poet and recitalist of folk ballads as well as a skilful accompanist on the guitar. Like Lincoln he kept contact with the common people. I well remember once inviting him to join me at dinner at a hotel only to have him express a preference for "some workingman's joint."

Sandburg is a tall, gaunt man like Lincoln, somewhat stooped from hard work in his youth, and the years spent over a typewriter. His face is lined and wrinkly, his expression kindly and suggestive of sly humor. Two unruly locks of stiff gray hair, which he persistently pushes back, just as persistently fall again across his forehead. When he works he wears thick glasses and his teeth clutch a thin cigar which, more often than not, juts out cold, sodden, and forgotten. He is a muscle worker who graduated to brain work, just as Lincoln did.

He grew up in the same part of the country where Lincoln spent most of his life; and he must have been attracted to him early. Like Lincoln, he is a common man with an uncommon mind. He has the same ideas about America that Lincoln had. When Sandburg wrote about Chicago, it was not the Chicago of the imposing lake front. It was the brawling, teeming, panting, bustling, sometimes stinking hinterland. That was what made Chicago great to him. His was the Chicago where the heavy work is done— where men take off their coats, roll up their sleeves, spit, cuss, and produce. Lincoln would have liked Sandburg's Chicago.

As Sandburg came to know Lincoln, he feared that "our youth were hearing too many preachers, sycophants, politicians, ignoramuses talking about Lincoln in a way to make you writhe." The real Lincoln was too great a treasure to lose. So Sandburg began his *Prairie Years* with the idea of writing a children's book. But the material guided him into something different.

Sandburg was working on the Chicago *Daily News;* but about three months out of the year he devoted to platform engagements. Soon he began to plan those performances according to the probability of finding Lincoln material. Places which boasted libraries where such material might be found, or places where some one lived who might be able to divulge some Lincoln information, won priority on his speaking schedule. Having fulfilled his engagement, he would stay over for a day or two to see what he could find about Lincoln.

Having collected his material, he presented it by what might be termed the impressionistic method, trying to recapture the aura of a bygone day by piling up his data, allowing the personages of that day to speak for themselves as much as possible. The New York *Times* reviewer found *The Prairie Years* "as full of facts as Jack Horner's pie was of plums." "Here is God's plenty indeed," gasped Mark Van Doren, when he reviewed it for *The Nation*. "Here is the lining of the old Mid-Western mind. Here are the songs all people sang, the poems they recited, the proverbs they spoke, the superstitions they could not discard, the machines they used, the clothes they wore, the facts they learned in the newspapers, the gods they swore by, the dishes they ate, the jests they laughed at. As Mr. Sandburg goes on he becomes drunk with data, and in true Homeric fashion compiles long lists of things."

More than one reviewer was reminded of Homer by the "disarming simplicity of his style" and the directness and economy of his narrative; to another his work seemed "as detailed as Dostoevsky, as American as Mark Twain." Sandburg's style is reminiscent of all these classic writers; yet it is modern too; and to still another reviewer it suggested the Hollywood technique, with its "shift," "cut-back," and "fade out." Mixed with the classical were "jazzy spots," "with occasional lapses into pure Sandburgese."

The icy reception which the purist historians accorded *The Prairie Years* was more than counteracted by the enthusiasm of literary critics. The *New Statesman* considered it "a masterpiece"; and what was even more remarkable, "a masterpiece which suits its subject." *Bookman* regarded it as "a veritable mine of human treasure from which to read aloud or to pore over by oneself." As William Allen White read the book, he felt Lincoln take on reality, "strong, rank, pungent, gorgeous reality." John Drinkwater, Lincoln dramatist, thought it not unlikely that Sandburg "will be found to have given the world the first American epic." Drinkwater had already read a dozen Lincoln books and never expected that anyone could beguile him into reading another thousand pages about Lincoln—and least of all, Carl Sandburg. The Sandburg Drinkwater knew was tough, hard, realistic—"the bleak poet of Chicago"; and as he read the first few pages he asked himself how Sandburg could write such "romantic frippery." But as he read on, he found it was not frippery at all, "but a quite sincere, and cumulatively very touching reversion of a mind, closely disciplined in an almost savage candor, to a natural grace and leniency of sentiment. Confronted by epic character of action, we find, this least compromising of realists can stand up and prophesy with revivalist fervor."

Other reviewers besides Drinkwater noted that while Sandburg was studying and depicting Lincoln, Lincoln had done something to Sandburg. Here was Sandburg's "noblest" work, the *Independent* asserted. "It has done us good to read this able, rugged book," declared the Boston *Transcript*. "We doubt not that it has done Carl Sandburg much good to write it. Such is the blessing which Abraham Lincoln bestows on his biographers." Stuart Sherman liked Lincoln "the better for it and Carl Sandburg and myself and my neighbor. And that result . . . is the living virtue that streams out of Lincoln forever."

If Lincoln brought out the sentimental in Sandburg, he did not emasculate his style. His conversational vocabulary includes "ain't," "gink," "hobo," "bum," "bunkshooter"; and one finds "strange kettle of fish," "lingo," "hillbillies," "huggermugger," in his books. His characters are "rare birds," "croakers," who play "peanut politics," "become plumb disgusted," "get sore," "get lit up," emit "horse-laughs" and "gabble."

Sandburg did not write for the professors; he aimed at the ordinary man. If a colloquialism best expressed what he wanted to say, he used a colloquialism; if what he had in mind came out clearest in the vernacular, he used the vernacular. Like Lincoln, he sacrificed literary perfection to literary effectiveness. According to W. O. Stoddard, Lincoln "didn't care a cornhusk" for the literary critics; and Sandburg seemed equally indifferent. "Among the biographers I am a first-rate poet," he observed, "and among poets a good biographer; among singers I'm a good collector of songs and among song collectors a good judge of pipes."

"Mr. Sandburg's prose is like the molten steel flowing into a vessel," one reviewer of *The Prairie Years* observed. "It fits the subject. It sparkles. It dreams. It pulls. It strikes the eye with a hot blast . . . [He is] a master of strong, moving prose as it is written and spoken on these shores." If Sandburg's prose had a smell, "it would be leaf smoke on an Illinois dirt road in November."

Even the literary critics noted a few mistakes. A quotation from De Tocqueville was attributed to Montesquieu. The chief justice of the Supreme Court of the District of Columbia spelled his name "Cartter," not "Carter" as Sandburg had it, stuttering "in his spelling as well as in his speech." Sandburg should not have had Nancy Lincoln singing "From Greenland's Icy Mountains" when she died before Bishop Heber wrote it.

But most critics were inclined to grant Sandburg a large measure of poetic license. One should not look for completeness or exactness in this type of work; the ensemble justified the flaws and lapses. Ida Tarbell—whose influence on Sandburg we have already noted, and whose books, so he told her, "I handle regularly while working"—wrote that she was hugging his book to her heart. "I feel as if the thing was made for me personally."

In 1932 Sandburg and Paul M. Angle collaborated to write *Mary Lincoln: Wife and Widow*—a biography by Sandburg, substantiated by documents edited by Angle. All previous books about Mrs. Lincoln were by persons biased one way or the other. Sandburg and Angle tried to be realistic and at the same time sympathetic. In the documentary section correspondence between Mary Todd and her friend Mercy Levering and between Miss Levering and her fiancé was published for the first time. Written during the period from July, 1840, to June, 1841, these letters illuminated the "fatal first of January." From this new evidence the authors were able to show rather conclusively that Lincoln, uncertain of himself, as he had been once before in his affair with Mary Owens, had confided his perplexity to his betrothed, who released him from his engagement. To mutual friends it appeared that Lincoln had been jilted; and they accepted this as explanation of his queer behavior. The letters also showed that Mary felt no bitterness toward Lincoln, as a girl of her vehement nature would, had he broken the engagement, much less left her waiting at the altar. It also appeared that she was anxious for the reconciliation that eventually took place.

Sandburg and Angle concluded that Mrs. Lincoln was psychopathic long before a Chicago court adjudged her insane in 1874; and with that fact understood, she became deserving of more sympathy than she had usually been accorded. Her case could best be analyzed by a physician; and appropriately enough, *Mrs. Abraham Lincoln* by William E. Evans, a Chicago physician, was published the same year the Sandburg-Angle book appeared.

In 1939 Sandburg's *Abraham Lincoln: The War Years,* in four volumes, completed his Lincoln story. It was a mammoth work, eleven years in the making, whose production led Sandburg to "read more Lincoln material than any other man living or dead." It took him to every part of the country, through mountains of newspapers, floods of letters, diaries, pamphlets, posters, proclamations, handbills, pictures, cartoons. He floundered neck-deep through official records and Congressional debates. He bought books by the hundreds; ripped them apart to obtain the pages he would use and stacked the gutted remnants in his barn. Two copyists worked on a glassed-in porch at his home while his wife and three daughters helped file and organize. "As I look at what the completed work will be," wrote Sandburg in the midst of all this labor, "I say to myself that if I had not faithfully plodded through every last piece of essential material that I could lay my hands on, I would feel guilty."

With part of the proceeds of *The Prairie Years* Sandburg had bought a home at Harbert, Michigan, and here where he could look out beyond the shifting dunes to where the red sun sank below the far rim of the lake, this greatest of his Lincoln books was written.

In his attic workshop a visitor noted a "bare, unpainted floor, no ornaments except a life mask of Lincoln beside the desk, and on the wall an old top hat from Lincoln's day. Books stand on open shelves of rough lumber around the four sides, lie in neat piles on tables and boxes, fill cases and bins. A stovepipe zigzags from the wood stove in the center of the room to the chimney. There's a big old battered woodbox, with a little heap of kindling beside it, and a pile of gray driftwood from the beach. A fire-extinguisher stands near the top of the stair."

Surrounded by these heaps of unprocessed ore, Sandburg applied his own peculiar method of extraction. He sat on a small chair with his typewriter before him on a cracker box. If Grant and Sherman could conduct campaigns from a cracker box, a cracker box was good enough for him. There was something uniquely American about a cracker box. Beyond his typewriter were his notes, and pages torn from books, thumbtacked to an upright screen. And as he swept them with his gaze, Sandburg applied his magic touch, transposing the essence of this raw material to paper.

In pleasant summer weather he took his work outside, stripping down to a pair of sandals, a loincloth, and a green eyeshade, brushing off his pure-bred goats when they became too inquisitive or affectionate.

His technique was essentially the same as in *The Prairie Years*. It was panorama through minutiae. The reader was infused with detail until suffused in atmosphere. Interpretation came by subtle suggestion. After finishing his first draft, Sandburg wrote to a friend: "The finish of the book is symphonic—life made it so. But there are throughout periods and passages of that war and that time which *must* be handled, and they are involved reading or they deal with cheap motives or with days dusty and gray with monotony—Yet they belong. If Lincoln had to endure these, the reader, seeking Lincoln, will have to endure in imagination what Lincoln went through in reality." Thus Sandburg explained the essence of his method.

"What lifts the book above mere stupendous anecdote," an appreciative reviewer observed, ". . . is the thoughtful searching comment of the collector. Each anecdote and incident is fastened to the growing pyramidal monument by the cement of Sandburg's particular feeling for the form of words—and of Lincoln's character. The method enables the author to pile up, along with the monument to Lincoln, another one—one to the people of the time." As in *The Prairie Years,* Sandburg seemed to have transposed himself back to an earlier day; to have lived with a man of that day until both the man and the times came alive in his mind.

Three-fourths done, Sandburg stopped to revise and rewrite, "in order to feel the scale and proportion better for the final quarter." The past eight months, he told Miss Tarbell, "I have had a detour into a long poem (very free verse!) titled THE PEOPLE, YES which I am sure holds some of your heartbeats about democracy and these times."

He had been at work seven years; had hoped to finish the year before; but it would still take four years more.

When this book appeared the historians were fore-warned; and while still amazed at Sandburg's methods they were slower to condemn; indeed, several of the most competent of them accorded unstinted praise.

As a matter of fact, Sandburg had profited by their previous criticism, and his work was more carefully done. Errors could still be found; but no major mistakes marred the work. Sandburg sacrificed nothing of his style; but he was less sentimental and imaginative. He did not invent thoughts to put in Lincoln's head, as he did in the earlier book.

Professor Randall, reviewing the book for *The American Historical Review*, criticised Sandburg's discursiveness —the book was "a kind of gargantuan Civil War omnibus" —his over-use of quotation, his neglect of some significant material, several factual slips. But he appreciated the author's rare feeling for Lincoln, his pithily descriptive adjectives, and his scintillating sketches of contemporary characters.

Professor Charles A. Beard, mellow, wise, learned in historical lore, thought nothing like it had ever yet appeared on land or sea. Strict disciples of Gibbon, Macaulay, Ranke, Mommsen, Hegel, or Marx would "scarcely know what to do with it. It does not enclose the commonplace in a stately diction appropriate for Augustine pomp. Its pages do not stand out in the cold formalism which marks the work of those historians who imagine that they are writing history as it actually was." Specialists would quarrel with it "more or less gently." Yet, when Beard compared their work with some of Sandburg's chapters, "with the best will in the world, I should not like to say on oath which is the truer," he asserted, "that is, which more clearly corresponds with the recorded and unrecorded emotions, thoughts, tempers, and actions in the case. But when specialists have finished dissecting, scraping, refining, dissenting, and adding, I suspect that Mr. Sandburg's work will remain for long years to come a noble monument of American literature."

Beard seemed ready to concede that there was more than one way to write history, and that the way of the academician was not necessarily the most excellent.

As for Lincoln, Sandburg made no evident effort to expound him, yet he was omnipresent, now in the forefront, now recessive. One sees Lincoln guiding when he can, biding when he must; coaxing, persuading, inspiriting; breathing on the heartstrings of the people. Sometimes exultant, more often he is disappointed. Harassed, let-down, thwarted, he is seldom outmaneuvered or outwitted.

Sometimes he seems bewildered and confused; yet always he holds steadfast to high purpose, seeing in the agony of war the testing of man's capacity to order his own destiny. A shrewd man, one watches him apply the cunning of the Illinois circuit to the business of holding together the diverse elements of a heterogeneous party. A kindly man, he eases the burdens of the humble and endures the arrogance of the vain. A peaceful man, he hurls the thunderbolts of war even when his own soul writhes in torment at their havoc. Magnanimous, he pardons when he can find reason and often without reason. Knowing no bitterness, he offers sympathy to friend and foe.

Suffering personal affliction, misunderstood, reviled, assailed, he exhibits qualities of patience, tolerance, and forgiveness such as no other national leader has ever shown, taking upon himself the sufferings of a whole people, holding to faith in the basic virtues of those people.

Indifferent to social conventions, plain, unprepossessing, sometimes even crude, still his very simplicity and friendliness attest the gentleman.

From doubt he comes to inner piety and faith, moving in the mid-ground between the seen and the unseen, seeming to hold mystic communicn with another world, seeing in the tragedy of war the hand of Providence working to great purpose through inscrutable means, bringing remission of sins through bloodshed.

A truly American product, he embodies the national traits, combining the rugged independence, the easy freedom, the boisterous humor, the loamy philosophy of the frontier plains with the granitic soul fiber of the mountains.

Thus Sandburg pictured Lincoln with his calm and solemn face masking deep sensitivity; breaking easily into mirth; lapsing quickly back to melancholy; marked early by the prairie years; becoming more careworn, weary, furrowed; taking on new depths, new shades, new highlights as the war years wrought upon it.

Its sentences crowded and compact, *The War Years* moves irresistibly, as befitted the times and their impact on Lincoln. Uncritical, with little attempt at analysis and with acceptance of unauthenticated reminiscences that the schoolmen would not have used, yet Sandburg's book is convincing and compelling in its mass effect. Its pace is geared to events; battles moving swiftly, office-seekers and favor-seekers passing through Lincoln's office with a monotony and insistence that wears on the reader as it must have worn on Lincoln. Watching events through the eyes of the people of that day, one experiences the fumbling military failures of the early years; defeat; discouragement; the search for generals who could fight; war weariness; the insidious borings of the Copperheads; patient heroic sacrifice; eventually the sure crunch of the Northern military machine as it wears down the dogged will of the South; then victory; assassination; mass sorrow welling from a war-worn people as the book concludes like a dirge.

Much more than a life of Lincoln, the book sets forth the whole society of the time. "It somehow gives you a sense of the immense tumult and confusion through which Lincoln was working his way," Miss Tarbell thought, "gives you the feel of the times better than anybody. I do not know that it could be done in any other way excepting by pouring in, in what seems to be an almost helter-skelter fashion, this tremendous accumulation."

Writing to the author, Miss Tarbell said she was trying to find a name for the book. "There is The Lincoln Book of Knowledge; the Lincoln Encyclopedia; the Lincoln Dictionary; the Lincoln Thesaurus. But they are all obvious, too commonplace. There is the Lincoln Pageant, but one does not want to use Pageant in connection with Lincoln, does he? I'll hit on something one of these days, I am sure." Meantime she found herself dipping into the book to see what Sandburg said about this person or event; and in every case she was delighted and amazed. The book was a guide and consolation; it was fun! He must pardon this "jubilant" letter! That was the way she felt!

It was an epic story, so replete that one reviewer thought Sandburg at some places would have done well "to sow by hand rather than the bag." Another critic, while recognizing the merit of the work, compared Sandburg to the painters of the primitive school whose work had that curious one-dimensional look because they lost perspective in detail. Stephen Vincent Benet, a fellow poet, felt some bathos and some rhetorical broodiness in an otherwise great work; but what was the use of criticising it? "To chip at it with a hammer is a little like chipping at Stone Mountain." It was "a mountain range of a book."

But what of Sandburg's position in the battle of the realists and idealists? Did he becloud the portrait for those who sought the truth? Drinkwater thought him sentimental; and Quaife disliked his "imaginative poetry and historical fiction." Would one whose poetry was so starkly realistic reverse the trend of Lincoln writing and turn it back to romanticism when he tried his hand at biography?

No. That is not the case. Sandburg is as realistic about Lincoln as he is as a poet, in the sense that he does not make Lincoln a better man than he was. His Lincoln is not perfect. He is very much like Herndon's Lincoln. Sandburg's imaginative touches are not those of the moralist. They are those of one who senses the grandeur of his theme.

Chapter Thirteen

THE EMERGING PORTRAIT

Thus we have our portrait emerging as posterity will see it. Still unfinished, it is not yet certain and sufficient. What we have is a composite. Touched by many brushes, it is the joint product of several different draftsmen whose combined efforts have given us an essentially faithful portrayal of a subject so difficult to comprehend that no artist could have done the job alone, although each has made some brush marks that endure.

Surely the real Lincoln was not the man Chauncey Black thought he perceived through Herndon and the Herndon manuscripts. Yet Black did not miss the meaning altogether; for an earthy alloy was a part of Lincoln's make-up. Herndon, too, descried these loamy elements, and to Lincoln's human qualities added mystic overtones.

But to accept Herndon's conception as being all there was of Lincoln would be to miss essential qualities—the magnificence and sublimity discerned by Nicolay and Hay, the spiritual depths that Holland rightly recognized.

Much of the disagreement about Lincoln has been due to his amazing growth. The Lincoln of Kentucky and Indiana was not the Lincoln of New Salem; nor was the New Salem Lincoln the Lincoln of Springfield and the circuit.

Lincoln changed markedly between 1849, when he returned from Congress, and 1854, when the repeal of the Missouri Compromise aroused him as he had never been aroused before. The change continued to 1860; and then, under the stress of war, his mind and spirit burgeoned.

Thus the Lincoln that Herndon knew was not the same man with whom Nicolay and Hay were familiar; and the Lincoln they knew had grown, in some respects, beyond Herndon's comprehension. Yet none of them was too far wrong in what he saw. The boy grew up to be the man, and the circuit lawyer and small-town politician was the president in embryo, although the growth processes were no less wonderful and mysterious than those of biology. Moreover, none of Lincoln's contemporaries enjoyed the perspective that only time would bring and without which understanding and proper appraisal of men and events are difficult, if not impossible.

Every Lincoln biography reflects the biographer. In the plenitude of Lincoln's personality Lincoln students are disposed to see most clearly—and perhaps to overstress—those qualities akin to their own natures. The evangelistic Holland was impressed with indications of Lincoln's piety; while the unorthodox Herndon saw the evidences of doubt. Nicolay and Hay viewed Lincoln as a great leader of a great party; Black never overcame his partisan bias.

Similarly, in later times, Miss Tarbell sensed the glow of a great spirit, but could not suppress a womanly romanticism. Barton solved some puzzling uncertainties, but by his own admission fell short of full comprehension. The painstaking Beveridge added factual fidelity and might have surpassed all others had he lived, although temperamentally he was probably more closely attuned to Douglas than to Lincoln. The academicians excel in analysis but have

suffered the constraints of an inhibiting technique. Sandburg's revitalizing genius grasps the subtle and impalpable;
but his poetic instinct sometimes tempts him to indulge
poetic whimsy.

The composite nature of our Lincoln portrait is strikingly illustrated by *The Lincoln Reader*, recently published under the editorship of Paul M. Angle, and itself
the outgrowth of another volume—*A Shelf of Lincoln
Books*—in which Angle attempted to "winnow the permanent from the inconsequential" in the vast domain of Lincoln literature, and to show in what respects the fifty-eight
authors whose work he thought worthy of appraisal had
contributed to our knowledge and understanding of Lincoln.

As Angle and the head of his publishing house read the
galley proof of *A Shelf of Lincoln Books* together, the publisher was amazed at the number of authors to whom one
must go in order to see Lincoln entire. Who except the
specialists could spare the time to read the work of fifty-
eight authors whose product sometimes ran to several
volumes?

Surely the man who could devote only a moderate
amount of time to Lincoln deserved to have an authoritative, up-to-date biography available to him within the
compass of a single volume.

And then there came an idea!

Why not bring *A Shelf of Lincoln Books* alive? Why not
prepare a sort of Lincoln anthology embodying the best
that had been written on the various phases of Lincoln's
life?

So *The Lincoln Reader* was conceived—to appear later
as a biography made up of one hundred seventy-nine selec-

Paul M. Angle

tions from sixty-five different authors, so arranged and integrated as to form a continuous narrative.

All the major biographers are represented—together with others; and the book not only demonstrates that none of them, unaided, could have given us our present conception of Lincoln, but also confirms the fact that, while they often disagreed, none of them was altogether wrong in what he saw.

Here is Lamon's Lincoln, mimicking the backwoods preachers; and here is Charnwood's Lincoln, doing justice, loving mercy, walking humbly before God. The gnarled hands of Herndon's Lincoln earn him welcome athletic repute; Nicolay and Hay see those same hands make history with fateful, enduring, pen strokes. The crossroads store at Gentryville rocks to the guffaws of the farmer boys as Beveridge's Lincoln leans against the fireplace, cracking his boisterous jokes; the blue haze creeps down from the hills at Gettysburg, as Sandburg's Lincoln brings a message to the living from the dead.

Here are many Lincolns, contrasting yet not incongruous; the same man seen in different points of time and from diverse vantage points; one man in many aspects. And Lincoln's manifold aspects explain, in some degree at least, the seeming perpetuality of his popular appeal.

Earlier Lincoln books—those written during his presidency or shortly afterwards—tended to stress the poverty to fame motif. Then came the theme of the Great Emancipator, followed by that of the saviour of the Union. After the turn of the century, with these themes about worked out, Lincoln literature became spotty and static until World War I brought challenge to Democracy and its ideals.

For a long time Lincoln had been regarded as the prime

example of the opportunities that Democracy affords the ordinary man, but now he began to be viewed, not only in this light, but also as the most powerful personal force behind the democratic movement.

Lincoln had seen himself in both these roles. Speaking to an Ohio regiment in the latter days of the war, he said: "I beg you to remember this, not merely for my sake, but for yours. I happen, temporarily, to occupy this White House. I am a living witness that any one of your children may look to come here as my father's child has." And re-marking upon his larger role of Democracy's champion, he explained to the youthful John Hay that the central idea of the national struggle, as he saw it, was the necessity of proving that popular government was not an absurdity, that the question to be settled, perhaps for all future time, was whether, in a people's government, a minority has the right to break up the government whenever it is so dis-posed. If the majority verdict could be flouted at will, then he saw no hope for Democracy as a workable form of government.

Repeatedly in public utterances he voiced the same idea; notably in a message to Congress on July 4, 1861, when he said: "And this issue embraces more than the fate of these United States. It presents to the whole family of man the question whether a constitutional republic or democracy— a government of the people by the same people—can or cannot maintain its territorial integrity against its own do-mestic foes. It presents the question whether discontented individuals, too few in numbers to control administration according to organic law . . . can . . . break up their government, and thus practically put an end to free gov-ernment upon the earth."

Lincoln saw clearly that if it were once conceded that in

a democracy there is any right of appeal from ballots to bullets, then government of the people, by the people, for the people would perish from the earth.

Extreme eulogists of Lincoln sometimes go so far as to compare their hero with Jesus Christ; and while some realists may scoff, there is a valid comparison, in one respect at least, and it goes far to explain why books continue to be written about Lincoln and why they will continue to be written. For both Christ and Lincoln symbolize great vibrant, living forces—the one Christianity, the other Democracy—and so long as these forces remain vital there will be no cessation of interest in either man.

Washington is different from Lincoln in that his fame is associated with a movement accomplished and done. His greatness is recognized, but not much thought about. But the movements which Christ and Lincoln personify are still vigorous and cogent, moving toward the fulfillment of their destiny. So it is not strange that the volume of literature dealing with the one man is exceeded only by that dealing with the other.

In the Lincoln story, moreover, there are other compelling themes. There is drama, romance, tragedy, war, hate, conspiracy, murder. And then too, there is the element of mystery that has always enshrouded the man. More than one writer has been led into the Lincoln field by the detective instinct, and the several Lincoln "Groups," meeting periodically in various cities throughout the country to discuss different phases of Lincoln's life and personality, have many things in common with the Sherlock Holmes cult of "Baker Street Irregulars."

In 'so far as realism and idealism in Lincoln literature are concerned, they should be complementary rather than antagonistic. Neither the realists nor the idealists have been equal to the task of portraying Lincoln conclusively. Those biographers like Tarbell, Charnwood and Sandburg, who combine realism with a measure of imagination, have come closest to success. Yet both the realists and idealists have left essential marks. To purge the human clay from Father Abraham is to sunder that intangible communion that the people hold with him. And to deny his idealistic attributes is to disparage his greatness.

Both realism and idealism have a place in Lincoln literature.

The realist's ruthless searching gives the necessary facts. Yet the realist is ill-advised to scorn the idealist's sensitivity to those soul-qualities of Lincoln which documentary facts alone may not disclose.

The idealists, on their part, need not fear facts; time has shown this fear to be ridiculous.

For as our portrait of Lincoln becomes true, it also becomes more superb.

BIBLIOGRAPHY

Manuscript Sources

Abraham Lincoln Association, Files, Springfield, Illinois.

Isaac N. Arnold Collection, Chicago Historical Society.

William E. Barton Collection, Library of the University of Chicago.

Albert J. Beveridge—William E. Connelley Correspondence, Illinois State Historical Library, Springfield, Illinois.

Albert J. Beveridge—William L. Patton Correspondence, in possession of William H. Patton, Springfield, Illinois.

George P. Hambrecht Correspondence, in possession of Ralph Newman, The Abraham Lincoln Bookshop, Chicago, Illinois.

John Hay Collection, Illinois State Historical Library.

John Hay Letters, Henry E. Huntington Library, San Marino, California.

William H. Herndon—Jesse W. Weik Collection, Library of Congress, Washington, D. C. (Photostatic copies at the Illinois State Historical Library.)

Ward Hill Lamon Collection, Henry E. Huntington Library.

Stephen T. Logan Manuscripts, Illinois State Historical Library.

A. A. Sprague Collection, Chicago Historical Society.

Judd Stewart Collection, Henry E. Huntington Library.

Ida M. Tarbell Collection, Riis Library, Allegheny College, Meadville, Pennsylvania.

Jesse W. Weik Papers, Illinois State Historical Library.

Books

Angle, Paul M., ed., *Herndon's Life of Lincoln*. New York: Albert and Charles Boni, 1930.

—— *A Shelf of Lincoln Books*. New Brunswick: Rutgers University Press (in association with The Abraham Lincoln Association of Springfield, Illinois), 1946.

—— *The Lincoln Reader*. New Brunswick: Rutgers University Press, 1947.

Arnold, Isaac N., *The History of Abraham Lincoln and the Overthrow of American Slavery*. Chicago: Clarke & Co., 1866.

—— *The Life of Abraham Lincoln*. Chicago: A. C. McClurg & Co., 1885.

Barton, William E., *The Soul of Abraham Lincoln*. New York: George H. Doran Co., 1920.

—— *The Paternity of Abraham Lincoln*. New York: George H. Doran Co., 1920.

—— *The Life of Abraham Lincoln*, 2 vols. Indianapolis: The Bobbs-Merrill Co., 1925.

—— *A Beautiful Blunder*. Indianapolis: The Bobbs-Merrill Co., 1926.

—— *The Women Lincoln Loved*. Indianapolis: The Bobbs-Merrill Co., 1927.

—— *The Lineage of Lincoln*. Indianapolis: The Bobbs-Merrill Co., 1929.

—— *Lincoln at Gettysburg*. Indianapolis: The Bobbs-Merrill Co., 1930.

—— *The Autobiography of William E. Barton*. Indianapolis: The Bobbs-Merrill Co., 1932.

—— *President Lincoln*, 2 vols. Indianapolis: The Bobbs-Merrill Co., 1933.

Basler, Roy P., *The Lincoln Legend*. Boston and New York: Houghton Mifflin Co., 1936.

Beveridge, Albert J., *Abraham Lincoln, 1809–1858*, 2 vols. Boston and New York: Houghton Mifflin Co., 1928.

Bowers, Claude G., *Beveridge and the Progressive Era*. Cambridge: Houghton Mifflin Co., 1932.

Carpenter, Francis B., *Six Months at the White House*. New York: Hurd and Houghton, 1866.

Charnwood, Lord, *Abraham Lincoln*. New York: Henry Holt & Co., 1917.

Dennett, Tyler, *John Hay: From Poetry to Politics*. New York: Dodd, Mead & Co., 1933.

—— *Lincoln and the Civil War in the Diaries and Letters of John Hay*. New York: Dodd, Mead & Co., 1939.

Detzer, Karl W., *Carl Sandburg—A Study in Personality and Background*. New York: Harcourt, Brace & Co., 1941.

Evans, William A., *Mrs. Abraham Lincoln*. New York: Alfred A. Knopf, 1932.

Herndon, William H. and Weik, Jesse W., *Herndon's Lincoln: The True Story of a Great Life*, 3 vols. Chicago and New York: Belford, Clarke & Co., 1889.

—— *Abraham Lincoln: The True Story of a Great Life*, 2 vols. New York: D. Appleton & Co., 1892.

Hertz, Emanuel, *The Hidden Lincoln*. New York: Viking Press, 1938.

Hitchcock, Caroline Hanks, *Nancy Hanks, The Story of Abraham Lincoln's Mother*. New York: Doubleday & McClure Co., 1899.

Holland, Josiah G., *The Life of Abraham Lincoln*. Springfield, Mass.: Gurdon Bill, 1866.

Lamon, Ward Hill, *The Life of Abraham Lincoln*. Boston: James R. Osgood & Co., 1872.

Lea, James Henry and Hutchinson, J. R., *The Ancestry of Abraham Lincoln*. New York: Houghton Mifflin Co., 1909.

Lewis, Lloyd, *Myths after Lincoln*. New York: Harcourt, Brace & Co., 1929.

Lincoln, Waldo, *A History of the Lincoln Family*. Worcester: The Commonwealth Press, 1923.

McClure, Alexander K., *Abraham Lincoln and Men of War Time*. Philadelphia: The Times Publishing Co., 1892.

Monaghan, Jay, *Lincoln Bibliography, 1839–1939* with a Foreword by James G. Randall, 2 vols. Springfield, Ill.: Illinois State Historical Library, 1943.

Newton, Joseph Fort, *Lincoln and Herndon*. Cedar Rapids: The Torch Press, 1910.

Nicolay, John G. and Hay, John, *Abraham Lincoln: A History*, 10 vols. New York: The Century Co., 1890.

—— *Complete Works of Abraham Lincoln*, 2 vols. New York: The Century Co., 1894.

O'Neill, Edward H., *A History of American Biography, 1800–1935*. Philadelphia: University of Pennsylvania Press, 1935.

Parrington, Vernon Louis, *Main Currents in American Thought*, 3 vols. New York: Harcourt, Brace & Co., 1927–1930.

Pease, Theodore C. and Randall, James G., eds., *The Diary of Orville Hickman Browning*, 2 vols. Springfield, Ill.: Illinois State Historical Library, 1925.

Phillips, Isaac N., *Abraham Lincoln*. Bloomington, Ill., 1901.

Plunkett, Mrs. H. M., *Josiah Gilbert Holland*. New York: Charles Scribner's Sons, 1894.

Randall, James G., *Lincoln the President: Springfield to Gettysburg*, 2 vols. New York: Dodd, Mead & Co., 1945.

Rankin, Henry B., *Personal Recollections of Abraham Lincoln*. New York and London: The Knickerbocker Press, 1916.

—— *Intimate Character Sketches of Abraham Lincoln*. Philadelphia and London: J. B. Lippincott & Co., 1924.

Raymond, Henry J., *The Life and Public Services of Abraham Lincoln*. New York: Darby & Miller, 1865.

Rice, Allen Thorndike, ed., *Reminiscences of Abraham Lincoln by Distinguished Men of His Time*. New York: The North American Review, 1885.

Sandburg, Carl, *Abraham Lincoln: The Prairie Years*, 2 vols. New York: Harcourt, Brace & Co., 1926.

———— *Abraham Lincoln: The War Years,* 4 vols. New York: Harcourt, Brace & Co., 1939.

Sandburg, Carl and Angle, Paul M., *Mary Lincoln: Wife and Widow.* New York: Harcourt, Brace & Co., 1932.

Tarbell, Ida M., *The Early Life of Abraham Lincoln.* New York: S. S. McClure, 1896.

———— *The Life of Abraham Lincoln,* 2 vols. New York: The Doubleday and McClure Co., 1900.

———— *In the Footsteps of the Lincolns.* New York: Harper and Brothers, 1924.

———— *All in the Day's Work: An Autobiography.* New York: The Macmillan Co., 1939.

Teillard, Dorothy Lamon, ed., *Recollections of Abraham Lincoln by Ward Hill Lamon, 1847–1865.* Chicago: A. C. McClurg & Co., 1895.

Thayer, William Roscoe, *The Life and Letters of John Hay,* 2 vols. Boston and New York: Houghton Mifflin Co., 1915.

Trent, W. P.; Erskine, John; Sherman, Stuart P.; and Van Doren, Carl, eds., *The Cambridge History of American Literature,* 3 vols. New York and Cambridge: The Macmillan Co. and Cambridge University Press, 1933.

Warren, Louis A., *Lincoln's Parentage & Childhood.* New York: The Century Co., 1928.

Weik, Jesse W., *The Real Lincoln.* Boston and New York: Houghton Mifflin Co., 1922.

Whitney, Henry Clay, *Life on the Circuit with Lincoln.* Boston: Estes and Lauriat, 1892; also Caldwell, Idaho: The Caxton Printers, Ltd., 1940. The latter edition has an introduction and notes by Paul M. Angle.

Articles, Brochures, etc.

"Abraham Lincoln's Religion: His Own Statement," *Abraham Lincoln Quarterly,* March, 1942.

Angle, Paul M., "Lincoln's Lost Speech," *Abraham Lincoln Association Bulletin,* No. 21, December, 1930.

———— "Lincoln's First Love?" *Lincoln Centennial Association Bulletin,* No. 9, December, 1927.

———— "New Light on Lincoln and Ann Rutledge," *Lincoln Centennial Association Bulletin,* No. 12, September, 1928.

———— "The Beveridge Lincoln," *Lincoln Centennial Association Bulletin,* December 1, 1928.

———— "Logan Hay," *Abraham Lincoln Quarterly,* September 1942.

Baringer, William E. and Bonzi, Marion Delores, "The Writings of Lincoln," *Abraham Lincoln Quarterly,* March, 1946.

Barton, Robert, "William E. Barton—Biographer," *Abraham Lincoln Quarterly,* June, 1946.

Beveridge, Albert J., "The Making of a Book," *Saturday Evening Post,* October 23, 1926.

Black, Chauncey F., "The Life of Lincoln: Lincoln, Lamon, Holland and Reed," *The New York World,* July 26, 1873.

Donald, David, "Billy, You're Too Rampant," *Abraham Lincoln Quarterly,* December, 1945.

Eisenschiml, Otto, *Reviewers Reviewed.* Ann Arbor: William L. Clements Library, 1940.

Herndon, William H., "An Analysis of the Character of Abraham Lincoln," *Abraham Lincoln Quarterly,* September, 1941 and December, 1941.

———— "The Patriotism and Statesmanship of Mr. Lincoln," *Abraham Lincoln Quarterly,* December, 1944.

———— "Abraham Lincoln, Miss Ann Rutledge, New Salem, Pioneering and the Poem," Springfield, Ill., 1910.

———— "Lincoln's Religion," broadside published by the *Illinois State Register,* December 13, 1873; also published by The Black Cat Press (Chicago, Ill.), 1936.

House, Albert J., "The Trials of a Ghost-Writer of Lincoln Biography: Chauncey F. Black's Authorship of Lamon's Life of Lincoln," *Journal of the Illinois State Historical Society,* September, 1938.

Lawson, Evald Benjamin, "That Man Knows Lincoln," *The Lutheran Companion*, February 12, 1942.

Lewis, Lloyd, "The Many-Sided Sandburg," *The Rotarian*, May, 1940.

Lincoln Kinsman, The, published by Lincolniana Publishers, Fort Wayne, Indiana.

Lincoln Lore, edited by Louis A. Warren and published by the Lincoln National Life Foundation, Fort Wayne, Indiana. Numbers 9, 718, and 739.

Massachusetts Historical Society Proceedings, Volume 51, 1918.

Monaghan, Jay, "New Light on the Lincoln-Rutledge Romance," *Abraham Lincoln Quarterly*, September, 1944.

——— "An Analysis of Lincoln's Funeral Sermons," *Indiana Magazine of History*, March, 1945.

Nicolay, Helen, "The Education of an Historian," *Abraham Lincoln Quarterly*, September, 1944.

"One Biographer About Another: A Criticism by John G. Nicolay," *Abraham Lincoln Quarterly*, September, 1940.

"Recollections of Lincoln: Three Letters of Intimate Friends," *Abraham Lincoln Association Bulletin*, No. 25, December, 1931.

Reports of Committees of the House of Representatives, 2d session, 37th Congress, 1861–62.

Strevey, Tracy E., "Albert J. Beveridge," in *The Marcus W. Jernegan Essays in American Historiography*, edited by William T. Hutchinson. Chicago: University of Chicago Press, 1937.

Teillard, Dorothy Lamon, "Lincoln in Myth and in Fact," *World's Work*, February, 1911.

Tilton, Clint Clay, "Lincoln and Lamon: Partners and Friends," *Transactions of the Illinois State Historical Society*, 1931.

Warren, Louis A., "Herndon's Contribution to Lincoln Mythology," *Indiana Magazine of History*, September, 1945.

Magazines and Newspapers

American Historical Review
Athenium, The
Atlantic Monthly, The
Bookman
Books
Century Magazine
Chicago Daily Tribune
Christian Science Monitor
Congregationalist
Critic, The
Dial, The
Galaxy, The
Harper's New Monthly Magazine
Illinois State Journal
Illinois State Register
Independent, The
Literary World, The
London Times Literary Supplement

McClure's Magazine
Mississippi Valley Historical Review
Nation, The
New Englander and Congregational Review
New Republic
New York Herald
New York Herald-Tribune
New York Sun
New York Times
New York Tribune
North American Review
Outlook, The
Saturday Review of Literature
Scribner's Monthly
Time
Virginia Quarterly Review
Washington Daily Globe
Yale Review

INDEX